AWAKENING THE
PLANETARY MIND

"Compulsive understandir ness. Essentia dition to our an conscious-

ns, author of
Gateway to Atlantis and *From the Ashes of Angels*

"Between lines of text exists an unseen world. Barbara Hand Clow, with her inimitable ability, peered into this world with laserlike vision and has thrust it before us in a way that cannot be ignored. As an engineer who is grounded in three-dimensional reality, *Awakening the Planetary Mind* reads between my lines with insight and clarity."

Christopher Dunn, author of *The Giza Power Plant*

"It takes a mind versed in interdisciplinary studies to fully understand, integrate, reassemble, and then accurately teach this complex subject. Barbara has that kind of mind. And her detective work is conveyed admirably."

**Freddy Silva, researcher, photographer,
and author of *Common Wealth***

"In *Awakening the Planetary Mind*, Barbara Hand Clow, with a perceptive voice, invites us to explore the unknown crevices of the past through her uncommon spiritual eye."

Rand Flem-Ath, author of *When the Sky Fell*

"I find this book mind-expanding, provocative, and offering an important contribution to our self-understanding as a species, especially as we face important decisions in these critical times."

Matthew Fox, author of *Original Blessing*

"Grandmother Sky (Barbara Hand Clow) has captured the essence of Mother Earth as a living energy within the Universal Circle in *Awakening the Planetary Mind*. The book reveals some universal dynamics that help us understand our connection to the past here on Turtle Island. We can truly learn from the past that we have the ability to change and to begin again."

**J. T. Garrett, Ed.D., M.P.H., member of the
Eastern Band of Cherokee from North Carolina and author of
The Cherokee Herbal and *Meditations with the Cherokee***

Other Books by Barbara Hand Clow

AWAKENING
THE
PLANETARY
MIND

Beyond the Trauma of the Past
to a New Era of Creativity

BARBARA HAND CLOW

Illustrations by Christopher Cudahy Clow

Bear & Company
Rochester, Vermont • Toronto, Canada

Bear & Company
One Park Street
Rochester, Vermont 05767
www.BearandCompanyBooks.com

SUSTAINABLE FORESTRY INITIATIVE   Certified Sourcing
www.sfiprogram.org
SFI-00854

Text stock is SFI certified

Bear & Company is a division of Inner Traditions International

Library of Congress Cataloging-in-Publication Data
Clow, Barbara Hand, 1943–
  Awakening the planetary mind : beyond the trauma of the past to a new era of creativity / Barbara Hand Clow ; illustrations by Christopher Cudahy Clow. — Rev. ed.
    p. cm.
  Previously published under title: Catastrophobia: the truth behind the Earth changes in the coming age of light.
  Includes bibliographical references and index.
  Summary: "Completing our conscious evolution by releasing our collective fear of catastrophes"—Provided by publisher.
  ISBN 978-1-59143-134-3 (pbk.) — ISBN 978-1-59143-938-7 (e-book)
  1. Catastrophes (Geology) 2. History, Ancient 3. Mythology. 4. Archaeoastronomy. I. Clow, Christopher Cudahy. II. Title.
  BF1999.C587 2011
  904—dc23

                                                                    2011031691

Printed and bound in the United States by Lake Book Manufacturing
The text stock is SFI certified. The Sustainable Forestry Initiative® program promotes sustainable forest management.

10 9 8 7 6 5 4 3 2 1
Text design and layout by Priscilla Baker
This book was typeset in Garamond Premier Pro with Trajan Pro and Agenda used as display typefaces

To send correspondence to the author of this book, mail a first-class letter to the author c/o Inner Traditions • Bear & Company, One Park Street, Rochester, VT 05767, and we will forward the communication; or visit the author's website at **www.handclow2012.com**.

CONTENTS

This book is dedicated to Matthew Clow
(November 15, 1968–June 26, 1998)
and his generation.

FOREWORD

The past three decades have seen a spate of books on the subject of world catastrophes. Of variable quality, these books have ranged from considerations of the believedly traumatic termination of the reign of the dinosaurs at the end of the Cretaceous times about 63 million years ago, to that which evidently brought the so-called Pleistocene Ice Age to an abrupt close approximately 11,500 years ago, when, in the opinion of some, the legendary island of Atlantis was cataclysmically swallowed by the sea.

These studies have focused chiefly on the physical evidence for the one-time reality of those events, on the mechanisms that apparently caused their irruption, and on some of the multifarious long-term aftereffects they unleashed.

Very significantly, the presence in the Pleistocene calamity's dossier of an impressively varied mass of ancient, globally scattered, human "eyewitness" accounts of the event (now preserved as traditions and legends), complementing the associated field evidence, is a factor understandably absent from the file on the far older Cretaceous catastrophe. Such legends and traditions, of course, are themselves very much a part of "catastrophism" in its wider sense. The resultant Pleistocene "mosaic" is thus an especially fertile one for in-depth scholarly investigation.

It is, therefore, somewhat curious that comparatively few writers have dealt to any extent with the now deeply etched psychological scars and subsequent social reactions (phobias) generated by early humanity's *en bloc* experience of the disaster 11,500 years ago—that is, until now, through the visionary writing of Barbara Hand Clow.

For those already familiar with this author's previous writings, it will be superfluous to emphasize her breadth of scholarship or facility in expressing succinctly otherwise naturally complex data. But for those to whom Clow will be a new author, *Awakening the Planetary Mind* should prove a most enlightening read, offering coherent explanations of many vexed aspects of humankind's past beliefs and social behavioral patterns, and how that has in turn led to the stultifying conservatism and orthodoxy sadly all too commonly still with us.

Using the latest findings of Earth science, of prehistorians, and of what may now best be termed "new wave" archaeology, *Awakening the Planetary Mind* traces the evolution of human psychology during the past 15,000 years or so, and concentrates on how that has been modified by the horrendous benchmark event that, around 11,500 years ago, cut short an older benign terrestrial regime, disrupted much of the adjacent solar system, and ushered in the harsher and more disturbed one of present (Holocene) times.

The marauding cosmic agencies responsible for such dire devastation are now identifiable with reasonable accuracy and are still graphically remembered as the hydras, griffins, dragons, and Medusas, the world-encircling serpents and vast "monsters" of popular mythology (the aforementioned traditions and legends); they actually symbolized cosmic phenomena. *Awakening the Planetary Mind* relates this cosmic event to a coincidental change in Earth's axial tilt and the inception of the calendrical precession of the equinoxes—an element of great importance for Holocene Man, and one linked to the newly discovered planet Chiron, which Clow argues may, like zodiacs, have been influential in the development 10,000 years ago of astrology. The destruction of an ancient equable world regime, the so-called Golden Age of precataclysmic days, gave rise among the survivors to the notion that its loss was, along with the coeval Noachian Deluge or Great Flood, a vengeful god's punishment of a sinful antediluvian humanity.

During the ensuing millennia, that idea spawned a great and varied raft of penitentiary and propitiatory practices, which were often expressly tied to equinoctial dates in the then-new Holocene precessional cycle. Thus guilt, penance, and sacrifice became mainstays of practically all the many religions and cults that arose following the initiation of the Holocene epoch—assumed "guilt" (to explain the "need" for a retributional catastrophe), voluntary "penance" (to atone for the imagined "sin"), and eager "sacrifice" (to hopefully avert a repetition of "divine cleansing")—themselves each long-established facets of "catastrophobia" itself. ["Catastrophobia" is Clow's term for the inherited aftereffects of catastrophes.]

Clow examines these and other psychological human changes in relation to what she terms the bicameral mind, its one-time degeneration, and its later reawakening. Citing several leading authorities on the subject, she posits that in terms of a general awareness of nature, precatastrophic humans possessed a more highly developed sense of it than their Holocene descendants, and that the terrible cataclysm that separated prediluvial from postdiluvial humankind produced a "perceptual narrowing" of that awareness. The original ancient awareness, Clow contends, has only lately begun to reemerge, and then not universally.

Clow emphasizes the important point that almost every ancient civilized society recognized to date not only first appears at a surprisingly advanced technological level, with, furthermore, connections to some thriving, globally active, maritime culture, but that such expertise and sophistication must originally have been acquired before the onset of Holocene times, that is, prior to the Pleistocene catastrophe. Clow wonders if this primal font was the fabled Atlantis of Plato's writings.

In that connection she duly acknowledges the late Charles Hapgood's pioneer work in *Maps of the Ancient Sea Kings* (1966) on the series of enigmatic early maps, yet extant, depicting *bygone* topographical conditions both north and south of the present equator; and, like Hapgood, Clow believes that these maps represent a legacy of this self-same ancient maritime race. She then goes on to consider some of the technological achievements of these mystery mariners, and the original location of Plato's lost continent.

The suggestion advanced by the Flem-Aths' *When the Sky Fell* (1995) that Atlantis occupied part of presently ice-smothered Antarctica—an idea mooted many years ago in an unpublished manuscript by Harold T. Wilkins about a now-ice-covered prehistoric Antarctic metropolis called

Rainbow City—is reviewed in connection with the actual portrayal of a partially ice-free Antarctica on several of the aforementioned ancient maps.

Mirroring the opinions of older writers such as Lewis Spence and D. S. Merekhovsky (1933), Clow concludes that Plato's Atlanteans were culturally associated with the gifted Magdalenian and Cro-Magnon peoples of so-called Upper Paleolithic times, and, with Mary Settegast (1990) and Richard Rudgley (1999), suggests that the numerous similarities between the primitive scripts of the slightly younger Vinca culture and the Cretan Linear A, the early Indus Valley, and the pre-Hellenic alphabetical signs are links in a long chain uniting the fabled primeval Atlantean civilization with the preclassical Indo-Mediterranean examples just listed.

On this basis the age-old belief of the Greeks, Romans, and various medieval chroniclers in a lost but formerly inhabited southern continent conceivably rests on a foundation of fragmented fact, while the many curious cultural similarities between ancient Old and New World civilizations—especially those of South America, significantly the *closest* southern landmass geographically to Antarctica—are very possibly explicable as pieces of the same ancient puzzle and for similar reasons.

Clow's wide-ranging evidence embraces the changing climatic history of the Nile Valley of the past 12,000 years or so, the fluctuating water levels and actual course of the Nile River during that period, and the detail that the Valley Temples of the Sphinx and the Second Pyramid were once situated nearer the Nile than today. Such factors, and the progressive desertification and impoverishment of an originally more densely wooded Nile Valley, from about 4000 BC onward, materially affected early Nilotic culture and its development. This culture, we are told, allegedly derived from the legendary "First Time," or Zep Tepi, when semidivine sages, the Shemsu Hor, reputedly ruled Egypt and instituted all the principal elements comprising ancient Egyptian Dynastic civilization.

Attention is drawn to the Egyptians' claim that their records extended back to 36,525 BC, and that it was Egyptian priests who, in Greek times, first told Plato's ancestor Solon about the former existence of Atlantis.

In that connection, and the possibility that Atlantis's original site was Antarctica, the fact that the massive cut masonry of the Osireion, a temple of unknown but exceptional antiquity at Abydos, is remarkably like some long known from pre-Incan Peru and Bolivia in Andean South America—the very continent nearest to Antarctica—and that the Osireion, like the Sphinx, is now believed to be a much older structure than the general 3300 BC date commonly awarded the beginning of the First Egyptian Dynasty, are collectively highly suggestive of common cultural links underscoring all these enigmatical wonders of the past.

Clow's acceptance of the Great Catastrophe that, as a benchmark event, separated a prediluvial from a postdiluvial world around 11,500 years ago should henceforth serve prehistoric chronology well. Her reworking, within the resultant new chronological framework, of so many previously contentious aspects of prehistory permit the perception of exciting new perspectives. Likewise, her analyses of the crucial psychological aspects that have until now largely constricted the realization of a truer world picture are equally meritorious. Indeed, both unquestionably merit extended applause.

J. BERNARD DELAIR
OXFORD, DECEMBER 2000

J. B. Delair, B.Sc., is an Oxford-based geologist with wide international and commercial field experience. An anthropologist, he has a special interest in animal and plant distribution and in tribal traditions. He is the museum curator of Geology at the University of Southampton, England. He is also the co-author, with D. S. Allan of *Cataclysm! Compelling Evidence of a Cosmic Catastrophe in 9500 BC* and *When the Earth Nearly Died: Compelling Evidence of a World Cataclysm 11,500 Years Ago.*

ACKNOWLEDGMENTS

I honor my Celtic/Cherokee grandfather, Gilbert Hand, for his teachings and wisdom, which are bearing fruit fifty years later. He instructed me in the oral tradition of ancient civilizations by guiding me through the mythological, archaeological, and geological sources when I was age five through seventeen. His Cherokee mother passed the Cherokee Records to him, and then he passed these teachings to me. Grandfather Hand was also a thirty-second-degree Mason, and I will never know which of his teachings are Cherokee or Masonic, or both. Thank you, Grandmother Mabel Austen Hand, for the songs and stories of the Celtic people.

Thank you, J. T. Garrett, Hunbatz Men, Alberto Ruiz Buenfil, Don Alejandro Oxlac, White Eagle Tree, Heyoka Merrifield, Abdel Hakim, Frank Aon, Sam Kaai, and Felicitas Goodman for knowing the medicine and sharing it so graciously with me.

My greatest joy while writing this book was working with the illustrator, Christopher Cudahy Clow, who is my third son. Thank you, Hampshire College in Amherst, Massachusetts, for the first exhibit of these illustrations for his senior project in May 1999. The edge of joy has also been the edge of sorrow: In 1998 my second son (Chris's older brother), Matthew Clow, drowned in Lower Red Rock Lake near Dillon, Montana. Chris encouraged me to keep writing, and his artwork also helped him with his sorrow. Chris, the illustrations are beautiful!

Thank you, D. S. Allan and J. B. Delair, for writing *Cataclysm! Compelling Evidence of a Cosmic Catastrophe in 9500 BC*, and for your assistance with this book; and J. B. Delair, I am deeply honored by your foreword. Thank you, anonymous donor, for the illustrations, since your generosity enabled Chris to do more than we had originally planned. I also am very grateful for the work of Anne Dillon and Jeanie Levitan at Bear & Company, for their careful and meticulous attention to detail, as well as the wonderful work done by copy editor Judy Stein. And thank you to Peri Swan, whose cover design I love, and to the book's designer, Priscilla Baker.

Thank you, Gerry Clow, for all your editorial work. You really helped me clarify my thoughts, and I am still writing because you always help me.

# INTRODUCTION

Awakening the Planetary Mind explores human evolution over the past 100,000 years based on the latest discoveries in archaeology, mythology, and Earth sciences. A recent global scientific data convergence reveals that a great cataclysm occurred only 11,500 years ago—the Late Pleistocene extinctions, according to geology, and the Flood, according to theologians. This was followed by massive crustal adjustments and flooding for thousands of years as human cultures struggled for survival while they were deeply traumatized. As this story comes forth, it emerges in a damaged world in which many people believe that the end of the world is coming soon. Because this recent catastrophe has been unknown, many people are afflicted with *catastrophobia*—an intense fear of catastrophes—the original title of this book. This new word is intended to name a psychological syndrome that causes individuals and societies to think an end is coming soon. Because they are always thinking something is coming, people are not caring for the earth. Crippled by unnamed fear that is carried in racial memory, our surface minds are filled with floating images of disaster, guilt, and suffering. To ease our inner minds, we project these painful thoughts onto outer moving screens, which could make a coming apocalypse into a self-fulfilling prophecy. But it already happened! Ten years have passed since the first edition of this work was published in 2001, and many more scientists and popular writers have brought forth the real story of these disasters. I noted in 2001, "Our attention is riveted when preachers and New Age prophets make predictions which sound true because they resonate with disassociated inner images." As this book goes to press in 2011, happily, these fanatics are striking a false note in many if not most people.

Many can also see that the probable cause of another catastrophe will most likely be an extinction caused by the human species, not by natural causes.

This book invites you to explore the probability that *we may have millions of years of peaceful evolution coming next.* I believe we are on the verge of a great spiritual and intellectual awakening just when popular culture is caught in a very silly obsession with the End Times. The current fad is waiting for December 21, 2012, when the poles will flip, Planet X will invade our planet, and/or the Matrix will take over—the newest versions of catastrophobia.

Today, many scientists are describing the real story of Earth's past: Based on geological, biological, paleontological, and archaeological knowledge from new dating techniques, ice-core drilling, ocean sediment cores, and computer-imaging technology, most scientists agree that a series of cataclysms occurred 14,000 to 11,500 years ago. We also know a lot about the follow-up Earth changes, such as the Black Sea Flood in 5600 BC and the eruption of Thera on Santorini in 1600 BC. During those terrible times, our planet was afflicted with floods, erupting volcanoes, earthquakes, and massive waves of death, and we were reduced to bare survivalism. Now, as a result of more data on cross-cultural global mythology, settlement patterns, and geoarchaeology, we are achieving a global memory of our recent past. Archaeological sites come alive because we know what happened and when, and we even know a great deal about the background of the sites.

Now that the date and the magnitude of the cataclysms are verified by science, we can see that it is a miracle anything survived, including ourselves. But in a way, we *didn't* survive, because our civilization and its cultures were obscenely obliterated; until very recently it was thought that we have always been progressively advancing. Since this book was first published, new research, discussed in this revision, has emerged that verifies Plato's date for the fall of Atlantis—the historical record of the fall of a previously advanced world. This new edition discusses these events more in terms of 14,000 to 11,500 years ago, because D. S. Allan and J. B. Delair's Vela Supernova hypothesis, described in their *Cataclysm! Compelling Evidence of a Cosmic Catastrophe in 9500 BC,* has now been adopted by more scientists. The Vela Supernova—the Blue Star in current Hopi knowledge—was probably visible on Earth and influenced its climate for a few thousand years before 9500 BC, the final great cataclysm. Now that other researchers have adopted this hypothesis, it is moving into the theoretical zone. For example, my original tentative discussion of the enigmatic Stones of Ica is supported by the growing acceptance of the Vela Supernova hypothesis, and so I was able to consider them even more deeply. I think the stones are records carved by an unknown race that knew what was coming and recorded it for posterity: I think the arriving supernova is depicted on the stone on this book's cover.

Awakening the Planetary Mind adopts the global maritime civilization hypothesis—the existence of an advanced global seafaring culture 25,000 to 8,000 years ago that some call Atlantis—and its prehistoric demise. Since the 1980s, many researchers, most notably Graham Hancock, have been analyzing the remnants of an advanced global maritime culture from more than 12,000 years ago that vanished almost without a trace. Any evidence of such a lost world is incredibly significant. In the first edition of this book, I creatively selected some evocative evidence of this lost world to open the reader's archaic or racial memory, and since then these remnants have been well accepted and are gaining wider credibility. I've been pleased to see that other writers have considered these remains, and their thoughts are considered here. The evidence for a lost global civilization has been compounding, especially in the Middle East. I strongly suspect that a brilliant civilization existed not long ago on Earth that flourished for 100,000 years, and I discuss this in detail in appendix E. Of course, a great deal of this time span is Neanderthal culture, so I have added this research, which is very thought provoking. Science says we use only around 10 to 15 percent of our DNA. I wonder if the unused DNA is the coding for a mixture of the global maritime culture's technological knowledge, psychic skills, and our emotional range that was shut down by the catastrophes. The new title of this book—*Awakening the Planetary Mind*—is a change I really like because I think we must access this dormant DNA as quickly as possible, so that we can take back our role as Earth's keepers. That is the essence of what my grandparents taught me.

Until very recently science investigated catastrophes that were comfortably at a distance, such as the extinction of the dinosaurs 63 million years ago. Lately, more scientists have been investigating the magnitude of the 9500 BC disaster—just as a tidal wave of apocalyptical fanaticism poisons the major world religions, including the New Age. We are waking up from *collective amnesia* as we hear the correct version of the past, which also stirs up repressed cataclysmic memory that lurks in the deep unconscious mind of each one of us. The whole world is in a very nervous mood, which bears all the signs of people dealing with terribly painful memories. Of course, the popular media stirs these murky fears with disaster scenarios and constant reports of violence and chaos. Why? Just so the Elite can prolong selling both pharmaceuticals and guns to get a few more corporate profits. People feel cornered, as if there is no future. Yet, events as great as the disasters described in this book probably occur about *every 30 million years or more* in our solar system.

Now that astronomers are exploring the Milky Way galaxy, they've discovered a long cycle when the solar system travels through the galactic arms. During our most recent passage 14,000 through 11,500 years ago, the whole solar system was disarranged, which may have been a unique event. By order of magnitude, this event for the *solar system* was probably even greater than the asteroid impact in the Gulf of Mexico off the Yucatan 63 million years ago that terminated the Cretaceous period. The public mainly hears that there are recurrent cyclical disasters caused by fields of meteors and comets and cycles in the solar system that influence Earth's climate. These things do happen, and they can cause big trouble, yet from a cyclical and galactic perspective, our solar system is probably in recovery mode. Meanwhile, science is infected with *catastrophobia for profit*—a big disaster is coming soon that could totally destroy the planet so we must spend trillions to build weapons to shoot things out of the sky—and this terrifies the public. Of course, the Elite manages what the public hears, and they want to dumb down the public. Meanwhile, I know our species is on the brink of the next evolutionary advance: a great spiritual awakening.

The data convergence described in this book is based on nearly incomprehensible amounts of scientific work and exploration done over 400 years that sped up exponentially 150 years ago and became a nuclear chain reaction 50 years ago. Considering this flood of information, I'd like to explain how I got into this field. During my childhood my Cherokee/Celtic grandfather educated me in the *real* story of Earth. My grandfather knew I would be here now to experience the scientific awakening, which he believed would make it possible for me to offer the Cherokee Records—Turtle Medicine. Searching for verification for the things he told me, I became a student of catastrophism, which posits that Earth experiences long periods of peaceful evolution that are periodically punctured by cataclysms. During the 1960s and '70s, the uniformitarian mind-set—that Earth changes have been slow and gradual—was finally being questioned by science. Finally, I heard ideas that agreed with my grandfather's seemingly improbable story. Uniformitarianism and social Darwinism—we are always evolving to a more advanced level by survival of the fittest—were the dogma of the day during most of my education. Attending school was very difficult because all this totally contradicted my grandfather's story—that Earth nearly died 11,500 years ago—a story that he insisted I would offer to the world someday.

In 1982 I was drawn to study with Matthew Fox for a master's program, which Fox called Creation-Centered Theology; I intuited I could escape the increasingly onerous dogma in schools, and I was right. Creation-Centered Theology celebrates our creative genius and posits that guilt and obsession with personal salvation is the natural result of the belief in "Original Sin." I was always disturbed by this prevalent belief in sin, since it is an idea that is very foreign to indigenous people. The ancient Cherokee Records are profoundly creation centered; so joyfully, during my studies with Fox, my early childhood training awakened. The reason for humankind's "fall" is obviously the cataclysms and not sin. Judeo-Christianity has taken advantage of suffering humankind's need for answers by saying early humans caused the Flood and must seek salvation.

I became the acquisitions editor at Bear & Company (initially working with Fox) in 1983, and my seventeen years of publishing healers and new-paradigm authors are deeply reflected in this book. In 1996, the British edition of D. S. Allan and J. B. Delair's *When the Earth Nearly Died* landed on my desk, and I was spellbound because it described *exactly* the same story as my grandfather's! In 1997 Bear published the U.S. edition—*Cataclysm! Compelling Evidence of a Cosmic Catastrophe in 9500 BC*—and I began discussions with Allan and Delair to explore the psychological implications of their study. My grandfather had said that the real story of Earth would be told once science described it, and suddenly I'd found a scientific book with the correct timeline and scenario. This has enabled me to investigate how our consciousness has been altered and molded by Earth changes. This new 2011 edition adds the many developments that have emerged since 2001.

Our species wounding from the cataclysms and the subsequent survivalism is the focus of other thinkers as well, such as the British writer Andrew Collins and the anthropologist Felicitas Goodman, and their work has deepened this text. Because of the rapidity and intensity of the global data convergence in science, theology, and consciousness, the research for this book has been daunting. I have analyzed and synthesized mostly nonacademic books based on primary sources, since this was the only way to avoid the assumptions of the old paradigm. In addition to reading Plato, Egyptology, and Aegean archaeology and related subjects, I used the secondary research of other writers, and I have checked all their primary sources carefully. I encourage readers to consult the books I call out in the Suggested Reading section, because I've barely touched on their genius. Attempting to summarize all the nuances of their arguments and ideas would necessitate many extra chapters and would not do justice to the power of these works. Yet I will quote them liberally, as I want readers to know their ideas. The new-paradigm movement is an exciting field because it lets you build things out of blocks, without having to first sculpt each block on your own. In that sense, this book is heavily sourced from these dozen or so writers, including myself. For instance, when I read *From the Ashes of Angels* by Andrew Collins, I felt as if Collins and I had visited the same library for years. Collins also uses Earth changes as a basis for understanding cultures and consciousness, and his thoughts have intensified and clarified my own arguments. It is so affirming to find another researcher who drew similar conclusions based on material that orthodoxy has defined so differently. We new-paradigm writers often feel like we are neck-in-neck in a horse race that is headed to the finish line of remembering the story of our species.

The Stargate Conspiracy (2000) by Lynn Picknett and Clive Prince ignited a firestorm of debates over Global Elite manipulation of the New Age movement. Having been a publisher for twenty years, I am well aware of the Elite's infiltration of the New Age, and The Stargate Conspiracy sheds much clear light on this process. The authors have exposed how the Elite manipulates people by their beliefs and fears. Their book invited me to assess my previous book The Pleiadian Agenda: A New Cosmology for the Age of Light (1995), a work that the Stargate authors might easily think is part of the Elite programming. To tell the truth, mind-control influence and the clarity of channeling really concern me. So in 2004 I wrote a scientific analysis of The Pleiadian Agenda titled Alchemy of Nine Dimensions (published in 2004 and revised in 2010), a hard-core analysis of channeled information. In Awakening the Planetary Mind, I offer further thoughts about these mysterious Pleiadians, the great mystery because there is evidence they have influenced humans for at least 40,000 years.

Awakening the Planetary Mind reverses everything we've been taught until very recently in Earth sciences and archaeology, since the real story of time is coming back to us now. The great challenge is to integrate this knowledge through deep spiritual intention, which was the basis of my grandfather's approach, since to him our story is sacred. To accomplish this, this book is a selection of detail from great spiritual wisdom traditions that activate the *intelligence of the heart.* I call out for the return to the spiritual life, because scientific materialism is a limited and deathly approach to knowledge. The spiritual realms are lost in the materialistic premise when spirit's rightful influence wanes—*the Fall!*

This book is a distillation of huge data banks that trace the thread back to spiritualism by many great thinkers. Pages could have been wasted on debates over Darwinism, old-paradigm geology, and scientific materialism, but this book bypasses these arguments because it is based on a perfectly credible premise: *Consciousness creates the material world.*

The latest discoveries in cosmology, biology, geology, and psychology are considered from this spiritual perspective. Chapters 3 through 7 revise ancient history by means of some incredible data banks that awaken very repressed memories, some from more than 12,000 years ago. Science is the language of our times, so I cover new-paradigm science with a spiritual perspective that softens the endemic materialistic bias of scientific orthodoxy that is seriously eroding *human intelligence of the heart.*

In the early stages of writing, I intended to use the cycle of the Great Ages—the precession of the equinoxes—to explore human consciousness over the past 40,000 years. But no matter how hard I searched, *I could not find any evidence for precession before 11,500 years ago.* Voluminous evidence for the Great Ages influencing human cultures and symbolism begins about 10,000 years ago. Allan and Delair think Earth's axis must have tilted only 11,500 years ago, and they detail the tilt mechanics during the 9500 BC cataclysm. In my 2001 edition, I included the possibility that Earth's axis tilted during the cataclysm, and I have added strength to this hypothesis in this 2011 edition because suddenly many new-paradigm writers are also looking at this very real possibility. Adopting this point of view has made sense of some really strange material in little-understood Egyptian sources, which are obsessed with axial tilt. These arcane and archaic Egyptian sources make more sense to others now, which enabled me to clarify my own thinking on them. We seem to be facing up to the actual fact of recent damage to our solar system, as well as how these cataclysmic events affected Earth, which is of great interest to both astrologers and astronomers. Allan and Delair hypothesize that Chiron assumed its current orbit in 9500 BC. I first wrote about Chiron's astrological influence in 1987. I now explore Chiron's orbit and the tilting axis as influences that are causing our species to become more emotionally complex. I've been amazed by the astrological importance of this planet or planetoid on its elliptical orbit around the sun; Chiron is our guide for healing post-traumatic stress.

Lastly, I discovered Carl Johan Calleman's Mayan Calendar hypothesis in 2004, and I wrote a book about it that was published in 2007 entitled *The Mayan Code: Time Acceleration and Awakening the World*

Mind. Calleman's idea is of profound importance to evolutionary and Calendar research, and so I have added it briefly to this text. With no further ado, let us take our journey through the story of time.

BARBARA HAND CLOW

MARCH 9, 2011

VANCOUVER, BRITISH COLUMBIA

1

SEIZING THE CYCLES OF THE STARS

Some say he bid his Angels turne askance
The Poles of Earth twice ten degrees and more
From the Sun's Axle; they with labour push'd
Oblique the Centric Globe
. . . to bring in change
Of seasons to each Clime: else had the Spring
Perpetual smil'd on Earth with vernant Flours,
Equal in Days and Nights, except to those
Beyond the Polar Circles.

JOHN MILTON[1]

The Galactic Winter Solstice

As we enter the twenty-first century, Earth is being stirred by an extraordinary series of astronomical cycles. New winter light pierces the heart of the galaxy, as Earth awakens to a new level of evolutionary potential. Our solar system is moving out of the Orion Arm into a dark region of the Milky Way galaxy; Earth is precessing out of the Age of Pisces into the Age of Aquarius as Earth's North Celestial Pole moves to the star Polaris; and the intersection of the plane of our solar system and the plane of our galaxy is in conjunction with the winter solstice sun. During the 26,000-year-long precessional cycle, called the Great Year by the Greeks, this intersection line—the galactic axis—is closely aspected by the winter solstice sun

10

for twenty-five years, from 1987 to 2012. This galactic alignment—the *Galactic Winter Solstice*—occurs when we enter the Age of Aquarius and the prophetic Mayan Calendar ends. This heralds the transfiguration of our species.

This Galactic Winter Solstice can be thought of as a stellar mystery play: The curtain rose on Harmonic Convergence on August 16/17, 1987, an Earth celebration when millions of people meditated at sacred sites all over the world. The final act is during 2011/2012, the mysterious end date of the Mayan Calendar. Approaching 2012, it's as if there is a *strange time-attractor in the sky*. We feel this pull instinctively, as if we are caterpillars undergoing metamorphosis and becoming butterflies; we are time-coded by evolution to change into new forms. What are we becoming? I have turned to the primordial wisdom for answers, because it contains many stories about other times when critical evolutionary leaps occurred on Earth. However, now a collective malaise—*catastrophobia*—insidiously limits the potential of our species, which is the collective fear of the End Times. The real truth is, in the midst of our evolutionary creative leap, beliefs that we are coming to the end of life are simply wrong. The destruction of our species is not the meaning of the end of the mysterious Calendar of the Maya, not at all.

This book is a deep exploration of the past 100,000 years of human consciousness, seeking earlier times when the primordial wisdom came forth to lead us forward. This book is guided by my deep contemplation of Egyptology, which became the center of my intellectual journey when my grandfather introduced me to the Egyptian temple reliefs when I was five years old. Egyptology inspires the intellectual journeys of many seekers; it is the focus of much new-paradigm research in archaeoastronomy, geology, and archaeology. Many journeys in Egypt have helped me integrate my Cherokee/Celtic grandfather's legacy—Turtle Medicine—with Egyptology. Until recently, much of the information in this book was closely guarded knowledge. Now millions worldwide seek the primordial wisdom, so it is time to share my grandfather's revelations. Many seek a new story of archaic human history, because the latest information suggests that human ancient cultures were globally connected and advanced.

Our planet is littered with very old sites that evidence inexplicable lost technologies, such as Baalbek in Lebanon, Tiahuanaco in Peru, and the Giza Plateau of Egypt. What happened to the people who invented those technologies? The latest evidence suggests that a highly advanced civilization was literally shattered in a great cataclysm. Our previous attainments were lost and forgotten until now, and as we remember this loss, we are processing deep emotional trauma. The latest discoveries suggest that archaic people once enjoyed a marvelous global civilization.

One thing we know about our ancestors is that they were deeply involved with the stars; for them the cycles in the heavens mirror the cycles on Earth. Yet, what were they really watching for in the sky? What did they mean when they said the cycles above mirror the patterns below? According to my legacy and those of many indigenous traditions, the stage is set again in the sky for big evolutionary breakthroughs. This mystery play has actually already begun, and we are ready to seize its creative potential by playing our own roles. As with any drama, the sooner we put on our costumes and learn our lines, the better. In myths and sacred teachings, the story of this expected awakening was very protected until now. What is this story? According to my legacy and the teachings of many sages, the new energy coming to Earth from the Galactic Center informs us that *we are a wounded species afflicted with global collective fear.* As we heal this fear, we remember the cosmic knowledge, and then the galactic waves can activate our brains.

Evolution occurs by cyclical time, not by clock time, which was invented around 500 years ago. There are hidden and influential time cycles, such as the precession of the equinoxes and the cycles in the Mayan Calendar, that guide human metamorphic processes. My astronomical discussions are mostly geocentric—viewing the cosmos from Earth—so simply allow your inner eye to contemplate this perspective. For thousands of years, early humans understood the sky very well without the perspective of modern scientific astronomy. In those days, the stars were living data banks of archetypal stories—*stellar mythology.* Knowing stellar patterns and how star emanations influenced cultural patterns on Earth was important for ancient humanity. We are in the midst of a deep and wonderful changing right now because we've switched to raw instinct, which is opening our minds. This happens when great evolutionary shifts occur. For instance, just as the mysterious Mayan Calendar is ending, the renowned Swedish biologist Carl Johan Calleman discovered how the World Tree organizes the physical consciousness fields of Earth.[2] He has discovered the stages of evolution in the Calendar, which will be discussed in detail after first considering how the precession of the equinoxes is influencing our times.

Precession of the Equinoxes

Precession occurs because our axis is tilted—not vertical—as it travels around the sun. From our vantage point on Earth, as we orbit the sun, the sun "eclipses" the stars behind itself, which is why the circle around the sun is called the ecliptic. Precession occurs because as Earth orbits the sun, it turns on its axis tilted at an angle about 23.5 degrees from the true vertical, and it also wobbles. This results in a 26,000-year-long funnel motion that causes Earth's axis to trace an imaginary circle in the stars around the North and South Poles. If Earth's axis were vertical, the stars about the poles would circle eternally in the same places. Instead, the polar stars move like huge serpents, and on today's horizon, the locations of the stars move about 1 degree every seventy-two years.

Precession is usually observed by tracking the sun rising in specific zodiacal constellations at the spring equinox, the Vernal Point on the ecliptic. For example, during the spring equinox 10,800 to 8,640 years ago, the Vernal Point was in Cancer—the Age of Cancer—when the sun "rose" in Cancer in the spring.

In the year 2000, on the first day of spring, the sun rose in the overlapping edges of the Pisces and Aquarius constellations, so people talk of the coming Age of Aquarius. Astrologers and astronomers give dates from AD 2000 to 2800 for the end of the Age of Pisces and the beginning of the Age of Aquarius. Pinpointing the exact time of the transition from one age to the next is arbitrary, because it is difficult to say when one constellation ends and another begins on the ecliptic. The Pisces constellation is a huge spread between stars seen as two fish. Right now the Vernal Point

Precession of Axis

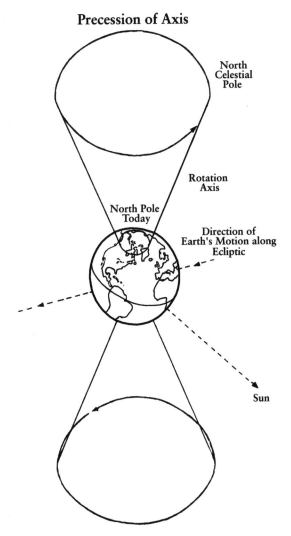

Fig. 1.1. The precession of the equinoxes

is near the end of the second fish of Pisces, but also *the Water Bearer is pouring water over the Vernal Point,* so the emotional nature of Aquarius is here now. Besides observing the Vernal Point in the constellations, the precessional influence is very clearly and simply described by the Platonic Great Year, a concept that was well defined by the early Greeks and exists in the Vedic scriptures. In the Great Year, the constellations are divided into twelve Great Ages or months that are each 2,160 years long. This is

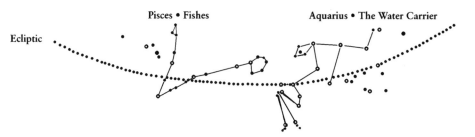

Fig. 1.2. Pisces and Aquarius on the ecliptic

a very useful tool because the division of the constellations is otherwise arbitrary if done on a visual basis. Constellations rising at the spring equinox gradually give way to the next ones, so where is the end or beginning? And how many constellations are there on or near the ecliptic? This is arbitrary, and thousands of years ago astronomers used fewer constellations, whereas the Maya divided the sky into thirteen.

In this book, I explore the possibility that precession began only 11,500 years ago, since before that some ancient texts suggest that the stars moved through the night skies in unchanging circles. This would be the correct description of the stars if there were little or no tilt of Earth's axis. I present evidence that humans began tracking precession's slow movement on the horizon only 8,000 to 10,000 years ago, when there is evidence for profound changes in cultures that may have been brought on by seasonality. Many others have suggested that precession is a *post*-cataclysmic phenomenon, so I'm going to use this possibility as a working hypothesis. (See appendix D for more scientific and anthropological data on axial tilt theory.)

Historians say that Hipparchus discovered precession around 2,300 years ago. However, Plato's Great Year and the Vedas describe precession, and they predate Hipparchus. Numerous modern scholars have concluded that Hipparchus used much earlier Babylonian data that was based on precession. In fact, precession has been tracked for many thousands of years; it was of immense importance to early human societies; and the discovery issue is actually an argument about the *mechanics of precession,* which is by no means scientifically certain because it is all a matter of perspective. For example, Walter Cruttenden of the Binary Research Institute notes that the precessional theory that is currently being used (and described herein) posits that precession is due to Earth completing a 360-degree wobble on its axis, meaning it is a movement of Earth, not the sun. Yet, Cruttenden notes, "The Ancients would tell us it just *seems* that way because the Sun (carrying the Earth with it) completed one orbit around a nearby star, meaning that it is mostly due to the movement of the Sun carrying the Earth on a journey through space, not Earth moving independent of the solar system."[3] I strongly suspect that Cruttenden is going to be proven right about precession, especially if astrophysicists sight the sun's probable binary star companion, but this is beyond the scope of this book.

My primary focus, whether the axis first tilted 11,500 years ago or not, is that *this was a time when a radical shift occurred in human cultures.* D. S. Allan and J. B. Delair's *Cataclysm! Compelling Evidence of a Cosmic Catastrophe in 9500 BC* offers convincing evidence that Earth's axis was pulled into its tilt by fragments of a supernova from the Vela star system that blasted into our solar system in 9500 BC.[4] According to these authors, before then Earth's axis was *vertical,* and we lived in the Golden Age. Many scholars have noted this distinctive shift in cultures 11,500 years ago when the Pleistocene epoch closed and the Holocene began. My working hypothesis is that the advent of precession in 9500 BC caused this cultural shift by fundamentally altering our experience of climate and time, and humanity was forced to adopt agriculture in response to the new seasonality. Regardless, it is virtually certain that a great cataclysm changed everything on Earth 11,500 years ago.

Archaeoastronomy

Archaeoastronomy, a relatively new division of anthropology, dates ancient human sites by star positions according to precessional analysis. Archaeoastronomers study how stone constructions at archaic sites align with the locations of stars at specific times in the precessional cycle, which enables them to date these structures. They cross-verify these dates with known history or other established dating systems, such as radiocarbon dating. They have established that the observable celestial effects of precession were being used to site temples by ancient astronomers at least 8,000 years ago; but archaic people probably did not understand the actual *mechanics* of precession.[5] New-paradigm researchers argue that these cultures were more advanced than was previously thought. For example, working with Egyptologist John Anthony West in 1991, the geologist Robert Schoch established that the Sphinx is *at least 7,000 years old,* and West believes it is probably much older.[6] And a researcher of ancient history, Edward F. Malkowski, has comprehensively examined the markings of granite machining processes that are far beyond the abilities of ancient Egyptians as described by Egyptology.[7] Beyond Schoch's analysis, if we consider precessional *symbolism,* which ancient people utilized, the Sphinx may be more than 11,000 years old. It has a lionlike body, and the lion is the symbol for the Age of Leo—10,960 to 8800 BC. No matter what new evidence is offered to them, most archaeologists simply insist the Sphinx is 5,000 years old, and their credibility with the public has been steadily dropping.

Ironically, the Sphinx is a great example of an artifact that is more accurately dated by geology and archaeoastronomy, but archaeologists just go on assuming it is the same age they offer for the Giza pyramids. The

Fig. 1.3. The Great Sphinx on the Giza Plateau

Valley Temple below the Sphinx is constructed very differently than the Sphinx, the pyramids, or other temples built during the early dynasties 2500 to 3300 BC. Both the Sphinx and the Valley Temple may be older, venerated monuments that determined the sitings of the later pyramids, and everything on the Giza Plateau may have been built over even more ancient buried constructions. Meanwhile, the refusal by archaeologists to reconsider these dating issues is very suspicious, since Egyptian esoteric science is the basis of Masonic rituals, and the Great Pyramid is plastered on the American dollar. By refusing to integrate recent scientific challenges, Egyptologists are discredited or accused of sinister cover-ups, such as being part of Elite power games. Such possibilities will be dealt with later in this book. For now, my focus is crafting a new story of time.

The Sphinx is the central enigma. Most people who see it crouching on the Giza Plateau sense it is the key to the ancient records, as if the ancient Egyptians created the Sphinx just so we'd keep asking questions about our past; so we are! I suggest that after the great cataclysm 11,500 years ago, suddenly the lionlike Leo constellation was rising at the new Vernal Point on the Giza Plateau. This would have been an amazing sight to the ancient stargazers, a veritable revolution in the heavens! This makes the Sphinx the ideal symbol for the cataclysmic Age of Leo. J. B. Delair recently noted that hundreds of winged sphinxes from Sumerian and Egyptian through Roman times have lionlike bodies with women's heads. They represented "one of the lethal destructive 'dragons of chaos' accompanying Phaeton/ Marduk," the agency of the great cataclysm.[8] The Sphinx reminds us of the

Fig. 1.4. Sekhmet

disaster as well as the long cycles of time. The fact that sphinxes so often have female heads is compelling, since the Egyptian lion-goddess, Sekhmet, is the force that brings chaos to Earth when humans are out of balance.

Proceeding with the axial-tilt hypothesis, if precession began 11,500 years ago and the Sphinx was carved as long ago as 11,000 years, then the insights of Robert Bauval and Adrian Gilbert in *The Orion Mystery,* who describe the Giza Plateau as a starclock, are very close to mine, even though my dating differs slightly.[9] Schoch's new geological dating and Bauval and Gilbert's Orion hypothesis offer a strong case for driving back the dates for the site plan of the Giza Plateau. Bauval's Orion correlation—the pyramids by the Nile mirror the Orion star system by the galactic plane—is very important because it correlates the Pyramid Texts with the Giza Plateau structures. This connection greatly deepened my own understanding of Egyptology, and I hope I can add a few insights to the exciting work at Giza.

Using precessional *symbolism* in conjunction with precise astronomical alignments gives much information about extremely archaic monuments. This is because key symbols express the qualities of each Great Age; for example, the bull for the Age of Taurus—4480 to 2320 BC—was the central symbol for temple/city cultures such as the Minoans, Egyptians, and Indians during that age. By knowing the dates of the Great Ages and their main symbols, which existed in ancient cultures all over the world, we can see how symbols have directed cultures. There is much evidence that people have been greatly influenced by these changing archetypes expressed by symbolism for at least 10,000 years. *We are the ones who have forgotten how precessional symbolism influences cultures.* "For everything there is a season."

The Platonic Great Year

The visual division between one constellation and the next on the ecliptic is arbitrary, so to describe the long precessional cycles, the neo-Platonic Greeks devised the Platonic Great Year of twelve months and four seasons. This helps us consider long phases of time. Many people thought of time in this way until 2,000 years ago. In the Platonic Year, one "month" is 2,160 years, and one "season" is 6,480 years. The "Year" thus totals about 26,000 years. A key question is *where* does the 26,000-year-long Great Year begin? If the axis tilted 11,500 years ago, then that is when the Platonic Great Year began, but that still does not identify the beginning and end of this cycle. As you will see, it has been possible to answer this question only recently by knowing about the orientation of our solar system in the galaxy. Now we can see that *the current alignment of the winter solstice sun to the galactic axis is the opening of the whole Great Year.*[10] This means the whole cycle begins with the Age of Aquarius (as well as the completion of the Mayan Calendar), so then the four seasons of the Great Year begin with the fixed signs—Aquarius, Taurus, Leo, and Scorpio. This model totally synchronizes with astrology, which posits that the fixed signs are where energy *culminates.*

Poised to enter the Age of Aquarius, we can test this model by looking into what happened during the opening of the *previous season,* the Age of Taurus, since the Vernal Point moves *backward* on the ecliptic, as illustrated. This "season" would have been a previous phase when major cultural patterns flowered. In fact, around 4480 BC the Taurus constellation rose at the spring equinox and opened a whole new Great Age. Early groups, who later developed theocratic city cultures, appeared, such

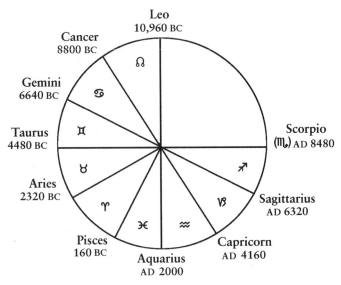

Fig. 1.5. The Platonic Great Year

as the Sumerians, Egyptians, and Vedic Indians. A monumental shift in human culture began. Then, around 3500 BC, highly advanced civilizations flowered with the bull as the central symbol. This "season" was when cities developed. According to the Platonic Great Year, a 6,480-year season is more foundational than the subsequent two 2,160-year ages, when the central issue of the fixed age matures. For example, during the Age of Aries—2320 to 160 BC—wars between the city cultures were the main theme. During the Age of Pisces, the main theme has been to find ways to handle the emotional implications of city cultures. Of course, the beginning of the whole 26,000-year wheel, which we are experiencing now, is the *most* foundational.

The Galactic Winter Solstice—1987 to 2012—is the turning point of the whole Great Year: The winter solstice at 0 degrees Capricorn points closely to the Galactic Center at 27 degrees Sagittarius, which means that this influence is cosmic. Macrobiologist Michio Kushi, who also believes that Earth's axis shifted about 12,000 years ago, says about this phenomenon, "When the earth's axis points directly through the Milky Way we receive much more energy radiation than we do when the earth's axis points away from the Milky Way."[11] *The Great Year describes how the Galactic Center influences Earth.* I then ask, where is the sun in the galaxy itself? Our solar system takes 200 to 250 million years to orbit the Galactic Center. The sun is our source of solar radiation (our biological fuel), and the Galactic Center is our source of cosmic radiation (our spiritual fuel). Our current awakening is spiritual because of the alignment of the galactic axis to the center of the galaxy. This awakening is also biological, since reptiles appeared on Earth approximately 200 to 250 million years ago, the same location of our solar system in its orbit around the Galactic Center. Something truly momentous is going on.

According to galactic astrophysics, this cyclical shift is an astronomical fact; however, what does it mean? My previous book, *The Pleiadian Agenda: A New Cosmology for the Age of Light,* contains some of the answers. In 1994 my brain was blasted open by nonphysical beings from the Pleiadian star system, and I "channeled" their information. Now, I think that this classic mystical breakthrough must have been triggered by the building galactic alignment, which I knew nothing about at the time. This kind of reception has often been the source of the perennial wisdom, yet conscious evaluation of it often deepens and even verifies such purely intuitional insights. As I've struggled to comprehend this new cosmology, galactic astronomy has been a great challenge. Regarding the Pleiades as a source for perennial wisdom, the Parthenon on the Acropolis in Athens was oriented to the Pleiades rising in 1150 BC. In ancient lore, the Pleiades are associated with the goddesses of wisdom—Athena of Greece and Neith of Egypt—so the reemergence of the feminine is a central theme in this book. The Pleiades are part of our local galaxy, so perhaps the Galactic Winter Solstice alignment makes it easier for us to receive information from stellar realms in general. The influence from the Pleiades may be the ultimate source for the Platonic Great Year, which was initially called the Great Year of the Pleiades.[12]

Fig. 1.6. Observing the Milky Way River of Stars

A direct way to access these ideas is to visualize the beautiful stellar geometry that forms in the skies and follow the cycles of the stars and planets. For this book, it's not really necessary to understand celestial mechanics heliocentrically. After all, we live on Earth and look at everything from our perspective. For thousands of years people studied the patterns in the sky without using celestial mechanics. Ancient people were very much in touch with Earth by viewing the sky patterns in relation to monuments or topographic features located in their personal bioregions. The Galactic Winter Solstice can be felt by contemplating the River of Stars—the edge of the Milky Way—which has a shamanic effect. As you observe the edge of the galaxy shining in the dark night sky, the galactic plane and the ecliptic cross at a near-60-degree angle, forming a *sextile*—the perfect harmonic. When you attune to these cycles, you may find yourself having mystical visions that carry you into other dimensions. Contemplation of time and cycles is a psychedelic experience without needing drugs, which is how I get high. We are going to explore the archaic mind experientially in this book, because that is how I've been able to enter it myself. It is important to consider that if the Great Ages first began only 11,500 years ago, then we are only just beginning to get used to this new orientation. When you look for it, the influence of the Great Ages on human experience is very apparent for the last 10,000 years.

There is irrefutable evidence of a global maritime civilization from before the great cataclysm. Just like today, many people preferred living by the sea. For thousands of years after the disaster, the seas were rising, and we suffered great climatic, geophysical, and social instability. World civilization became possible again only during the Age of Taurus. After the cataclysm, the Age of Leo was a partial age when *humans began their first experience with an altered sky and landscape*. As is widely reported in mythology, sages as gods assumed authority amid chaos, and they assisted the survivors. Due to the desperate conditions on Earth, sages emerged to lead the traumatized people, and their royal symbol was and still is the lion. Then during the Age of Cancer—8800 to 6640 BC—the moon is the main symbol. The goddess was venerated because birthing was ruled by lunar phases, and humans needed to repopulate Earth. The Mother

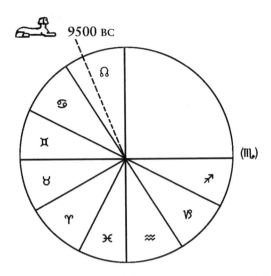

Fig. 1.7. The beginning of the Great Ages in 9500 BC

Goddess is one of the earliest primordial archetypes in the human psyche; it seems to recede back into the darkness of time and triggers memories of our birthing by monthly cycles of blood. After this age ended, in the middle of the Age of Gemini—6640 to 4480 BC—a great flood in the Black Sea region killed many people, and the struggling survivors migrated to other lands.[13] The Age of Cancer balanced the power of woman with the gods and sages of the Age of Leo. Winged sphinxes with lion bodies and the heads of women combined the symbology of both these ages, and then when the Age of Gemini began, cultures began exploring the meaning of time. Sages such as Zarathustra appeared.

Individuation by Celestial Archetypal Forces

We are ready to become conscious of how we have been individuating through the cycles and symbols of the Great Ages, the archetypes that inspire culture. These archetypes, which exist in the *collective unconscious,* as described by C. G. Jung and within *racial memory,* as described by Sigmund Freud, contain the memory of all human experience. We have arrived at a unique point: Many people are now realizing that they have been inspired by and also manipulated by archetypes, such as the emphasis on Christianity's cross during the Age of Pisces, instead of the subtlety of two opposing fishes. We are *collectively questioning how we humans affect Earth,* and I don't think most people considered this until recently. The more perspective we can get on this the better, since the collective unconscious is time-coded to respond by cycles. There is no reason that we cannot fully understand how we are changing Earth, especially since Aquarius is to be the age of enlightenment.

The story of the evolution of consciousness is wonderful: During the Age of Leo, we separated our identities into gods and humans. During the Age of Cancer, we discovered that Earth's women are the goddesses of eternal birthing with their consorts. During the Age of Gemini, we became fascinated with order and time. During the Age of Taurus, we organized ourselves in cities. During the Age of Aries, we fought for control over these cities and temples. And during the Age of Pisces, we sought connection with spiritual realms to heal our species. While we lived these experiences, we worshiped gods while being controlled by their representatives. As we went through these phases, each agenda was piled on the agenda of the next age, so now *our collective consciousness is like a layer cake.* Consider this: We rolled into the Age of Taurus imbued with our experiences with god-kings, the Mother Goddess, and the great Gemini sages, and then during Taurus this rich archetypal pool was deposited as a matrix in the great temples in the centers of commercial city cultures. Once the cities grew, they were like great organisms fed by the surrounding fields in which the farmers toiled. Then, during the Arian Age, the cities warred with one another while the country people stayed out of the way as best they could. Finally, the people suffered and became empathic during the Piscean Age; they became mystified by their emotions.

Just as the sacred king, goddess, and sage archetypes rolled into the Age of Taurus, now as we roll into the Age of Aquarius, will we bring along war, suffering, and emotional obsessions into cyberspace? The fate of Earth encourages us to question ourselves, since religions claim that God said we are the stewards of our planet. We go about our daily lives assuming that everything will go on as it always has, yet few people believe this, and they nervously mark time. *During great seasonal shifts, passivity is lethal.* To survive during rapid and chaotic change, we must invent new ways of living that will sustain the new reality that is emerging. Furthermore, we must recover our precatastrophic ability to harmonize with Earth, an ability we've been gradually losing since 9500 BC. Michio Kushi says that with the new galactic orientation, our mental images will begin to synchronize: "We think in terms of the whole planet united in a time of peace, creativity and harmony by the descending (centripetal) energy which formed the galaxy, the solar system, and this earth."[14]

For thousands of years, we lived more in darkness. The night sky was a fluid movie—star lore—that revealed our individual roles in the mythical story of Earth; it was the library of our thoughts. *The tilting axis has been causing us to discover ourselves in a field of great mythological dualities that have radically complicated our sense of self.* Various spiral patterns, such as the dramatic rise and fall of the Orion star system and the undulating north polar serpent, Draco—brought on, perhaps, by the recent phenomenon of axial tilt—inspired great myths about sages, kings, mother goddesses, and family sagas. Luckily the Egyptians and other cultures, which understood sacred science, saved the stories of the stellar library. Ancient cultures *used storytelling to communicate the legends of the gods and great sages.* These memories exist eternally in the star libraries, and now the nectar from the Galactic Center incites us to remember our connections with ancient wisdom. For thousands of years before the Age of Reason, the subtle realms unfolded in a vast drama that played out in the skies. We had a personal relationship with these worlds in the Dreamtime, and these contacts are recorded in temple reliefs, in sacred art, and in mythology all over the planet.

Access to the star libraries was severed in AD 221, when the Synodic Vernal Point was fixed at 0 degrees Aries, since the constellations move by precession from Earth's perspective. This needs to be noted here, because this fixing distorted geocentric viewing, and astrologers can't easily use the stars to locate planets in the sky. By losing the visual connection with the stars as a backdrop for planetary locations, human alienation has become progressively more profound. The planets rule primary psychology, so mental processes are more emphasized without the backdrop of stellar influence. This *astral alienation* has enabled us to observe and reflect on our own behavior, so now we see a resurgence of astrology. By mastering psychology first, we rather easily comprehend the planetary influences in our lives. Yet, for thousands of years humans experienced the planets located by the star background as archetypal forces—as well as psychological forces—that influence behavior. According to astrology, the planets exemplify the structural nature of our inner feelings. For example, Mars reflects our ability to use power, and Venus reflects our ability to express love and devotion. The planets mirror our own ecstasy and pain back to us, which makes it easier to recognize what is going on inside ourselves in relation to events outside ourselves. We now know that we do not act alone in this world. The planets motivate us to evolve and understand our real purposes in life amid the collective passions of humanity. The temporary alienation from the stars has brought a new facet of human awareness into being—*self-reflective consciousness.*

As the Age of Pisces closes, a keen awareness of astrology may be a good tool for moving beyond war and suffering. Mars rules war and the personal mastery of power. Neptune, which rules the Age of Pisces, rules suffering and personal mastery by compassion. With awareness, many can choose their own personal power to become radically compassionate, and then they won't be nailed to the cross as soldiers. The laws of astrology are based on the concept that the larger realm (macrocosm) mirrors our inner experience (microcosm). As already shown, the macrocosm is priming us to transfigure so that we might become enlightened in the microcosm. Understanding our urges by planetary archetypes helps us objectify the personal morass we live in. Stellar separation during the Age of Pisces has enabled us to see how much we are influenced by psychological patterns, yet *we feel the disconnected stellar archetypal powers.* Many wonder if puppeteers pull our puppet strings. Yes, they do, and I think they manipulate humanity by means of stellar archetypal powers.

Many sense that we must identify these controllers, lest we seek "aliens" out there, simply because we are alienated within. I suggest "control" instead of "influence," because the cycles of the planets *do* control those who are unaware of their influence. As we've seen, precessional cycles inspire cultural processes. These cycles are great control tools of the powers-that-be, the Elite. I've watched the planets influencing collective humanity, and I'm sure the Elite controllers use planetary patterns to create events. Their stated agenda is to bring in the New World Order, which is a cover label for the Age of Aquarius. As you will read later, manipulation by cycles *is* how cultures are controlled, and the mysterious Mayan Calendar is part of this grand story. Let's move back in time to find this record.

Cataclysmic Theory

The new-paradigm descriptions of the past 15,000 years support the timeline of this book. Moving back a few hundred years, we were torn out of simple village life by the Industrial Revolution, and science came forth to describe human history. Previously, history had been the preserve of theologians, who pondered the cataclysms and the Flood in the Bible, and they said Earth was created about 6,000 years ago. Meanwhile, science was proving that Earth is billions of years old. The newly emerging sciences invented a theory for Earth's evolution called *uniformitarianism*—geological and biological change is very slow and gradual. Now, science has shifted to *catastrophism*—periodic instantaneous geological and biological cataclysms occur in between long periods of slow change. Next, by means of a global data *convergence* during the 1990s, we know that Earth was nearly destroyed only 11,500 years ago. Thus, with the new millennium, galactic alignments are stretching our minds way out into the universe, just when many people are flooded with memories of previous advanced cultures and their horrific destructions. This is happening as the theocratic city cultures of the last 5,000 years are breaking down and industrial civilization is ending. Cataclysmic science, with its media soapbox system, is stirring up a potent stew of traumatic memories. For example, the film *Deep Impact* depicts an asteroid hitting Earth and turning the crust into Jell-O. This triggered great unease, and viewers feared something terrible was coming soon. The public feared the Y2K technology crash, while Microsoft made billions. Now the Global Elite scientists want to scare the public into paying for a weapons system that will shoot asteroids out of the sky so that they can rule space.

Many people have become keenly aware of the control systems that operate through schools, banks, governments, and even museums—the Elite. Humanity is being led down a road that few people want to travel, and people move passively along, not realizing that they are powerless only because of their unresolved fear. *The disaster is the past, not the future.* The disasters discussed in this book were not described by science until very recently. Most people have been deeply troubled by free-floating anxiety about the sky falling; they literally feel an apocalypse is coming soon. Well, the sky *did* fall within recent memory, and then the recovery period from 9000 to 1500 BC was filled with periodic upheavals. These fearful memories will lurk in our subconscious minds. *We are a wounded species on the verge of recovery, and we're poised to undertake the brave journey back to our previous brilliance.* We will cease cowering before the Elite and remember how to use our personal power.

In 1994 twenty-two fragments of the comet Shoemaker/Levy slammed into the viscous surface of Jupiter, which people watched on television. This media event awakened memories of a time when similar monsters in the sky pummeled Earth. Many reported they felt awe, dread, and sadness for Jupiter when they watched the impacts. Like adults who have unrecalled childhood abuse or trauma, we are deeply fearful, paranoid, and easily drawn into collective fear. Religious fanatics, who intuitively know how to activate our inner fear complexes, use them to manipulate us. Some of them truly believe the world is coming to an end, so they'd rather convince us we should end it all right now. *This is a collective insanity that could destroy human civilization.*

Cataclysms *did* cause the Late Pleistocene extinctions, when woolly mammoths, saber-toothed tigers, and many other species and human clans were decimated.[15] This massive wave of death lies deeply buried in our psyches. Cities have become huge economic machines fueled by people who desire material comfort at any cost. The fear of scarcity drove us to invent agriculture, and now we connect to each other in cyberspace. Previously we *aligned* with nature as hunter-gatherers and horticulturalists. What has been accomplished materially since 9500 BC is amazing.

We have proved that we can create almost anything, yet why are we so worried about the future? *We fear potential scarcity during this time of awesome plenty.* Anthropologists have demonstrated that cultures that retained their stories of origin do not want, need, care for, or use so many things. In comparison to modern Western culture, people in indigenous cultures often enjoy plenty of nonworking time. In our civilized, technological world of nanoseconds, we are all smothered in gadgets, and we are all linked up and work constantly. What's next? I think we are on the threshold of a massive *dematerialization* after becoming more dense and material for 11,500 years, and I believe this will be the central theme of the Age of Aquarius. Yet *how* can we do this?

Generational Change and Dematerialization

How could we lighten up and do things differently? Seeking answers to this question, I've been hanging out with younger people, because they exhibit emerging characteristics of the new world to come. They will raise their families in the new times, and what they are thinking about offers some clues about where we're headed amid the dizzying changes. Many people who were born since 1965 seek ways to live in a less material world. They know this is the only possible next step, since Earth can't sustain the current level of technological overload. Meanwhile, based on precessional laws, we will be less materialistic in the next cycle as we remember how to align with Earth's forces instead of callously *using* Earth. The remnants of cultures that have retained simple ways of life are suddenly being rediscovered and valued as critical resources, such as the precataclysmic cultures of the Australian Aborigines.

Precataclysmic cultures were using currently unknown technology, and nobody has figured out how they cut and moved huge stones. One of the best examples of this technology is the Osireion in Egypt, which has precisely cut and placed stones that weigh hundreds of tons. These are called cyclopean stones, because they seem to have been forged by giants. Their forgotten builders must have known how to work in alignment with Earth's forces, and there must be ways to recover these forgotten

Fig. 1.8. The Osireion of Abydos

skills. For example, the anthropologist Felicitas Goodman discovered how people in shamanic cultures gathered information to solve their problems for thousands of years. They went into trance while assuming very specific postures that helped them access spirits in the alternate reality for advice.[16] The alternate reality is a world that coexists with ordinary reality that contains shamanic wisdom and powers. We can visit it to recover archaic methods, healing techniques, and even lost technologies. Maybe the spirits could explain how the Great Pyramid and Osireion were constructed? I will report extensively on my work with Dr. Goodman throughout this book.

The most painful situation in this last stage of materialization is health and wellness. Many people, even many young people, are very ill in the midst of the rapid changing. It is good news that the Age of Aquarius promises to rejuvenate our bodies. The ruling planet of Aquarius is Uranus, which activates *kundalini energy,* the power that acupuncturists and healers stimulate and spiritual teachers awaken. In striking contrast to those who use solely alternative wellness, those who depend on materialistic medicine are plagued by chronic disease. They are *nailed on the medical cross* as the suffering Age of Pisces closes. Newtonian physics has caused people to think of their bodies as machines that periodically need new parts. The health of people in modern Western countries has deteriorated; their kundalini energy is weak, and they are losing their life force and genetic integrity. Chemical and nuclear medicine toxify the environment and people's bodies, and we need the vibrational repatterning that comes with strong kundalini energy flow. Individuals with awakened kundalini are very psychic and energized. As the Aquarian influence builds, many people are seeking healing methods that enhance kundalini flow to reduce this wave of chronic disease. For thousands of years before Western medicine, enhanced kundalini energy was used to revitalize people, and these medicines are legacies from even *before* the great cataclysm.

Growing up after the Second World War in Michigan, I watched the ecosystems around my childhood home deteriorate when American culture was in decline. According to my grandparents, these destructive traits were taking over because the people had totally forgotten their origins. My parents' generation—born between 1910 and 1930—did not think in terms of meaningful origins. They had lost hope in the future because they were disheartened by the Great Depression and living through two world wars. They were convinced they had only one life to live, possibly the most lethal Christian dogma. What a life! This life was their *only* life, and it was battered by global and economic trauma. For them, Earth was a torture chamber. The term *Great Depression* caught on because it describes the psychological condition of a generation.

Grandfather said the darkest hours on Earth during the past 10,000 years were during the Second World War when the climb to enlightenment also began. My parents' generation believed their one life was all they had to live, so they frantically pursued security. Meanwhile their children—born between 1940 and 1960—watched Earth dying. Herded like sheep into concrete "shelters" during nuclear alerts and taken to the doctor to be inoculated with traces of disease, the children concluded the plan was to kill them. They knew there was something very wrong with the radioactive mushroom clouds exploding on the television screens. In light of such a limited future, these "war babies" dedicated themselves to facing and healing their own emotional scars to avoid passing on negativity to their own children. These children—born during the 1960s and '70s—are assuming roles in the world, and many of them possess great emotional strength.

Turtle Medicine

In the midst of the awesome death of life and culture after the Second World War, my grandparents' greatest gift was an unshakable vision of the future that protected me from the depressed attitude of my parents. Still in touch with their own origins and marvelously educated in Egyptology and other ancient cultures, they knew the great awakening would come after they were gone. They knew my father would not live to see it happen, so they passed their legacies to me. Together we studied Plato and other classical sources, Egyptology, and Cherokee and Celtic stories. My Celtic grandmother taught me how to see the nature spirits in her garden and the wee spirits in the house, and my Cherokee/Celtic grandfather taught me how to hear the sounds of the stars in the wetlands, to see the spirits (Little People) in the forest, and to read the messages from animals and insects, the numinous Earth. They shared their knowledge of the long time cycles, and they taught me how to work with the Ancestors—unseen teachers who are symbiotic with Earth and who commune with all receptive humans. In this book, the Ancestors are also called the Elders, and sages are humans who work with the Ancestors and Elders. As a result of studying with Felicitas Goodman, I believe sages are humans who work *consciously* with the Elders and Ancestors who inhabit the alternate reality. In my grandparents' home, modern culture was not thought of as enlightened or superior in any way. Instead, they explained that *we are the descendants of an advanced culture that disappeared in a day.* Plato saved the record of these days before the Flood, and my grandfather began directing my study of Plato when I was eight years old. These long cycles of time are in the Celtic myths, which my grandmother still remembered. This is their legacy—Turtle Medicine.

Turtle Medicine is about Earth changes. Earth's surface is made of twenty great plates, just as Turtle's back is the skirt of twenty plates around thirteen central plates. Sometimes the plates move when Turtle walks, as do Earth's plates while we live on the surface influenced by the bodies in the heavens. The three stars in Orion's belt are Turtle's spine and the four outer stars—Saiph, Rigel, Betelguese, and Bellatrix—are Turtle's feet. We are happy on Earth when we contemplate these correspondences, which open pathways that connect us with our spiritual vehicles, the stars. *The stars are the home of our souls.* Turtle's back is the home of our body—Earth—where I am assisted by the Cherokee Little People. Grandmother introduced me to the wee folks, who would always be around to tell us where to go if the sea were to rise and the land submerged. They taught me to trust Earth and her subtle realms, and to realize that whether we are in or out of body really doesn't matter much. But if we cling to life too much, we get stuck in our material form. These subtle realms support everything that is material, yet they are invisible to us if we do not believe in them and trust Earth. My grandparents were symbiotic with these other worlds, and so they are still with me now. Their house was filled with allies who still live with me today. Turtle Medicine means you exist intentionally and consciously in many worlds while you're alive; then life is never boring, and there is no desire to make it more than it is. Grandfather also was a Mason who had attained a very high degree, which may be why he loved Egyptology. He helped me develop a living relationship with my *ba,* my body of consciousness that lives in the stars.

Fig. 1.9. Turtle Medicine

We *all* need to recover our connection with the stars, because we cannot exist on Earth if we conceive of ourselves as unloved creatures born to suffer through one life, and then just die at the whim of avenging gods. Mayan teachings are very similar to Cherokee knowledge, especially regarding Turtle Medicine, and the Mayan legacy is their calendars. Mayan calendars are weavings of thirteen days and twenty glyphs or modalities, and the longer calendar works with thirteen Days and Nights that accelerate by factors of twenty. Hunbatz Men of the Yucatán and Don Alejandro Oxlac of Guatemala graciously opened these teachings to me as an adult, when I was delighted to see how interconnected all the indigenous teachings are. The science of the twenty great plates that float in Earth's mantle is *plate tectonics,* and Turtle Medicine explores how these modalities create change. The indigenous Maya have retained the knowledge of the Day Calendar, which describes our personal unfolding day by day, but they lost the meaning of the *tun-based* Calendar, hereinafter capitalized as the Mayan Calendar. This Calendar, which was found on a stele at Coba, describes cycles of time over *16.4 billion years;* it was very recently recovered by Carl Johan Calleman. The ancient Maya knew this moment in time would be very important, so we will consider what Calleman has found in the complete Mayan Calendar. This is a very brief summary of a very complex idea, so curious readers should consult Calleman's books or mine on the Mayan Calendar.[17]

The Mayan Calendar and Time Acceleration

According to Calleman, the Mayan Calendar describes Nine Underworlds of Creation that began 16.4 billion years ago, and all nine complete simultaneously on October 28, 2011. The length of each Underworld is twenty times shorter than the previous one, which has caused time to accelerate twenty times faster in nine increments. These *time accelerations* kicked in whenever the previous Underworld attained a division of itself by twenty, which is a great mystery because the stages of these accelerations match up very closely with critical evolutionary stages. For example, 820 million years is 1/20 of 16.4 billion years. The First Underworld of 16.4 billion years represents first creation (maybe the Big Bang), and the Second Underworld of 820 million years is the evolution of mammals. Each one of these Underworlds develops through thirteen equal stages (Heavens) that seed, grow, and mature each theme. For example, if you divide 820 million years by 13, you get 13 *alautuns* (Heavens) that are each 63 million years long. The most recent evolutionary leap was 63 million years ago when dinosaurs went extinct, which made space for mammals to evolve, the maturation phase of the Second Underworld.[18]

Calleman's idea is mind boggling, and Elite science has so far greeted

Fig. 1.10. The Nine Underworlds of Creation. Based on Calleman, The Mayan Calendar and the Transformation of Consciousness.

him with utter silence, even though he is a respected biologist. Even when their own research later matched what Calleman had found in the Calendar, they ignored Calleman's findings. For example, in March 2005, physicists Richard Miller and Robert Rohde announced they'd found 62-million-year-long cycles of extinction since 542 million years ago in the "Compendium of Fossil Marine Genera" that happen to correspond almost exactly with Calleman's 63-million-year-long alautuns during the Second Underworld.[19] Calleman was the first to detect and describe this cycle in detail; however, his e-mails to Miller and Rhode after he sent a copy of his book went unanswered. The hard facts are, the dates for the Nine Underworlds and the divisions by thirteen Heavens were carved on a stele at Coba around AD 750—Coba Stele 1—and they closely describe biological cycles that science was able to catalog only in the last 100 years! The progressive phases of evolution, such a mammals, hominids, and cultural stages, kicked into gear exactly when the next time acceleration in the Calendar occurred, and the Maya figured all this out at least 2,000 years ago!

This wild idea is easier to comprehend if we go forward to the time phase this book covers—the last 102,000 years—which is the Fifth Underworld, the Regional Underworld. This is when we find humans that resemble us, because they've discovered art and the soul—the Neanderthals, who buried their loved ones with red ochre and held rituals in ceremonial caves. Then in 3115 BC, the Sixth Underworld began, and suddenly we see the simultaneous rise of civilization all over the world, an acceleration that moved us totally out of the Regional mind, the part of us that longs for Eden. The great cataclysms happened during the Regional Underworld before the advent of civilization, events that also distanced us from Eden. The Seventh Underworld began in AD 1755 when industry went into gear all over the planet, and we were wrenched out of simple country and village life. The feelings from these accelerations linger in our bodyminds, and I've found that Calleman's interpretation of these evolutionary stages is healing and empowering. *This is not about the past; it is about how far we've come.* The Eighth Underworld began in January 1999, when we were suddenly accelerated by technology. You will remember the intensity of that acceleration if you recall what 1999 felt like when people were sucked into the Internet and started using cell phones. Incredibly, the Ninth Underworld unfolds during less than one year in 2011, when our species is evolving again twenty times faster. Some might think this book published in 2011 is dated, yet I rewrote it to offer more perspective on what's happening to us right now. Remembering our story is the path to wholeness, and seeing our long climb from single-celled animals to complex modern humankind is the essence of our journey.

After the 9500 BC cataclysm, which indigenous people all over the world reported accurately, we peered into the haze of the destroyed world and saw the faces and bodies of leaders who'd assumed authority, and we believed they were gods. They said that they would punish us unless we worshiped the gods correctly, so we made sacrifices to them. Banished from the primordial garden by an avenging deity, we became a traumatized species. By this fall from grace, we lost the ability to feel nature and to see the spirits. We were profoundly lonely, and the skies had changed. During the long years of survival under an altered sky, we adopted agriculture to harness nature, which separated us from Earth. This occurred during the Fifth Underworld. For more detail about how the cataclysms fit into the cycles of the Mayan Calendar, see appendix E. Thousands of years would pass before we could wake up, while Earth bided her time. Earth knew a potent cosmic infusion of energy from the stars would cause us to begin to vibrate with nature again, and we are. The Ninth Underworld during 2011 rips open the full vibrational response to nature, so our unresolved inner traumas are arising like great monsters in our hearts and minds.

Like gossamer tendrils of silicate light, new waves come from deep space as gamma rays, which trigger massive increases of photons that incite chaos and change. *During such intense change, you can avoid energy depletion by detecting the qualities of the new wave and participating in it.* We can activate our energy bodies and center that force in our *hearts*. We can be less material and more emotional, which is where technology is leading us if we use it as a tool to get what we want. To get there, we are becoming self-reflective and opening our hearts, which is exposing our hidden fears. Unprocessed trauma has limited our creativity, which will return if we see how it binds our emotions and separates us from love.

2

THE GREAT CATACLYSM AND THE FALL

Precession took on an overpowering significance. It became the vast impenetrable pattern of fate itself, with one world-age succeeding another, as the invisible pointer of the equinox slid along the signs, each age bringing with it the rise and downfall of astral configurations and rulerships, with their earthly consequences.

HERTHA VON DECHEND AND GIORGIO DE SANTILLANA[1]

Hamlet's Mill and the Precession of the Equinoxes

The precession of the equinoxes is an astronomical cycle that shapes the timing and qualities of cultural patterns by symbols, as introduced in chapter 1. This chapter investigates how this subtle symbolic force influences human cultures and how the great cataclysm fits into this process. Each Great Age is represented by a symbol that is derived from a constellation located on the ecliptic. For example, the symbol for the Piscean Age, when Christianity was founded, was the fish, and the Pisces constellation is drawn as two interweaving fishes. These symbols go far back into prehistory and still leave their traces today.

How might this symbolic weaving still influence us and even direct our lives? Even today, indigenous people are usually members of clans that have animal totems, which is intriguing, since the zodiac is a circle of animals plus a few human images in the sky. The zodiac consists of the constellations on the ecliptic—twelve out of eighty-eight constellations—and all eighty-eight star systems were thought of as spiritual influences. I am sure that the animal totems are vestiges of precessional knowledge, just as modern bullfights are lingering vestiges of the Age of Taurus, the bull. Besides the wonderful creative potential in these connections, does this subtle factor still direct the collective unconscious? If so, did the ancient people use these powers intentionally, and how can we? Judging by the amount of work they put into building and maintaining their temples to showcase these symbols, we would be foolish *not* to consider whether the precessional factor actually affects us now. At the very least, we can understand the past better by understanding what these symbols meant to people in the past. Then it would be apparent whether precessional cycles may now influence human cultures, even if they are not consciously aware of the moving circle in the sky. What if secret societies, such as the Masons, know all about these influences and noninitiated modern people are ignorant of them?

Traces of precessional influence are found in sacred scripture and mythology, which were passed down in the oral tradition for thousands of years and then were eventually written down. *Hamlet's Mill: An Essay on Myth and the Frame of Time* by famed scholars Hertha Von Dechend and Giorgio de Santillana is the consumate study of mythology by precession. The authors determine that archaic mythology and art cannot be fathomed without understanding its underlying complex celestial basis—precession of the equinoxes—and I agree. *Hamlet's Mill* was initially labeled as a wild and radical tome that few could understand. However, it was widely read and discussed during the early 1970s because it was written by two otherwise highly esteemed scholars. It is now *the* foundational source for researchers who are investigating how archaic cultures understood precession. It explores how the core myths contain elements from earlier times layered over by later times. Like a household of family antiquities mixed with new furniture, the archaic fragments are mixed in with more recent stories. The bards rescued them, even if they didn't know what they meant, just like treasured family heirlooms. Bards are keepers of the oral tradition, and the bardic tradition reveals that time is *the essential structural format of myth.*

Von Dechend and Santillana decoded these factors by investigating the linguistic variations and archaic elements in the myths that reflect various periods of time, discovering that *mythology is a veritable mathematics of consciousness.* Their book examines the ancient sagas, stories, epics, and dramas and deciphers them by means of precessional cycles and symbolism. These stories often begin with phrases such as "Once upon a time," or "Once in the days long ago . . ." The core myths are filled with stories of origin that span extremely long cycles of time in specific places. Often without even realizing it, we perceive events by time. Try telling a story to somebody without using time and place.

Mythology is an archaic time-coded system, a treasure hunt back into prehistory through thousands of years. We can use it to figure out how people remembered and dealt with what happened to them over the Great Ages. The most noticeable thing is that *extremely similar myths of the great cataclysms exist in all ancient cultures.*[2] I contend that the universal desire to comprehend and remember the days of disaster inspired the post-catastrophic storytellers and astronomer-priests as long as 10,000 years ago; very early on they told stories of startling changes in the sky. This alteration in the cosmic order probably caused by axial tilt would have been very disturbing to them. They probably did not understand *why* precession began, but they came up with some very accurate mythic images, such as Atlas holding the globe or the goddess Nut holding up the sky. They would have immediately noticed the new seasons, and soon they would have seen that star positions were moving on the horizons and around the poles. Naturally, they also feared more disasters, and there *were* follow-up adjustments as Earth settled down. Thus, archaic people offered sacrifices to the gods from earliest times, hoping that the sky would not fall again.

The possibility that precession began only 11,500 years ago is a radical hypothesis, which could only be *proven* by a very detailed analysis and synthesis of geological and paleontological records, as well as complex astrophysical calculations. I've provided some of this data in appendices

B, C, and D. Astrophysicists would need to study the current orbits of bodies in the solar system to determine if a new pattern began 11,500 years ago. Certainly, this is what the cross-cultural legends describe, which Allan and Delair catalog in *Cataclysm!* Regardless of exactly when precession began, humans have been obsessed with cyclic time for the past 10,000 years. There must be a reason, since tracking precession requires advanced astronomy and lots of leisure time. Many excellent technical books establish that people tracked precession at least 8,000 years ago, such as *The Dawn of Astronomy* by J. Norman Lockyer, *The Secret of the Incas* by William Sullivan, and *Stonehenge* by John North.[3] Later, I will present evidence from Çatal Hüyük in Turkey that archaic people were contemplating the precessional influence as long as *9,000 years ago* during the Age of Gemini—6640 to 4480 BC. Considering how far back this way of viewing reality may go, core myths and archaeological sites can be used as time tunnels that open our eyes to the brilliance and exquisite creativity of the preliterate cultures that haunt and fascinate many people.

The great cataclysm occurred in the middle of what became the first Great Age—Leo—so the current shift into Aquarius is an entry into the sign that is *opposite* Leo. According to astrological principles, an oppositional phase is like the full moon, which brings things to fruition. Therefore, the Aquarian Age will bring to completion all the things we've created since the Age of Leo and the cataclysm. This *is* happening as we observe waves of barbaric warfare and personal psychosis breaking out, as if someone has opened Pandora's Box. In this book, I am focusing on the final event in 9500 BC, but there were disturbances in our solar system for a few thousand years before the most destructive event. The physicist Paul A. LaViolette published *Earth Under Fire* in 1997, right after the English edition of Allen and Delair's *Cataclysm!* LaViolette describes a series of explosions in the galactic core (superwaves) that unleashed a barrage of destructive cosmic rays. He calculates that the superwave front passed Earth around 14,200 years ago, which triggered a series of great changes, such as the Gothenburg Flip and the Younger Dryas.[4] To recover our true past, we must remember these cataclysms. Who were we then? What happened to us?

The Terrible Days of Flood, Wind, and Fire

Cataclysm! Compelling Evidence for a Cosmic Catastrophe in 9500 BC describes the recent cataclysm that disarranged our solar system and tilted the axis of Earth. Allan and Delair theorize that fragments of a supernova in the Vela star system crashed into our solar system 11,500 years ago and then approached Earth.* What follows is a replay of the day Earth nearly died based on *Cataclysm!*, and readers who question or respond powerfully to this description would be well advised to read this monumental work. My intention here is to awaken your own inner memory of this event, since it is deeply buried in the subconscious minds of all people as the *core source of modern collective fear.*

The Supernova fragments approached Earth and our atmosphere became electrically supercharged, our waters and winds began to heat up. Earth was becoming hot and fetid as a horror unfolded for all living things on Earth: Lurid monsters appeared in the sky that looked like giant birds, writhing serpents, or dragons that kept changing shape and color. Whatever it was, it was the most terrible thing that had ever appeared in the skies. It even seemed to be moving against the passage of the Sun through the sky, and people fell

---

*D. S. Allan and J. B. Delair, *Cataclysm! Compelling Evidence of a Cosmic Catastrophe in 9500 BC* (Santa Fe: Bear & Company, 1997), 207–11. To summarize Allan and Delair's theories of the cause, they say on page 209, "Although it is impossible at this juncture to positively pinpoint Phaeton's [supernova] real identity, we can merely state what it was *not.*" Then they list the "nots": meteors, asteroids, and conventional comets; satellites, such as moons; planets; passing stars; and giant interstellar comets. Finally, they offer details on the cloud of aluminum-26 in space surrounding the solar system, which makes a supernova the likely candidate. According to astronomy, at least five supernovas exploded near our solar system 15,000 to 11,500 years ago, and one of them—the Vela supernova—erupted sometime between 14,300 and 11,000 years ago (D. K. Milne, "A New Catalogue of Galactic SNRs Corrected for Distance from the Galactic Plane," 32:83–92 and G. R. Brackenridge, "Terrestrial Palaeoenvironmental Effects of a Late Quaternary-Age Supernova," *Icarus* 16:81–93). Of course, they say "It is impossible at this juncture to positively pinpoint Phaeton's real identity." Likewise, LaViolette's superwave would have caused supernovas such as Vela that were in its path to explode. So, a few years after the release of Allen and Delair's cataclysmic hypothesis, LaViolette is in agreement with it, and we see that Earth was stressed over a few thousand years.

down on their knees in terror. The thrashing fire in the sky got bigger and bigger for many days, and as it came closer, it looked like it would pass over the North Pole as it moved inside the Moon. Then terrible sucking winds came as Earth began to tip toward the chimera in the sky.* There was a deafening explosion in the vault of the sky and Earth shuddered.† Within hours, blocks of ice, hail, and gigantic masses of water pummeled our planet.‡ What was coming? What could it be? asked all who stared at the frightening sky.

The atmosphere imploded and all living things were terrified of the deafening sound that was like a great ringing bell. Great electromagnetic storms overwhelmed the bioelectric fields of animals, humans, plants, and even rocks. On that day, fear was so deeply imprinted in human consciousness that ever since our minds have tried to suppress and deny this memory. Chaos reigned next as volcanoes exploded and spewed, as the oceans and lakes boiled, as Earth shuddered and cracked insanely.

---

*Allan and Delair, *Cataclysm!* 250–54. The authors comment on page 250 that the Persian legends report that this phenomenon went on for many days, and the weird shapes must have been caused by the electromagnetic activity and changing positions within the fragments and debris. On page 252, they say, "Earth/Moon gravitation now begins to affect the course of the intruders, while Earth, tilting axially away from the vertical, starts to align itself toward Phaeton and Kingu."

†Allan and Delair, *Cataclysm!,* 254. The authors speculate that Kingu (a moon of Tiamat that is a destroyed planet in the asteroid belt) disintegrated in Earth's Roche Limit, the area around Earth that will expel or destroy objects approaching the planet.

‡Allan and Delair, *Cataclysm!,* 281–89. Judging by the swarms of craterlike depressions in the Atlantic Coastal Plain, the Carolina bays, the craterlike shallow depressions in the Alaskan permafrost near Point Barrow, and other such formations in Bolivia and the Netherlands, the authors constructed a global schema and map of this falling matter that seems to indicate by the debris that Phaeton was passing over the North Pole and opposite Earth's rotation. On page 221, they speculate that the fragments could have ruptured the Kuiper Belt, a belt of tiny planetoid objects that orbit around the solar system or occasionally inside Pluto's orbit. Decaying aluminum-26 surrounds the solar system in this general region. If the fragments did shatter the Kuiper Belt, on Earth there would have been visual effects of an explosion but no sound. My sense that the solar system would vibrate like a bell comes from some of the findings science garnered from research on Supernova 1987A. For example, according to astronomer Alfred K. Mann, "During the 12 seconds, SN 1987A generated an amount of power in the form of neutrinos that dwarfed all power production on Earth by about 34 powers of 10" (*Shadow of a Star: The Neutrino Story of Supernova 1987A* [New York: W. H. Freeman and Company, 1997], 103).

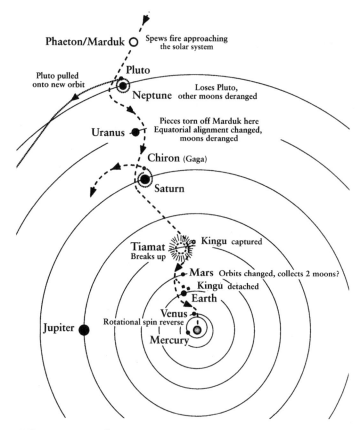

Fig. 2.1. The great cataclysm in 9500 BC. Figure 4.13 of Allan and Delair's Cataclysm! Compelling Evidence of a Cosmic Catastrophe in 9500 BC.

The following extract contains more details of this story from *Cataclysm!* The authors use Ovid's Phaeton to represent the fragments of the supernova and Kingu (a moon of a destroyed planet, Tiamat, from the Akkadian epic, the Enuma Elish) to name the mass that moved along with the supernova fragments toward Earth.

The combined separation of Kingu from Phaeton and the stopping or slowing of Earth's axial spin caused terrible havoc on Earth. The waters of the world's rivers, lakes, and oceans were drained from their original basins and drawn gravitationally to the point on Earth nearest (opposite) Kingu and Phaeton. Worldwide traditions remember the awesome effect.

The retarding of Earth's rotation also resulted in the world's winds blowing with a ferocity and intensity never experienced by modern people—winds which flattened whole forests, whipped ocean billows to mountainous heights, moved giant rocks and removed incalculable volumes of loose surface materials to very great distances. It was, in fact, remembered as a veritable diluvium venti.

Meanwhile, the internal magma tides continued to flow below the tormented terrestrial crust. Through the united gravitational influence of Kingu and Phaeton, they will have been slowly pulled towards that aspect of Earth nearest those celestial bodies. This inevitably resulted in geoidal deformation, huge portions of the lithosphere buckling, fracturing, subducting, collapsing, or overriding one another as simultaneously numerous mountain ranges were upheaved. Rivers of molten lava, rains of red-hot ash, and vast clouds of volcanic dust and gas swirled over enormous regions. Elsewhere rampant fires will have consumed all living things in their path.

*At some localities volcanic gas clouds—*nues ardentes*—transported large boulders many miles, scored rock surfaces with striae closely resembling effects often ascribed elsewhere to glacial action, and, in company with high-pressure grit-charged steam, polished and carved rock surfaces and excavated entire valleys. Concomitantly, avalanches of boiling mud ejected from volcanic vents and fissures poured down hillsides and along valleys, transporting more boulders and producing further rock striations.*

Crustal Shifting Models

Science historian D. S. Allan and geologist/anthropologist J. B. Delair drew their description of the cataclysm from their comprehensive analysis of worldwide accounts of the disaster in the voluminous geopaleontological and astronomical data. It seems impossible that a disaster of such magnitude could have *ever* happened, much less only 11,500 years ago, yet the scientific records of Earth and the solar system confirm this, as do the ancient legends. Modern science is only putting all this data together now. Meanwhile, this memory was kept by indigenous people all over the world; cross-cultural records that tell the same story verify modern cataclysmic theory.[5]

The magnitude of the cataclysm calls for serious thought about the accuracy of accepted geological mechanisms, such as crustal shifting. For example, scientific data from 14,000 to 11,500 years ago indicate that the *topography of Earth was almost completely rearranged.* "The former disposition of land and sea was changed," Allan and Delair write, "a new world mountain system came into being, the number of active volcanoes was augmented enormously, a legacy of seismic activity was bequeathed which is far from over, a new land drainage pattern was instituted, and completely different oceanic and atmospheric circulatory regimes were established."[6] Ocean basins collapsed and global rift valleys and fracture complexes formed that can only be explained by plate tectonics—the movements of Earth's crustal plates—that *dislocated Earth's lithosphere both vertically and horizontally.*[7]

The major tectonic plates of Earth are divided by great faults, such as the San Andreas fault in California, where Earth's crust has actually fractured. A popular theory for the presence of these great seismically active faults has been Wegener's continental drift theory.[8] However, recently some researchers have begun to question continental drift as the only factor in the formation of these major tectonic plates. Allan and Delair point out that the global *pattern* of tectonic plates is actually icosahedral—a polyhedron of twenty faces—suggesting that *Earth expanded hemispherically very recently,* "cracking apart like the shell of an overheated egg."[9] The authors give voluminous evidence that this incredible geometrical faulting had to have been caused by a uniformly exerted *external* stress, such as

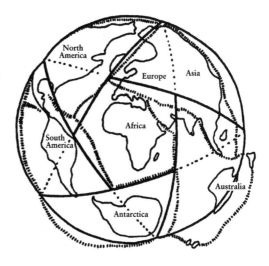

Fig. 2.2. The icosahedral Earth. Figure 5.9 of Allan and Delair's Cataclysm! Compelling Evidence of a Cosmic Catastrophe *in 9500 BC.*

Phaeton, and the pattern of the faulting indicates that this stress markedly slowed the speed of Earth's rotation and caused longer days.[10] "The sudden slowing of Earth's rotation, therefore, inevitably caused severe crustal fracturing worldwide," they write. "The continued rotation of the semi-molten magma below Earth's halted or decelerated crust resulted in vastly increased thermal energy and, not improbably, in temporary geoidal deformation."[11] In a letter, J. B. Delair wrote, "The plates formed more or less simultaneously and suddenly under violent conditions."*

This analysis of the cataclysm may be the only possible explanation for what happened so recently to our planet. After consideration of various radical catastrophic geological mechanisms, such as Rand and Rose Flem-Ath's crustal-shifting theory in *When the Sky Fell* and Charles Hapgood's theories in *Path of the Pole,* I've adopted Allan and Delair's model.[12] Astute readers will realize how mind-bending their hypothesis is, yet Allan and Delair have thoroughly cataloged the worldwide Late Pleistocene data, carefully considered forces required for such great destruction, and then found a logical candidate for the mechanism—fragments from the Vela supernova. Allen and Delair's theory calls for serious consideration, and also for questioning many ideas about the recent past. The voluminous physical evidence for recent cataclysms is throwing science into great turmoil, because theoretical models for the past 20,000 years just don't work very well. There have been a number of new cataclysmic models for this period since this book came out in 2001, which I have carefully reviewed: I continue to think the Allan and Delair models are the most accurate. We are in the middle of a huge paradigm shift that is following the classic stages as defined by Thomas Kuhn in *The Structure of Scientific Revolutions*[13]: Tired of being pigeonholed in specific fields and denied an overview, many young scientists are looking at new mechanisms for cataclysmic change. The existing theories do not make sense now in light of the magnitude of the obviously recent disaster, and even the holy grail of geology—the geologic column—is being scrutinized.

---

*J. B. Delair, letter to the author, August 3, 1999. He also noted that the plates would *not* have moved as a single unit, as once advocated by Charles Hapgood, and Hapgood admitted this to him during conversations in London a few years before he died.

The Geologic Column

Scientific analysis of layers of rocks—stratigraphy—assumes that these layers were created by gradual processes over millions of years. Yet, Allan and Delair suggest that gigantic and geologically very rapid *relocation and reconstitution* of many rocks has occurred by *crustal shifting,* a mechanism that is not even under consideration by orthodox geologists, at least officially. For a geologist to discuss crustal-shifting theory is anathema, similar to a historian mentioning Atlantis or an archaeologist saying the Sphinx is more than 7,000 years old. It is extremely difficult to imagine the crust of Earth being pressed, rolled, liquefied, upthrusted and downthrusted, and/or pushed up sideways in an instant. It's even harder to conceive of these cataclysms as relatively recent events. However, in light of Allan and Delair's research, *all geological descriptions of the landscape based on uniformitarian models must be reconsidered.* This includes the geologic column, which correlates and dates rock and coal layers and alluvial deposits. This column, invented by uniformitarian science, is used to date sedimentary rocks in all the Earth sciences. Supposedly, these sequential layers represent millions of years of geological deposits found all over the planet. It is the basis for the *global geological timeline:* The lower layers are older, the upper levels are more recent, and the thickness of each layer is a record for specific lengths of time. Then the fossils found in the sedimentary layers can be dated whenever they are found in layers that are datable according to the geologic column.

A hypothesis that seriously calls the geologic column into question is from the French geologist Guy Berthault, who was investigated by the new-paradigm science reporter Richard Milton. Milton reports that in 1985, Berthault conducted an experiment that seriously challenges sedimentation theory and the validity of the geologic column. Berthault crumbled samples of rocks and reduced them to their original constituent particles. Then he sorted and colored them for identification purposes. He mixed them all together and flowed them into a tank, first in a dry state, and later into water. He found that when the sediments settled on the bottom *they reformulated into layers that are exactly the same as the layers of the original rocks from which they had come.* Berthault said, in summary,

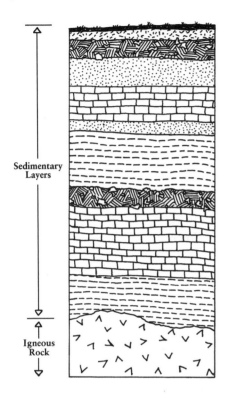

Fig. 2.3. The geologic column

"These experiments contradict the idea of the slow buildup of one layer followed by another. The time scale is reduced from hundreds of millions of years to one or more cataclysms producing almost instantaneous laminae [layers]."[14] That is exactly what happens during crustal shifting and massive flooding. So what if the geologic column is a record of how soil usually deposits when its constituent particles settle out over millions of years, yet it also is a record of how they settle instantaneously after they've been broken down by water? This would more accurately explain some features of the landscape that settled out after massive flooding 11,500 years ago.

No matter how this hypothetical turmoil flushes out, we have been educated by—and are still being educated by—flawed geological theory. This makes it very difficult to consider new theoretical geological mechanisms or reconsider the age of the landscape. Meanwhile, there is mounting evidence that something is wrong with the geologic column. Berthault's experiment may indicate what would happen when crustal shifting and floods periodically reconstitute the rock layers. Considering the magnitude of the devastation 14,000 to 11,500 years ago, the geologic column may better describe the features of landscapes that were altered by crustal shifting and global flooding. It may explain more about the Late Pleistocene deposits, which *contain the remains of plants and animals from a spectrum of 29 million years ago to the cataclysm.* As mentioned above, the stratified layers are dated by the ages of the fossils deposited in them, which calls the geologic column into serious question. Possibly *much of Earth's present topography is only 11,500 years old, especially in locations that were the most devastated.* Of course, Earth's rocks are millions and billions of years old, but the *layers* of rock may not be a datable record in all cases. The next question that arises in light of the awesome magnitude of the destruction: What was the world like *before* the cataclysm?

The Prediluvial Landscape

The world before the cataclysm is often referred to as the *prediluvial world*—Earth before the biblical Flood. It is very difficult to imagine what the world was like before it was nearly destroyed. However, Allan and

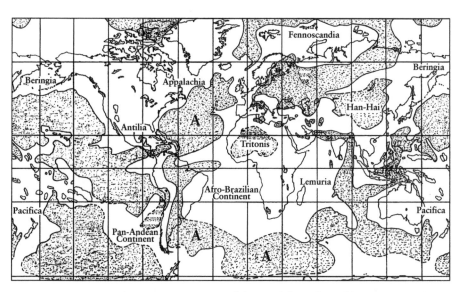

Fig. 2.4. Tentative reconstruction of the prediluvial world. Map 2A of Allan and Delair's Cataclysm! Compelling Evidence of a Cosmic Catastrophe in 9500 BC.

Delair examined the global fauna and flora and the geological data and they have proposed a tentative precataclysmic map of the world. Also using the rare fragments in myths that describe the world before the Flood, Allan and Delair hypothesize that before the cataclysm (1) Earth must have been a stable planet over a long span of geological time; (2) the continents were more horizontal than vertical; (3) mountains were fewer and lower, and deserts were less extensive and seas shallower; and (4) polar ice caps, if they existed at all, would have been of modest size. They surmise that there was more carbon dioxide and oxygen in the atmosphere; storms were infrequent and modest; humidity was high with mostly dew instead of rain; and vegetation was luxuriant. In those days, some writers have alleged that Earth was perpetually springlike when we were "in the prime of life, with no aging or senility."[15] Based on his analysis of very old Japanese documents, Michio Kushi says the prediluvial world had a system of global transportation—boats as well as airplanes—and natural agriculture based on the idea that Earth would produce all that was needed if it was "untouched." He says, "People in Paradise had freedom without the concept of freedom, health without any idea what health was, happiness without the need to speak of happiness."[16] This was *the Garden of Eden during the Golden Age,* a utopia that lives in the subconscious minds of many people along with the memory of the time when this primeval earthly paradise was abruptly destroyed.

Allan and Delair have cataloged worldwide sources that indicate Earth's axis changed from vertical to a significant tilt since the cataclysm. See appendix D for more detail on this. Before the axial tilt, during the Golden Age, there was little seasonality, and through the year the stars revolved in a *tholiform* manner—always on the same horizontal plane as Earth's spin. The stars rose and set in the same location on the horizon, making a perfect circle around the vertical celestial poles in a day.[17] With no axial tilt, there would have been no equinoxes or solstices, and this alteration in the sky explains humanity's virtual obsession with the sky after 9500 BC. During the early years after the cataclysm, the stars—especially the prominent Orion star system—rose and set seasonally in the heavens. Such alterations in the sky and the new seasonality affected our consciousness in ways that still influence us today and are explored throughout this book.

Table 1A: The Tertiary and Quaternary Periods

The conventional subdivisions of the **Tertiary** *and* **Quaternary** *periods with their estimated duration shown in parentheses. Not to scale.*

Period	Epoch			Millions of Years
Quaternary	Holocene			**.011**
	Pleistocene	Upper	Ice Ages	**2**
		Middle		
		Lower		
Tertiary	Pliocene	(10,000,000 years)		**12**
	Miocene	(17,000,000 years)		**29**
	Oligocene	(12,000,000 years)		**41**
	Eocene	(10,000,000 years)		**51**
	Palaeocene	(9,000,000 years)		**60**

Table 2C: *Revised chronology for the* **Tertiary** *and* **Quaternary** *periods in the light of the Phaeton disaster.*

	Period	Epoch	Stages	General Conditions	Approx Dates (in years BP)
Era: CAENOZOIC	**Quaternary**	Holocene *(Later)*	Historic	As at present	2300–today
			Sub-Atlantic	Dry mild	2700–2300
			Atlantic	Wet mild	3450–2700
			Boreal	Dry cold winters Warm summers	5500–4900
				Glaciers Melt	
		Holocene *(Earlier)*	Pre-Boreal	Dry cold	8000–7500
			Sub-Arctic	Wet cold	11,400
			Pleistocene	Severe. Rapid development of glaciers	11,500
		PHAETON DISASTER			
	Tertiary	Pliocene		Equable	14,000,000
		Miocene		Equable	29,000,000

Fig. 2.5. Revised Chronology of the Euro-American Quaternary Subdivisions. Tables 1A and 2C from Cataclysm! Compelling Evidence of a Cosmic Catastrophe in 9500 BC.

The Holocene Epoch: Earth After the Cataclysm

The period after the cataclysm is the Holocene epoch, according to the Euro-American quaternary subdivisions, which vaguely divide the Upper Pleistocene and Holocene at about 9000 BC.[18] Allan and Delair call for a *revised chronology* that says the Pleistocene epoch was a short transition phase between the end of the Pliocene and the beginning of the Holocene to emphasize *exactly* when the disaster occurred and its magnitude. This emphasizes how different the world was during the chaotic early Holocene epoch, when there was rapid glaciation and deglaciation and crustal settling.

They call for this correction because the cataclysmic debris found all over the planet from 11,500 years ago contains Miocene, Pliocene, and Pleistocene epoch deposits.[19] They conclude from this that "extraordinary speed, huge scale, great violence and indiscriminate action are therefore equally prominent factors in *both* the geological and biological records of the period under review."[20] These biological remains or *drift* are easily datable because they are organic, and they show that the drift deposited 11,500 years ago contains plants and animals from all three epochs—Pleistocene, Pliocene, and Miocene; that is over 29 million years. These plants and animals were still alive 11,500 years ago, which suggests *a tranquil and peaceful world for 29 million years.* Readers must read *Cataclysm!* to consider the magnitude as well as the accuracy of these staggering conclusions. Allan and Delair's theory fits with the Cherokee Records that my grandfather gave to me. It is the first satisfactory hypothesis to explain the Late Pleistocene drift deposits, which Grandfather Hand said are the ultimate proof of the magnitude of the cataclysms. He shared this ancient knowledge with me when he took me to the La Brea Tar Pits in Los Angeles by train from Michigan when I was eight years old. Both the Pliocene and Miocene epochs were very favorable for the development of species, which thrived until the sudden end 11,500 years ago. Allan and Delair posit that the Pleistocene is better described as a very brief cataclysmic *stage* in the beginning of the Early Holocene, not as a real epoch between the Pliocene and the Holocene.[21] This revision makes more sense of the Early Holocene archaeological sites and the Pleistocene drift deposits. We next need to look at the Holocene epoch itself.

In the beginning of the Holocene, survivors emerged and attempted to comprehend the destroyed landscape and shifting sky. There is evidence that we were *more* advanced at the end of the Pliocene epoch (using the revised chronology), and we had significantly *de*volved at the beginning of the Holocene. Darwinism posits that humankind has been progressively evolving from apehood to modern computer human. Another important alternative source on the Holocene times is cartographer Charles Hapgood's 1967 book, *Maps of the Ancient Sea Kings: Evidence of Advanced Civilization in the Ice Age* (often referred to just as *Maps*), which is an analysis of thirty maps that are thousands of years old.[22] Hapgood argues that the maps he examined were the tools of a *scientifically advanced global civilization that sailed the oceans more than 6,000 years ago*.[23] He got the cold shoulder from academia, but he built an airtight case, which is receiving wide attention now because so much evidence for this global maritime civilization is being discovered. Regarding who the mapmakers were, J. B. Delair has suggested that they were "all-knowing culture-heroes who helped stricken mankind to begin again."[24]

Mapmaking requires mathematical expertise and global assessment. *Maps of the Ancient Sea Kings* has essential information on Earth's geography during the Early Holocene, a period that is difficult to assess because Earth's crust was continually readjusting and the seas were rising. Without Hapgood's research, all we have from 11,500 to approximately 6,000 years ago are scattered archaeological sites, mythological fragments, and big gaps in the records everywhere. Of course, any suggestion that there were mapmakers who charted the planet globally before 6,000 years ago goes against all conventional historical models! Graham Hancock comments on the rising seas and Hapgood's research: "The combined effect of the Piri Re'is, Oronteus Finaeus, Mercator and Bauche Maps is the strong, though disturbing, impression that Antarctica may have been continuously surveyed over a period of several thousands of years as the ice-cap gradually spread outwards from the interior (of Antarctica), increasing its grip with every passing millennium but not engulfing all the coasts of the southern continent until about 4000 B.C."[25]

Hapgood concludes that the various maps *"argue for both the vast antiquity of the maps and for the displacement of the earth's crust.*"[26] About the mapmakers themselves, he says, "In geodesy, nautical science, and mapmaking, it [the global maritime civilization] was more advanced than any known culture before the 18th century of the Christian Era."[27] Along with cyclopean monument sites, such as Tiahuanaco in Bolivia and the Giza Plateau in Egypt, these maps are evidence for a scientifically advanced lost culture, a culture with a technology *that we are just beginning to discover ourselves!* Rand and Rose Flem-Ath in *When the Sky Fell* make a very good case that the Atlantean city described by Plato has not been found because Earth's crust underwent a monumental shifting approximately 11,600 years ago, and then ice grew over Antarctica. They believe that the city exists under this ice.[28] This theory may solve the biggest problem in Atlantology: The large and civilized island has not been found. Atlantis will be discussed later, because it obviously existed in the prediluvial world, and its descendants were still around during the Holocene epoch.

When the Sky Fell and *Cataclysm!* both describe the same scenario that is the basis of this work: *Earth cracked, undulated, and groaned when an intense paroxysm ended the Golden Age.* Early civilizations experienced a repeat of the trauma in 5600 BC during a massive flooding in the Mediterranean and Black Sea regions. On the continental shelves around the world, communities were swallowed when the land sank or the seas rose. In more recent memory, the volcano on Santorini in the Aegean erupted in 1626 BC, which triggered a minor crustal adjustment when, as Hapgood puts it, "a worldwide geological upheaval took place, and this was the final readjustment of Earth's outer shell to its new position after its last displacement."[29] This last major displacement caused great subsidence in the Aegean and western Mediterranean, north and equatorial Atlantic, and East Indies; while Siberia, India, the southwestern United States, the Caribbean, Peru, and Bolivia uplifted.[30] Regarding these reverberating disasters, it is wise to differentiate between the great cataclysm and the major disasters that occurred afterward. The event in 9500 BC terminated a whole geological era and ushered in a new one, which is why Allan and Delair devised a new chronology.

No matter how all the details wash out, *we are a multi-traumatized species.* Motivated and driven by fear, mass culture is profoundly disconnected from the past. My grandparents taught me that the twentieth century's mass global warfare was the natural result of these unrecognized inner fears. Now as these catastrophic memories boil to the surface, people do anything to avoid inner darkness. They park their awareness in the media and cyberspace and ignore the ecological and emotional damage the cyber-revolution causes. Unresolved inner trauma is projected out of dark minds, making the outer world into a theater for human-caused cataclysms. Wars and obscene killings are rampant because *outside events are being created by repressed images that lurk in the collective unconscious.* Our current situation has all the elements of the end of an age, yet the new paradigm is on the verge of supplanting the old one, and it heralds the possibility of peace returning to Earth.

A deeply connective river of inner knowledge flows within us. I've found that Carl Calleman's description of the Nine Underworlds takes us easily and deeply into the river of time. I find that people are really fascinated with time acceleration because *it reconnects our sped-up reality with the deep past.* We can understand who we are now if we understand where we've come from. Allan and Delair's revised chronology awakens archaic intelligence because it actually explains what really happened to us during a very short and recent time.

Still, our inner sense of time is horribly scrambled by the incorrect historical timeline, which robs us of our intelligence. The old paradigm data bank makes us stupid, whereas the new chronology is exciting. For example, when I gaze at the wavy and squeezed, crunched-up folding rocks that form the almost vertical mountains in many parts of British Columbia, they are full of life because they are so young. Professors and scientists had better revise the scientific paradigm, because kids won't go to school anymore to memorize false and boring data. As the winter solstice sun is activated by its alignment to the Galactic Center during the end of the Mayan Calendar, we are poised to attain our next stage of evolution. The revised chronology makes it easier to get in touch with the peaceful Pliocene and Miocene epochs, yet still the unprocessed horror from the recent global destruction is in the way. The next chapter explores the possibility that the cataclysm actually altered our brain function, because there is evidence for cranial narrowing in the Holocene epoch.

3 THE BICAMERAL BRAIN AND THE SPHINX

The very notion of truth is a culturally given direction, a part of the pervasive nostalgia for an earlier certainty. The very idea of a universal stability, an eternal firmness of principle out there that can be sought for through the world as might an Arthurian knight for the Grail, is, in the morphology of history, a direct outgrowth of the search for lost gods in the first two millennia after the decline of the bicameral mind. What was then an augury for direction of action among the ruins of an archaic mentality is now the search for an innocence of certainty among the mythologies of facts.

JULIAN JAYNES[1]

The Breakdown of the Bicameral Mind

In *The Origin of Consciousness in the Breakdown of the Bicameral Mind,* neurologist Julian Jaynes hypothesizes that consciousness is a learned skill that has emerged out of an archaic hallucinatory mentality. Jaynes examines historical and mythological sources for the emergence of consciousness over more than 6,000 years. In early literature, Jaynes says the gods spoke in our heads as if they *occupied our brains,* broadcasting from a relatively dormant area of the right brain, Wernicke's area.[2] Jaynes says that around 3,500 years ago we were bicameral, or split in two, with an "executive" part called god and a "follower" part called man.[3] Then we lost this facility as our left brain became increasingly dominant when we became "conscious." I prefer the term *self-reflective* to *conscious,* because using *conscious* suggests that archaic people were *not* conscious. Archaic people, especially before the cataclysms, seem to have been very conscious, albeit more so of nature, spirits, and community. They seem to have been less *self*-conscious or separate from many dimensions, very much like the rare vestiges of undisturbed indigenous people living on Earth today.

Jaynes characterizes this process of becoming conscious as an evolutionary advance; I argue that it was also a *perceptual narrowing.* Just like developing psychology while losing access to the stars, we *have* attained self-reflection during the past 3,500 years. Armed with a new sense of the separate "I," our left brains matured, which certainly is an evolutionary advance. However, the fullest range of human intelligence—a balanced right-and-left brain—is extremely dormant in most modern people. Jaynes traces his idea of the breakdown of the bicameral brain in detail, especially since 1500 BC, when Earth changes in the Mediterranean repeatedly traumatized humanity. His book is a great counterpoint to my book, because we both explore the same data banks, but from differing points of view. For Jaynes, consciousness is located in the left brain; but in my experience, consciousness emerges out of the right brain, and then the left brain organizes its data. The left brain is merely a tool, like a computer, whereas the right brain accesses intelligence from many dimensions. I am bringing Jaynes in here because orthodoxy adopted Jaynes as their golden boy in the 1970s, since his book is based on the premise that we are evolving out of a primitive mentality to a higher level; Jaynes seems to idolize rationality. Yes, we have become more rational, but is that such an advance? In Jaynes's book, people with bicameral brain skills—artists, channels, and prophets—come off as nutty skulls loaded with babbling gods, which has resulted in the pharmaceutical suppression of access to many dimensions.

Probing mythology and early literature, Jaynes detects great perceptual alterations in humans, and his examples are thought provoking. While reading him, I realized that I had inadvertently reactivated my dormant bicameral brain during the hypnotic sessions I undertook to research my trilogy, *The Mind Chronicles*. Maybe this is because past-life sessions under hypnosis are *experiential*. Clients move their consciousness fully into the real live bodies of past people, which is described in detail in chapter 9. Melding into these individuals with my full perceptual powers turned on, I awakened 100,000 years of archaic intelligence in my mind. Of course, I live during a time when I am not compelled to obey orders from the gods occupying Wernicke's area of my brain, so my experience of the inner voices was vastly different than it was for someone 4,000 years ago. I didn't get stuck in atavistic mentalities, because my left brain endures, yet I was able to access archaic consciousness. Recently, discovering time acceleration has awakened even more dormant memory, which makes whole phases in the past come alive like old movies stored in my brain. Considering the Nine Underworlds of the tun-based Mayan Calendar, I'm sure we were very right-brain dominant during the Fifth Underworld that spans the last 102,000 years. We became more rational during the Sixth Underworld (3115 BC–AD 2011), and even more rational during the Seventh (AD 1755–2011). Yet now, during the Eighth Underworld (AD 1999–2011) and the Ninth during 2011, all the dormant faculties in our brains are blasting wide open.

Bicameral skills seem to be reactivating in many people with well-developed left brains, which suggests some form of *super*consciousness is activating—the agenda of the Ninth Underworld during 2011. This is what is needed to balance our species with planetary ecology. The people of the Fifth Underworld, especially before the cataclysms, seemed to have been in harmony with nature. Remnants from Paleolithic times, such as Magdalenian cave art, suggest that in those days we were immersed, fused with, and totally enlivened by nature in the primordial Garden of Eden, the Golden World. I found verification for this possibility myself when I traveled far back in time under hypnosis, and James Cameron's film *Avatar* recently brought back this world for millions. Archaic humans experienced symbiosis with other life forms, and recovering this faculty could enable us to *release nature from human control*. I believe that long ago, phosphorescent in the waters of the Garden, our brains were open lenses to all of nature's intelligence.

Reawakening the Bicameral Mind

As science currently understands it, human perceptual access lies within the visible light spectrum (VLS) of the electromagnetic spectrum. Access to wider vibratory fields, such as seeing infrared or ultraviolet light, is probably what enables people to see and hear things that people normally are not aware of, such as hearing the voices of gods, or seeing phosphorescent plant light in *Avatar*. Back to Jaynes's analysis of human perceptual abilities over thousands of years: as our left brains have matured, the wider range has atrophied.

The human access range in the electromagnetic spectrum has narrowed, yet still, prophets, artists, schizophrenics, and channels are often bicameral. Since I wrote the first edition of this book in 2000, our perceptual range has again been widening very fast, which is intense and chaotic if people don't understand what is happening to them. Instead of encouraging this great perceptual awakening that's right on schedule, doctors

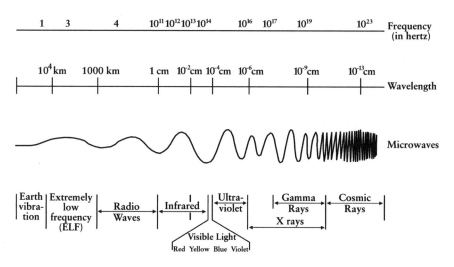

Fig. 3.1. The electromagnetic spectrum

prescribe mood-altering drugs to shut people down. Drugs can disable reality-check skills, so many people wander around in insane worlds while not at home in their bodies. Since Prozac was introduced in the 1980s, people either on or getting off antidepressants have committed approximately 85 percent of the random killings; the Columbine massacre in Colorado is just one example.[4] Meanwhile, regardless of how much anybody tries to stop it, the human perceptual range is again widening. Ironically, the airwaves are saturated with a wide range of electromagnetic frequencies—microwaves, radio and television waves, cell phones, and Internet. *Modern wave technology is stimulating latent cranial potential outside the VLS in the populace.* People are told they are bipolar, yet it might be more correct to say they are awakening bicameral perception.

When Plato wrote the *Timaeus* and *Critias* approximately 2,500 years ago, according to Jaynes, humans were losing the last vestiges of the bicameral brain.[5] Plato saved sources that reflect this archaic mentality, while he also seemed to value his awakening rational mind; Plato retained his right-brain access as he added left-brain skill. Plato's work is now respected because many archaic records that were thought to be silly myths have turned out to be real history, such as the worldwide myths of great floods and cataclysms. Finally, Plato is getting some respect as a historian. When I was working on this revision during January 2011, I received a remarkable new consciousness idea from the New Age musician Raymond Lynch in his soon-to-be-published *The Unreasonable Unity of God*. In the manuscript, Lynch has also adopted Allan and Delair's cataclysmic hypothesis and examined cultures before and after the disaster. He drew some really fascinating thoughts about left- and right-brain function out of *Mapping the Mind* by the science writer Rita Carter. Carter notes that each half of the brain has its own strengths and weaknesses, its own special skills, as if there are *two individuals in one skull:* The left brain is analytical, precise, and sensitive to time. The right brain is more emotional than the left, and it is responsible for fearful and mournful feelings and general pessimism. Carter considers some cases of people who have suffered right- or left-hemispheric damage that indicate that *a function of the left brain is to control and inhibit the negativity of the right brain.* This idea really caught Lynch's attention and mine!

Lynch wondered, "Why should the holistic, intuitive, and emotional right hemisphere harbor a miserable view of life, a view which is coupled with emotions of fear and sorrow?"[6] Like myself, Lynch argues that the most significant event in recent human memory is the cataclysm, which brought evil into the world that was incomprehensible to our forebears. He notes that in the right brain, things "just happen," so the cataclysm has a *metaphorical affinity* with the right brain because it also just happened. Lynch argues that during the Golden Age, our species would not have had a pessimistic and fearful right brain, and I am sure of that based on my own travels back into that time as well as my studies of the Paleolithic. The cataclysms profoundly changed us—possibly split our minds—and then we had to become more left-brain-dominant to inhibit right-brain pessimism. Lynch believes, as I do, that the strong survivors who later ended up becoming the Elite had been able to suppress the right brain in favor of the optimistic and busy left brain, just to get people to rebuild civilization. He notes that this did not have to be a permanent solution, yet it was until now because it allowed the Elite to control the people, who eventually forgot the story. Meanwhile, the Elite have been on the throne ever since because they knew the ancient story and harbored it as their secret. Well, the secret is now out, which means we all need to understand the contents of the right brain and come to terms with them; the only other alternative is antidepressants.

According to social Darwinism, modern rational culture is the most highly evolved, yet now we can see that this is a cover for hidden trauma. So, with the Elite in control when the awakening began, people got thrown into mental institutions in the 1950s for hearing voices in their heads. Now the looney bins have mostly closed down, and people wander around in the streets lost on legal drugs. Unresolved trauma from past cataclysms is erupting, which is the source of some of the hideous crimes we witness in modern times. This very serious issue seems to be getting out of control as hidden memory seeks the light. Freud discovered that the cause of amnesia was traumatic events, and then the amnesiac either denies the trauma or *makes an effort to relive it.*[7] This is one of the causes of violent crime and abuse, and then in the collective, the desire for the coming end comes out of the need for *psychic relief from repressed catastrophic memory*. We became almost totally left-brain-dominant, but by time acceleration, now the left brain can't block the feelings in the right brain.

Cataclysmic popular science stirs these memories, which actually may be a good thing in small enough doses. As with memory therapy for early childhood abuse, the real story of the past encourages people to recognize their inner fears. The more that people realize our forebears attained abilities that we have not yet achieved in modern times, the more they become suspicious of the prevailing historical orthodoxy. Meanwhile, the media, like a gigantic memory-fogging machine programmed by the Flintstones, repeats and repeats the false story of the past. Or, the media sanitizes information about ancient cultures, which bores the public. Whatever they do, *we are at the end of the progressive narrowing of human perceptual lenses.* Consensus reality is increasingly chaotic as the old patterns break down, and new sight into the deep past is changing how we think about our species.

The controversy over dating the Sphinx sheds new light on other mysteries. Çatal Hüyük in Turkey is an incredibly sophisticated archaeological site that dates back at least *9,000 years.* In the 1960s, only a small part of it—4 percent—was excavated, and then the funding of its discoverer, esteemed archaeologist James Mellaart, was terminated, and it was reburied! Excavations at Çatal Hüyük resumed in the mid-1990s under Ian Hodder, and other sites in Turkey that are even *older* than Çatal Hüyük, such as Nevali Çori and Göbekli Tepe, attract global interest. Advanced cultures in Turkey that go back 11,500 years support the greater antiquity of Egypt. Meanwhile, what happened to the people who built Çatal Hüyük and the Sphinx? As you will see, that question *can* be answered. As it turns out, Çatal Hüyük is a precursor of the Minoan culture, which was merely a myth until a hundred years ago. *We now know more about the ancient world than people knew for thousands of years!* A whole new story is waking up in our world, and the interpretation of these sites and artifacts is thrilling; this heritage is available to the public on the Internet. No one even knew these sites existed for thousands of years, so it is not surprising that archaeology concocted an incorrect timeline a few hundred years ago.

Suddenly stories that were merely myths for thousands of years are history; mythology illuminates artifacts, sacred texts, and ancient sites. Lost worlds emerge like the images of forgotten places, like images on film that materialize when it's soaking in the chemicals. It is exciting to remember who we were in the days long ago, and new theories about Egypt are excellent examples of how this process is working.

The Orion Correlation and the Riddle of the Sphinx

Dating the Sphinx is the starting point of all discussions about ancient Egypt, and now recent geological opinions contradict old-paradigm Egyptology. The greater antiquity of the Sphinx supports the Egyptologists of the last century, who thought the mysterious Pyramid Texts found in Fifth and Sixth Dynasty pyramids were already very old when they were first discovered. According to the highly respected Egyptologist Wallis Budge, the Pyramid Texts were carved on the granite walls of the Pyramid of Unas 4,300 years ago, but they were composed long *before* the reign of the First Dynasty Pharaoh Menes 5,300 years ago.[8] Were the writers of the Pyramid Texts from the same culture that carved the Sphinx more than 7,000 years ago? What happened to the people who wrote the Pyramid Texts and built the Sphinx?

Robert Bauval and Adrian Gilbert's controversial astronomical decoding of the Pyramid Texts in *The Orion Mystery* correlates the Pyramid Texts with the Giza Plateau complex, which they believe was developed in some form more than 12,500 years ago. These texts, as well as others—such as the Turin Papyrus from 1400 BC—describe the earliest know period, the "First Time," or Zep Tepi, from which dynastic Egypt was derived. The leaders of Zep Tepi, the Shemsu Hor, were semidivine sages who ruled Egypt for thousands of years before the dynastic times. Throughout all of dynastic history, Egyptians said that *all* their rituals and ways of kingship derived from the Shemsu Hor.[9] Manetho, who was an initiated Egyptian priest and scribe 300 years after Plato, was said to have recorded 36,525 years—dating back to *39,000 BC!*—for the duration of Egyptian civilization.[10] (See appendix A for an Egyptian timeline.) Manetho's history did not survive, but others quoted it extensively, and it was a common source in the ancient world. Manetho's dates are of the same magnitude as the Turin Papyrus, which says that the time before Menes went back at least 36,620 years. The quotes and summaries by other scholars of Manetho's history all match up, signaling that these dates came from him.[11]

There is no reason to doubt Manetho's veracity, because his historical chronology has been consistently verified by archaeology. Yet Egyptologists ignore Manetho's huge spans of early time while they use his dynastic records! Graham Hancock says about this absurdity regarding Manetho as an accurate source, "What is the logic of accepting thirty 'historical' dynasties from him and rejecting all that he has to say about earlier epochs?"[12] The fact is, Manetho described a First Time more than *39,000 years ago,* when semidivine rulers led Egypt. When Solon visited the Egyptian temples and libraries 2,500 years ago, the priests still retained these records of Zep Tepi. Solon passed this same information to Plato, who was privy to secret Egyptian temple information himself.[13] The Giza Plateau is the place to search for the abode of the Shemsu Hor of Zep Tepi, now that the age of the Sphinx has been pushed back at least 4,000 years before the First Dynasty of Menes.

We will search for the ancient Egyptians of the First Time using orthodox Egyptology and new-paradigm research. Also, the Giza Plateau has been the focus of strange conspiracy theories for the past fifty years, which I will discuss in chapter 8. I will not waste time here describing the explorations and measurements of the Great Pyramid, because this has already been done so many times. Nor will I discuss the pyramids-as-tombs theory, because this is just an old belief that has never been proven. It is patently obvious that usage as tombs was not the only or main purpose of the pyramids, if at all. Yet this claim is repeatedly thrown at the public, who end up bored and exhausted with little energy left for thinking about the real functions of the pyramids. Meanwhile, there are other critical issues to investigate that have gotten minimal attention, such as the mysterious Blank.

Cyclopean Non-incised Stone Monuments

Based on extensive archaeological digs near the Nile, there are no complex pharaonic sites from 12,500 years ago to approximately 6,000 years ago, a period known as *the Blank*.[14] The official story is that the unification of Upper and Lower Egypt occurred under Menes 5,300 years ago, when the First Dynasty entered history as an extremely complex theocratic culture with hieroglyphics, a pantheon, pharaohs, elaborate burials, and exquisite art. Egyptologists say this "instant-flowering model" just dropped out of thin air, as if they believe in magic! Recently ecologists and archaeologists have discovered many reasons for the Blank. For example, Robert Bauval and Thomas Brophy have just published an extremely fascinating investigation of Nabta Playa, a megalithic complex in the western desert of Egypt. Their investigations reveal a precursor culture of the Early Dynasties. The oldest parts of this complex are 11,000 years old.[15] Who's more right?

Fig. 3.2. The Valley Temple of Giza

According to the instant-flowering model, the Giza Pyramids, Valley Temples, the Sphinx, and the Osireion of Abydos are no more than 5,300 years old. They date these monuments by nearby dynastic constructions dated by cartouches at these sites. Non-incised cyclopean stone monuments, such as the Valley Temple, are constructed by similar methods as cyclopean monuments around the world that are thought to be much older, such as the cyclopean monuments in Bolivia and Peru. The truth is *the oldest non-incised structures located at the major sites on the Nile have never been dated.* For example, Abydos Temple was built during Seti I's reign about 3,300 years ago, and then this date was assigned to the adjacent Osireion, which is *fifty feet lower.* It is constructed of huge non-incised cyclopean stones, except for Seti I's cartouche, which marks his restoration of it. John Anthony West argues that the Osireion and the Valley Temple below the Sphinx were both significantly weathered by the heavy rains that occurred more than 10,500 years ago.[16]

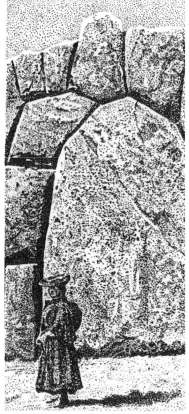

Fig. 3.3. Sacsayhuaman Temple in Peru

An examination of these temples with Nile ecology in mind indicates that they were heavily weathered by rain during the Neolithic Subpluvial, a period of heavy rain 9,000 to 6,000 years ago. These temples have to be at least 6,000 years old, and at least some of them may be more than 11,500 years old. To avoid such contradictions to orthodoxy, Egyptologists simply ignore the monuments that are radically different from the incised temples that have been dated by pharaonic cartouches. Meanwhile, when visiting the Osireion or the Valley Temple, anyone who has studied Nile ecology and has seen other cyclopean temples—such as Sacsayhuaman in Peru, which is constructed with similar cyclopean interlocking-stone construction—concludes that the non-incised temples are much older. It would seem the most logical that Seti I built Abydos Temple to venerate the already-ancient Osireion, a sacred temple from the First Time. The rooms in Abydos Temple that contain the King List and reliefs depicting the birth of Horus from Isis and Osiris lead right out to the Osireion. Like other cyclopean sites, the Osireion is one of Earth's great mysteries.

If archaeologists can't offer reasons for why the Osireion is fifty feet below the most sacred corner of Seti I's temple and is of such radically different construction, the instant-flowering model simply collapses. The truth is, Egyptian sites were used selectively to support a scenario that was concocted during the nineteenth century by British, French, German, and American

Fig. 3.4. The Osireion of Abydos

archaeologists who were beholden to their patrons—museums and wealthy individuals who looted Egypt. Precious remains have been lost or misunderstood because they were not correctly identified and valued. Now, the Osireion is filling up with water and sinking from seepage caused by the Aswan Dam. The silt that flowed downriver during the Inundation (the annual flooding of the Nile) lined the Nile bed, which prevented water seepage into the layers of the limestone beneath the temples. The silt no longer comes with the Inundation, so the water runs between these layers and threatens the Osireion. Now that many ancient sites are endangered, it is time for indigenous Egyptologists to critique the foreign archaeologists who destroyed the earliest evidence at the main sites while they looted dynastic remains and stocked their museums with artifacts selected to support their faulty analysis and dating.

The past is history. It is time to rethink the key sites based on the latest findings of Nile ecoarchaeology and geoarchaeology. Comparisons of construction styles of worldwide archaic structures are needed, as well as the latest correlations between sacred texts and history. Hard science is being offered a golden opportunity: Egypt has many remnants of texts and wall reliefs from dynastic Egypt that the dynastic Egyptians said reflect much earlier times that survived because of the low humidity. This claim was even reported to early visitors, such as Solon, who brought this information back to Greece according to Plato, who himself had a direct linkage with the Egyptian temple teachers. Plato says in the *Timaeus* that in his day (2,500 years ago) *complete records* of Egyptian institutions went back *8,000 years,* which of course is right after the cataclysm. Considering *all* Manetho's dates, the Turin Papyrus, and Plato's report, the undated cyclopean monuments must have been constructed thousands of years earlier by the Shemsu Hor during Zep Tepi. That is, *cyclopean temples in Egypt are from the First Time.* Floods caused by the Neolithic Subpluvial rains must have buried the Osireion. To properly venerate the Osireion, Seti I removed millions of tons of soil deposits in and around it, and restored it. Then when Seti built his new temple, he located the rooms with the King List of Abydos in the hallway that leads down to a passage to the Osireion. It is probably at least 10,000 years older than Seti's temple, which was known as the House of a Million Years, the Osireion.[17] Maybe it goes back 40,000 years, which you can see is possible according to appendix E. One thing is certain: The Osireion is much older than Seti I's temple, just as the Sphinx is older than the First Dynasty remains at Giza.

Assuming there was an exceedingly advanced civilization on the Nile more than 12,000 years ago, that still does not explain the Blank, which stands right in the way of crafting a new timeline. The fact is, outside of the obvious implications of the cyclopean stone remnants and ancient reports discussed here, there still is a serious lack of archaeological evidence for civilization from 12,500 to approximately 6,000 years ago in comparison with the dynastic sites, except for Nabta Playa. Regarding this gap, archaeologist Michael Hoffman says, "The Epipaleolithic-Predynastic Gap (Blank) remains one of the least known and most important research problems facing prehistorians and archaeologists working in northeastern Africa."[18] Where are all the cities, villages, temple complexes, and tombs on the Nile from this earlier civilization that would be the foundations for the protodynastic and early dynastic remains from 5,000 to 6,000 years ago? Even if *before* the cataclysms there was a high civilization in Egypt, considering the Blank, how could dynastic Egypt just appear more than 5,000 years ago? The Blank is the reason some Egyptologists *genuinely believe* that Egypt was in a primitive state until 6,000 years ago, and then civilization suddenly flowered. But now they have few reasons to cling to this fading paradigm: Ecologists have recently surveyed the Nile as a complex alluvial river system, which explains the existence of the Blank. Based on the recent findings of Nile ecologists, we can surmise there was a *precursor culture on the Nile,* or out in the western desert, that moved back to the current riverbed after they abandoned sites when the heavy rains ceased.

The Mysterious Blank Phase and Nile Ecology

During the Neolithic Subpluvial (9,000 to 6,000 years ago), the Nile basin was very rainy. Because of so much flooding, the precursor sites of protodynastic Egypt are buried either in deep silt or hidden in terraces far away from the current river. Or the Egyptians went far away for

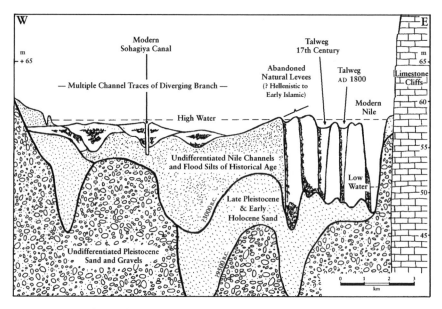

Fig. 3.5. Nile Valley cross-section near Tahta. Adapted from figure 1 of Butzer's Early Hydraulic Civilization in Egypt.

thousands of years and came back to the Nile, since the great river changed its course after the cataclysm and again after the rainy phase. The Nile flows from Lake Tana and Lake Victoria in central Africa down to the sea, and the volume of rain in Africa greatly affects Egypt. Ecoarchaeologist Karl Butzer says, "Major segments of ancient Egyptian history may be unintelligible without recourse to an ecological perspective."[19] Just as in Egypt today, stone temples, mud-brick villages, and tombs were located close to the Nile, away from the fierce aridity and heat of the desert. If the volume of the river decreases or the level of the Mediterranean drops, the water then cuts down through its old silt level, which *leaves the previous shores high and dry as terraces above its new course.* Therefore, generally the highest terraces are the oldest, and the lowest are the most recent.[20] Approximately 13,000 years ago, the Nile was extremely full and wide, and then it cut down deeper, becoming less wide after 11,500 years ago.* It is

---

*Michael Hoffman, *Egypt Before the Pharaohs*. This phase is called the Sahaba-Darau Agradation, from 13,000 to 10,000 BC. The later phase was a time of massive flooding.

extremely doubtful that the Nile course is in the same place now, as can be seen in figure 3.5, and precursor sites must be buried in terraces way out in the western desert or in silt. About early dynastic times, Karl Butzer says, "The axis of the Nile ran far west of its present course between Akhmim (north of Denderah temple) and Cairo."[21] One thing is certain: When the level and location of the Nile changes, people move to the new shores.

More can be understood about the moving and changing sites by studying records of how this process worked during protodynastic and early dynastic times, which Butzer examines in detail. The Abydos region is rich in layers from very early sites, because it is a huge alluvial valley between the mountains and the river; there the Nile was free to move and change. For example, today Abydos is located far away from a great curve of the Nile, but during wetter times, the Osireion was closer to the river. Another moist interval ended about 2900 BC, which caused the abandonment of desert-nomad sites like Abydos and Hierakonpolis.[22] The Osireion seems to have been designed for water to flow into it during the Inundation, because it contains inner pools and channels. The ancient Egyptians built sophisticated systems to channel the Inundation to the fields and lakes, and to temples like the Osireion.[23] Legends describe the fabled Mound of Creation, where Osiris was born when the Mound rose out of the waters after a great flood. The birth of Horus is depicted on the walls in Abydos Temple, yet by its name—Osireion—it is a temple of Osiris. Hence, it very well may be the sacred Mound temple. The Mound would reappear annually deep within the Osireion when the Nile receded after the Inundation, and probably a statue of Osiris was set on top. This was an important yearly ritual because it celebrated creation, so this temple was literally the rebirthing center for Osiris even if the river channel moved. The early dynastic Egyptians cut a canal to the Osireion from the Nile to continue the flow of the Inundation into it. For a few thousand years they built other temples and tombs around the Osireion because it was so sacred, yet they abandoned the site, most likely around 2900 BC. Then around 1300 BC Seti I revived the region again. Butzer shows in graphic detail how the abundant and lean times described in history correlate perfectly with changes in the course of the Nile.

This continual rebuilding caused by changes in the bed of the Nile can be seen all along the river even today. The Valley Temples of the Sphinx and the second pyramid were once closer to the Nile, and later the Nile dropped down, most likely after the moist interval around 2900 BC, possibly much earlier.[24] As the river receded, great limestone causeways that still exist were built to create new access to the Nile. Regarding these kinds of constructions, Butzer found the stone revetments, large piers, and extensive artificial basins—*harbor installations*—on the edge of the desert near Abusir and Abu Garob to be of great interest. Abdel Hakim and I visited this area in March 1996, and the only possible conclusion is that these massive constructions were a large harbor. *It's amazing to think of what must lie buried under the shifting sands of Egypt.* Saqqara, which now is high above and away from the Nile, has been extensively excavated and restored. It is possible to walk on the limestone causeways that once reached the Nile, which have mysterious deep pits next to them that once contained large cedar boats. In 1991, twelve 5,000-year-old large wooden boats were discovered buried in brick pits *twelve miles from the Nile* near a funerary enclosure for the First Dynasty Pharaoh Djer at Abydos.[25] This discovery supports the likelihood that the Nile dropped after the 2900 BC moist interval, when their boats were left high and dry!

Michael Hoffman explored the ecological approach of Karl Butzer and others, and he notes that conventional archaeological opinion is gradually moving again in the direction of locating the Old Nile, the *Ur Nil.*[26] Michael Hoffman, one of the most brilliant early Egyptian archaeologists, is to be commended for his attention to ecoarchaeology. *Ecoarchaeology is putting Egyptology to shame, yet its findings rarely get to the public.* I've had reservations about covering so much of this material in detail, but regardless of old-paradigm Egyptology, *Nile ecologists are driving the dates further back.* By studying the overall context of sites, attention shifts to the whole Nile basin and away from just the known sites on the present river. Adding the cataclysm 11,500 years ago and seeking a better timeline, the Nile course would have changed radically during the crustal shifting and flooding. People would have lived farther out into the desert and remained for quite a while. Then when the Neolithic Subpluvial ended about 6,000 years ago, they moved much closer to the river again. Egyptians who had gone to other places such as north and east may have returned. After 2900 BC, people migrated north out of Abydos, when the pharaohs became more organized. Nile ecology explains the absence of complex sites before 6,000 years ago, which ends the credibility of the instant-flowering model. Will Egyptologists keep on using the Blank as the basis for the instant-flowering-model as Nile ecologists and Nabta Playa prove them wrong? As the hard sciences come up with much better ideas, maybe Egyptologists hope that the public won't have the patience for detailed scientific analysis.

The bed of the Nile downcutted and shifted dramatically 11,500 years ago, and it continued to downcut and move until the rains decreased 6,000 years ago. Predynastic civilization arrived seemingly out of thin air, yet in fact a whole culture relocated its temples and villages, nome by nome, closer to the Nile. *Many sites from 15,000 to 6,000 years ago must be out*

Fig. 3.6. Round Head art from Tassili n'Ajjer with inset of Osiris and Nut in the Primeval Waters. Round Head art is adapted from figure 59 of Settegast's Plato Prehistorian.

in the western desert. How far west? The archaeological researcher Mary Settegast examines Egyptian influences in Tassili n'Ajjer artwork from 10,500 to 6000 BC that was found in the central Sahara. Regarding the Blank, she comments, "One of the many puzzles presented by the Tassili collection is how, at a time when the Nile Valley seems almost deserted, so many of the Round Head compositions could show what appears to be an 'Egyptian' influence."[27] The central Sahara was wetter during the Neolithic Subpluvial, and remnants of the Shemsu Hor probably sojourned there. The Nile might even have been totally swollen as a result of flooding then, and imagine the volume of silt and debris that came down from Central Africa after the cataclysm! Butzer says, "The Nile floodplain and delta are free-draining, seasonally inundated alluvial surfaces that have marked the focus of human settlement since Paleolithic times."* There is no reason *not* to accept Manetho's report of Egypt being ruled by the Shemsu Hor for at least 25,000 years before the cataclysm. There is no reason *not* to consider the possibility that the Sphinx, Osireion, and Valley Temple are more than 12,000 years old and are relics from the First Time. There may be many sites buried in the desert that are different from dynastic sites because the survivors would have been rebuilding their cultural models. A British team of archaeologists released news of a 6,000-year-old treasure trove of sophisticated carvings in the desert east of the Nile. Egyptologist Toby Wilkinson calls it "the Sistine Chapel of Predynastic Egypt" because the depictions of boats and representations of gods have all the elements of later Egyptian art and pharaonic culture.[28] Maybe the culture of the First Time could only be regenerated in full flower on the sacred river, the Nile.

On a much more speculative note, I'd like to offer two assessments

---

*Karl Butzer, *Early Hydraulic Civilization in Egypt,* 106. Some scholars suggest that the early dynastic Egyptians appeared in full flower because the Sumerians influenced them. However, these two cultures differ radically, and what influence there is comes from periods when people from the Fertile Crescent periodically sojourned in Egypt because famines forced them to. Such speculations often come from those who assume that the indigenous Egyptians could not have just evolved themselves (see Hoffman, *Egypt Before the Pharaohs,* 298–344).

of New-Paradigm ideas and discoveries that might advance this process of sifting out data that is coming forth. First, let's just rule out extraterrestrials as the founders of Egyptian civilization, the central thesis of *The Sirius Mystery* by Robert Temple, which tries to prove that extraterrestrials from the Sirius star system visited the Dogon of the central Sahara and gave them their ritual system.[29] I find nothing in Dogon, Egyptian, or Sumerian culture that could not have been accomplished by shamanic traveling in the sky and in the Dreamtime. The archaic Egyptians were masters at visiting other worlds with their minds whenever they wanted to. The Sirius star system is one of those worlds, and anybody can go there with their consciousness. Of course, Sirians or other extraterrestrials *could* come to Earth, but I think there are plenty of better candidates for the Shemsu Hor. I think they were indigenous people of the Nile, who were significant players in the global maritime civilization that flowered during the Edenic culture of the Fifth Underworld. When the stellar, environmental, and evolutionary conditions were just right, they blossomed and probably sailed their great boats around the globe. Maybe they left the Nile circa 10,000 BC and returned circa 4000 BC, which is further considered in chapter 7.

To believe that Egypt's advanced wisdom could have been delivered only by spacemen denigrates the Egyptians' extraordinary innate abilities. Another belief that clouds the minds of otherwise rational people is the search for the "Hall of Records," which comes from the so-called Sleeping Prophet, Edgar Cayce. Although I admire Edgar Cayce's skills as an intuitive healer and medical diagnostician, I've never found his channelings about Egypt to be that accurate or interesting. I have experienced many of these sessions myself and researched their contents, and such input is best evaluated by constant reality checks. It is time to stop looking for hidden rooms in Egypt as the source for enlightenment. It is time to study the remarkable findings of ecoarchaeologists such as Karl Butzer. With these reservations clearly stated, now let's explore some of the *credible* theories from new-paradigm Egyptology.

The Giza Plateau as a Cosmic Clock

The Giza Plateau is the geographic center of Earth's landmasses. It is more stable than areas to the northeast during geological cataclysms, which is exactly what the temple priests told Solon. Butzer says that the Nile alluviated (created silt barriers) rapidly between 7000 and 4000 BC to compensate for rising seas and marine incursion from the Mediterranean.[30] These are good reasons why some monuments on the plateau could be much older. Robert Bauval theorizes that the site plan of the pyramids was laid out in 10,450 BC, but his evidence for that *exact* date is not convincing. Strangely, it is the same as Edgar Cayce's date for the supposed high Atlantean civilization in Egypt, which Bauval admits.[31] As for my own thoughts on this dating, I think the Giza site plan was designed right *after* the cataclysm as one of the earliest systems to observe precession. Considering the oldest Egyptian records, the Giza Plateau and the delta would have been major habitation sites during the Paleolithic as long ago as 40,000 to around 13,000 years, when the Younger Dryas and Gothenburg Flip probably made the Nile inhospitable. Once Earth's axis tilted and survivors recovered enough to look at the sky, *the Leo constellation would have been rising at the new Vernal Point on the Giza Plateau.* The Giza site plan may mark *the advent of precession.* Divine kingship *began* during the Age of Leo. The double lions that support the pharaoh's throne in Dynastic times suggest this. A very archaic double-lion symbol, the Aker, may symbolize the ecliptic.

I am suggesting that the Giza Plateau is an observatory for the new astronomy based on precession. Bauval and his coauthor Adrian Gilbert have built a very solid case that the main pyramids by the Nile mirror the Orion constellation by the Milky Way galaxy in 9000 to 10,000 BC. Factoring in Egyptian records, the Osireion, Nabta Playa, and eco-archaeology, the site plan and the Sphinx are probably part of a site layered with tens of thousands of years of settlement. Bauval and Gilbert suggest the site plan was probably built as a system of mounds that mirror the Orion star system at its low-rising point approximately 12,500

Fig. 3.7. Tutankhamun's throne and the Aker

years ago.* The 9500 BC date for the great cataclysm is very solid, so I think the site plan was built very soon thereafter, because (1) the Orion constellation does not change its vertical angle much when it is reaching its low-rising point in the sky; (2) the mounds were covered by the later pyramids, making it difficult to pinpoint their exact original locations; and (3) if there was no precession before 9500 BC, there would have been no reason for the site plan before that time, which highlights the Sphinx as a marker of the new seasonal points.

The Shemsu Hor must have selected the spectacular Orion system to mark the effects of the new cycles because it is right above the equator, so at Giza, Orion's high- and low-risings are extreme during the 26,000-year cycle. As with the Osireion, if the Sphinx *predates* the cataclysm, it would have been restored afterward when the silt that buried it weathered away. Close to the geodetic center of Earth, the Sphinx would have been the

---

*Bauval and Gilbert, *The Orion Mystery,* 192. Orion's declination would have been about 48 degrees, 53 minutes, and its altitude at meridian about 11 degrees, 8 minutes, in 10,450 BC. In 9500 BC, it would have been about 48 degrees, 20 minutes, and its altitude at meridian about 11 degrees, 40 minutes.

perfect mythological symbol for the cataclysms during the Age of Leo. My intuition tells me it was built soon after the final cataclysm, and then the people had to leave. Could they have built the Sphinx as a reminder of their culture, in case anybody found their way back?

Bauval and Gilbert argue that the pyramids that exist today were built on the site plan mounds in 2550 BC when the shafts into the King's Chamber of the Great Pyramid were aligned to key star positions, an idea first posited by Egyptologist Dr. Alexander Badawy.[32] The authors of *Giza: The Truth,* Ian Lawton and Chris Ogilvie-Herald, discount the shaft-alignment theory because the shafts curve, as viewed from above.[33] That is, starlight would not be sighted through them, which J. Norman Lockyer demonstrated was a key part of Egyptian stellar technology.[34] I leave this to be argued over by others, but it is important because the shaft-alignment theory supports the traditional construction date for the pyramids, circa 2500 BC. Regardless of exactly when the site plan was first constructed by the Nile or when the pyramids were actually built, the Giza Plateau mirrors the Orion star system by the Milky Way galaxy around 11,000 years ago. It was the ideal place to observe precession: The Sphinx marks the constellations that rise on the spring equinox, the four sides of the Great Pyramid dramatically emphasize the four cardinal directions, and the high-

Fig. 3.8. The solar system between the Orion star system and the Galactic Center

and low-rising of Orion emphatically marks Earth's new galactic alignment. Robert Bauval and Graham Hancock move in this direction, possibly unconsciously, regarding the precession of the equinoxes, when they comment that the astrological ages were "believed to have begun to unfold after a kind of spiritual and cultural 'Big Bang' known as Zep Tepi—the 'First Time' of the Gods."[35] The Giza Plateau complex is a sophisticated precessional clock that started ticking around 11,000 years ago.

In the Pyramid Texts, the oldest sacred texts in the world, the pharaoh is guided to travel out in the sky to the Orion star system; *the pharaoh was star traveling!* This idea really struck me, because in Cherokee and Mayan traditions, Orion attunement is an essential doorway into cosmic consciousness. The ridges on the spine of Turtle's back are the three central stars of Orion that correspond to the three Giza pyramids, and the outer four stars are Turtle's feet. Assuming the pharaoh was actually star traveling, then *why* would a high priest want to move the pharaoh out through the Orion star system? Why not the ecliptic? The answer is *galactic:* Our solar system is located between the Orion system and the Galactic Center. If you were in the Galactic Center and you looked out to our solar system, you would see the Orion star system way out beyond this solar system in the Orion Galactic Arm. More easily comprehended from Earth's perspective, regardless of precession, the center of the galaxy is always in one direction and the Orion constellation is in the exact opposite. Then, once the axis of Earth tilted, from the Giza Plateau, during the solar year, this "stargate" exhibited a wild serpentine movement on the horizon, changing its position in the sky from summer to winter, as it still does today.

According to modern science, the Orion star system is where the greatest number of new stars is being born; it is a stellar nursery.[36] Bauval and Gilbert have shown convincingly that the Pyramid Texts describe the pharaoh becoming a star by his ascension to Orion, which makes his intelligence eternally available to Egypt as a cosmic data bank; archaic Egyptians found *another dimension or alternative reality populated by their ancestors.* As long as the pharaoh could go there for guidance about how to maintain a balanced and peaceful culture by the Nile—Maat—the stargate was open. I think the complex stellar technology of the Pyramid

Texts explicates this system, which also suggests that the pharaoh took these journeys during his life as well. Possibly the advent of precession has made it more difficult to access this star-traveling zone. Regardless of the few differences I have with Bauval and Gilbert on dates, they have established that the Pyramid Texts describe the pharaoh's ascension to Orion. Other highly respected researchers, such as the Egyptologist Jane Sellers, have come to the same conclusion.[37] In some way, ascension to Orion linked the dynastic pharaohs with Zep Tepi. Possibly the pharaoh's stargate initially deconstructed because of axial tilting and access was lost to Zep Tepi? Then the dynastic Egyptians rebuilt this access to the utopia by reinstating the rituals from Zep Tepi once the sacred river was habitable again. Temples were built again for the Shemsu Hor to access the stargate, and the rituals resumed.

Numinousness and Stellar Genius

Norman Lockyer catalogues complex star alignments of Egyptian temples from *6400 to 700 BC* that were constructed to capture the light of key stars. Yet because the stars were moving as a result of precession, they had to be constantly reconstructed.[38] This must have been a method for visiting the other reality as far back as 6400 BC. Other systems for capturing stellar, lunar, and solar light exist all over the planet, as if these ancient astronomers believed the reception of starlight was critical for humans, possibly to maintain direct links to other worlds. Could they have found a way to "read" stellar frequencies and developed some form of cosmic telepathy? This is not crazy, since these systems existed worldwide for thousands of years. Lockyer's earliest dates are found before the Blank ended, especially his findings at Karnak.

The Egyptian records say that there was a radically different *quality* of time during Zep Tepi that was unlike dynastic and predynastic Egypt. They say Zep Tepi was a formless eternity that was ruled by gods, not mortals, a time when the Egyptians were very happy. This suggests that Zep Tepi was a time before the cataclysm and before precession began. Later the pharaohs assiduously maintained a *kingship covenant* by their words and deeds, and Osiris and Horus connected dynastic pharaohs to the Shemsu Hor.[39] *Hamlet's Mill* portrays archaic myths as a code language based on highly technical astronomical knowledge. Based on sixty years of research as an Egyptologist, Jane Sellers offers impressive evidence that the Egyptians tracked precessional changes *as far back as 7300 BC,* during the Age of Cancer. Sellers goes back this far with precession because she locates the Golden Age between 7300 and 6700 BC, the beginning and end of Orion's rising at spring equinox.[40] Von Dechend and de Santillana say that humans and gods could meet during the Golden Age at *Time Zero,* about 5000 BC.[41] Regarding the unification of Upper and Lower Egypt under Horus, Sellers concludes, "It was an account constructed to explain the altered sky, and solve the consequent problems that the alterations posed."[42] The unification, as Sellers describes it, is *before* Menes, which was a predynastic union, as is evidenced by the Narmer Palette from Nekhen. These ideas suggest that the rebirth of an order from the First Time by *the unification was designed to deal with the changes caused by the tilt,* which I explore in depth in chapter 5. Sellers's statement suggests that Zep Tepi was a time before the axis tilted, and she contrasts the earlier and later periods by noting that during the First Time, "the skies had a magnificent balance," and during the later historical period, myths were created "to deal with distressing alterations in the sky."[43] The Pyramid Texts tell the story of Sekhmet, the lion goddess, who unleashed the Flood in a rage and nearly obliterated Earth during the Age of Leo. The dynastic Egyptians created a ceremony that involved rebalancing the skies, the erection of the Djed Pillar.

Maat and the Djed Pillar

The Egyptian line of descent was through the mother, so it was shocking when a female goddess, Sekhmet, created catastrophes on Earth. The sought-after order on Earth, Maat, was lost, which was a profound shattering. The sacred balance and access to the stargate had to be found again, so the dynasties were established to maintain order versus chaos by the Nile. A dynastic foundational ritual was the Djed ceremony, when the pharaoh erected a pillar to connect Earth and sky. This maintained the power of the pharaoh because *it gave him access to the sky.* In the Abydos Temple reliefs, the pharaoh is shown holding a tilting pillar that is capped by four sections, the four directions.

The Djed Pillar is a classic symbol of the cosmic vertical axis. The Djed Pillar is depicted initially tilting about 20 to 25 degrees off vertical, *the same as the axial tilt angle of Earth!* Then during the ceremony, it is erected to a vertical position, as if making Earth perpendicular to its orbital plane around the sun, a symbolic way to recreate Zep Tepi; the Djed ceremony seems to be a memory of the vertical axis during Zep Tepi. It suggests that the dynasties were founded by reerecting the pillar to the sky to rebalance Egyptian culture and reestablish Maat. Because of its central geodetic location, the land of Egypt—Khemet—is divine for the world; it is the bridge to the stars that maintains Maat. Divine harmony between the Earth and sky had to be reattained after the axis tilted, because balance is essential for human happiness. The advent of the seasons was a significant change for the people. The four sections on the top of the Djed Pillar are ideal symbols for the equinoxes and solstices as

Fig. 3.9. Seti I erecting the Djed Pillar

well as the four directions. People had to learn to live with Earth in a new way, so agriculture was invented and then venerated as a sacred way of life. The Djed ceremony of Abydos shows the New Kingdom pharaoh, Seti I, reestablishing Maat, his way to access the divine world.

Casting the Giza Plateau complex as a technology for pharaonic ascension through the Orion stargate is not as far-fetched as it may seem. Sometimes I think we are just too limited in the modern world to imagine what they were doing, so I will close this chapter with some speculations: Possibly unusual cosmic infusions came to Earth when Orion was at its low-rising cycle approximately 11,500 years ago. The dynastic Egyptians could have completed the early site plan to access vibrations from key stars more than 11,000 years ago, and then the time came to build (or rebuild) the Great Pyramid, around 4000 to 3500 BC, as a *multidimensional technological device.* Engineer Chris Dunn has written a very challenging book, *The Giza Power Plant,* which argues that the Great Pyramid and certain other pyramids were *sonic power plants that harvested the wave powers of Earth.*[44] After building a strong case that advanced power tools were used in Egypt at least 5,000 years ago, Dunn asked, where's the power source? Could Chris Dunn be right? If so, how can Chris Dunn's hypothesis coexist with Robert Bauval and Adrian Gilbert's Orion correlation? How could the Great Pyramid be both a power plant and a device that enhances human intelligence?

According to *Alchemy of Nine Dimensions,* nine dimensions of consciousness are available to humans while they are in physical bodies.[45] The Heliopolitan Mystery School, one of three ancient Egyptian theological schools, also taught that humans can attain these nine multidimensional levels.[46] During the past 3,000 years our perceptual range has become so limited that we perceive only this dimension—linear space and time. This has made us so left-brain-dominant that people think Egyptian sacred science is arcane nonsense. Based on vibrational resonance, many other dimensions exist, whether people tune in to them or not, as described by advanced mathematics. *Alchemy of Nine Dimensions* describes how modern humans detect these vibrations, just as the Heliopolitan Mystery Schools described how the ancient Egyptians also accessed many dimensions. In

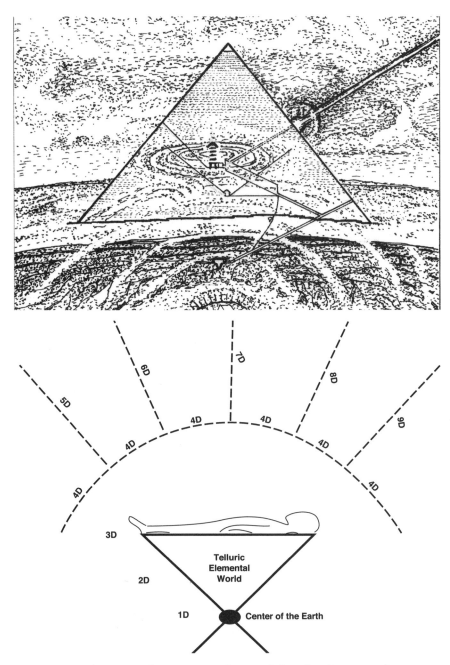

Fig. 3.10. The pyramid as a power plant and the Pleiadian Agenda energy model. The pyramid as a power plant is adapted from Dunn's The Giza Power Plant, *and the energy model is from figure 10 of Clow's* The Pleiadian Agenda.

my system, the higher dimensions—the fifth through ninth—all vibrate to stellar frequencies; the lower dimensions—the first and second—are the vibration of Earth; and the middle dimensions—the third and fourth—vibrate in Hertz frequency ranges that most people detect. The third dimension is linear space and time, while the fourth dimension is the aggregate of human emotions, which functions at the quantum level by means of probabilities; we may or may not act on something we feel. A remarkably innovative new researcher, Laird Scranton, has demonstrated that the Egyptian hieroglyphs are a scientific language that describes the composition of matter.[47] He shows that *they had discovered quantum and string theory thousands of years ago,* and they used this advanced mathematics as the basis of their language.

Chris Dunn says the base of the pyramid is a harmonic integer of Earth that taps Earth energy.[48] This is the same as tapping the second dimension in my system, which is the vibration of Earth.[49] The electromagnetic spectrum maps the field of frequencies from the lower frequencies all the way up to stellar frequencies, which are all potentially detectable by humans aided by technology. Now that we are inventing vibrational technologies such as ultrasound and microwaves, we can see that the ancient Egyptians could have attained such technological expertise as well, especially since they possessed the scientific language for it. We use math, and they used hieroglyphics. Chris Dunn and Laird Scranton are actually demonstrating that *sacred science is technological as well as multidimensional.* One dimension does not cancel out another one; they coexist in structures and bodies. I think the ancient Egyptians understood this because they even understood string theory, which is the basis of the Heliopolitan mysteries. Once our scientists get that far, a technology that accesses the hidden dimensions will open the multidimensional world for us. Imagine technologies based on string theory; stretch your minds! *The pyramid is a device that links lower and higher vibrational frequencies by tapping the vibrations of Earth, which broadcasts stellar frequencies.* That is why it was built on the geodetic center of our planet.

With more and more intense galactic particles penetrating Earth, such as gamma rays, more people are realizing that everything is vibrational. A specific range of frequencies causes physicality, such as massive stone pyramids or your body, but other creations coexist in other dimensions. *We are simultaneously material and vibrational.* Like a pharaoh, we can travel in space and also establish the other world on Earth, which is what our technology would do for us if it were based on many dimensions in harmonic resonance. Few modern people can imagine a device (much less their own bodies) that can exist in many dimensions simultaneously and also be a material technology, yet this is exactly what alchemy is. The severe lack of imagination in modern science causes them to theorize that the soul is a ghost in the machine; however, *the soul continuously manifests itself as the physical body.* Chris Dunn has come up with a great hypothesis for the material usage of the Great Pyramid, and his ideas merit serious consideration. Bauval and Gilbert offer fascinating ideas about higher-dimensional star traveling by the pharaoh. In my mind, the Great Pyramid can be both a power plant and a Giza Plateau star clock. In *Alchemy of Nine Dimensions,* the eighth dimension is the Orion star system—the abode of the Elders and the Ancestors, the sages who know cosmic wisdom. The pharaoh would want to go there after death so that he could continuously advise the living Egyptians. We are trapped in our physical bodies on Earth without developing multidimensional access powers. Like the pyramid, we have a physical form that vibrates with Earth while it also accesses higher frequencies while we live our daily lives. We have just forgotten we exist in the divine world—our human bodies—the access to the many dimensions.

4

THE STORY OF THE
PREDILUVIAL WORLD

*The racial memory of a species is a matter of fact: It tells
a wild creature how to build its nest, how to provide food,
how to find a mate for procreation, how to survive in
open spaces or in a long winter; but the most devastating
experiences are also the most deeply buried and their
reawakening is accompanied by a sensation of terror.*

IMMANUEL VELIKOVSKY[1]

Science Brings Back a Lost World

A great cataclysm in recent memory destroyed a highly advanced civilization in a paroxysm of massive crustal shifting and global flooding. Our
ancestors struggled to rebuild their cultures while the continents and seas
kept changing amid more disasters. Earth was a sea of change for thousands of years. These experiences lurk in the deepest recesses of the human
brain, and now science is resurrecting them. The renowned psychoanalyst
Immanuel Velikovsky, who was one of the early Freudian analysts, also
became widely known as a cosmologist and an ancient historian. He was
one of the first popular writers to bring public attention to catastrophic
theory in the 1950s. His bestselling book, *Worlds in Collision,* told the
story of the cataclysms in vivid and engrossing detail. It sold millions of
copies, probably because people resonated with his catastrophic version

of the recent past. Yet there was an intense negative reaction to his ideas, which really shocked Velikovsky. The scientific establishment was irate and attacked his publisher, Macmillan, because *uniformitarianism*—everything happens by slow change—was the only acceptable paradigm. The senior editor at Macmillan, who accepted the manuscript, was sacked, as well as the director of the Hayden Planetarium, who had proposed a display of Velikovsky's cataclysmic hypothesis. Many scientists refused interviews with Macmillan representatives for their upcoming books.[2]

At the end of his life, after publishing many other books exploring catastrophism that also sold millions of copies, Velikovsky attempted to understand this weird response to his ideas by writing *Mankind in Amnesia*. This time, using his analytical skills, he looked deeply into the hidden springs of human irrationality in both the minds of his detractors and those of his readers. During his long practice, he'd already delved deeply into the minds of his patients. He found most of them had inherited unconscious memory, or *racial memory,* and for some this was buried memories of the recent cataclysmic scenes amid unchained elements. In agreement with Freud regarding racial memory, Velikovsky says, "All ascendancy reaches back to the same generation that was exposed to the trauma."[3] That is, the recent cataclysm is in our minds and probably located in the right brain, as already discussed in the previous chapter. As the memory of the cataclysm comes back, we are participating in the recovery of a collective terror. Velikovsky is the father of modern catastrophism, and it is ironic that this new paradigm comes from a psychoanalyst, not a cosmologist.

Modern experiments in epigenetics are in agreement with these early analysts who said that traumatic experiences can pass to our children, and some researchers are seeking treatments for this problem. Back in the 1950s, Velikovsky's graphic descriptions of the unchained elements caused a big reaction because it stirred ancient memory in many people. While under hypnosis, I experienced great instinctual fear when I accessed a lifetime soon after the cataclysm. Reading *Mankind in Amnesia* helped me make sense out of that difficult session. He believes we need to recover the originating memories to move beyond this crippling fear, as I do. According to indigenous people all over the world, we need to know our stories to value life. Our lives become shared journeys with Earth when collective survival is valued over individual needs. When people focus on sharing instead of hoarding, and creativity instead of violence, they respond to life with courage instead of fear. This approach can release the grip of the controlling left brain so that whole-brain consciousness is available.

Mythology has many stories of life in the global maritime civilization, but few could understand them until geology and archaeology shed more light on what the past was really like. Recent discoveries of archaic sites that date back 9,000 years, such as Çatal Hüyük, and Göbekli Tepe in Turkey, suggest that some extremely old cultures were very advanced. In his day 2,500 years ago, Plato gathered historical accounts of global maritime cultures, such as Atlantis, Egypt, Greece, and the Magdalenians, and in the 1960s, Charles Hapgood in *Maps of the Ancient Sea Kings* analyzed the maps of the lost world. Even in Plato's day, only scattered stones and memory fragments of the lost world still existed, which he assiduously recorded. Aristotle said Plato was the last person in the ancient world who truly understood the difference between mythology and history. As if he knew how important these fragments would be someday, Plato carefully wrote these records down, even though many of his contemporaries already did not believe they were true. The philosopher Crantor, who was a contemporary of Aristotle and wrote the first commentaries on Plato's dialogues, went to Egypt to confirm Plato's report. Crantor reported that he saw the column of hieroglyphs that tell the story that Plato described.[4] During the Golden Age of Greece 2,500 years ago, the Alexandrian Library of Egypt was a repository for at least 10,000 years of the records of the leading minds of the ancient world, and many of them believed that Atlantis had existed. The library was partially burned by Julius Caesar in 48 BC, later by Christian fanatics, and then closed when the Arabs destroyed Alexandria in AD 642. Vandals sacked the Roman Empire in AD 455, Greco-Roman culture died, and memory of the old world sank into the gloom of the Dark Ages. If Plato's accounts had not survived, the Western world might have totally forgotten the prediluvial world. Indigenous people in the Western Hemisphere also retained these ancient stories for thousands of years, but they were brutally conquered, and their memories of origin were nearly destroyed during the "Age of Reason." The fact is, the myths of the conquered people were remarkably similar to the stories of origin in the Bible, so these stories had to be obliterated by the superior ones. Now the cataclysmic scenario is coming forth in the scientific discoveries of the last three hundred years, and the remaining *cross-cultural global records of indigenous people are being verified by science.* Folk memory lives a long time. For example, Australian Aborigines have described the locations of 8,000-year-old landmarks that are now deep underwater with such precision that modern divers have found them.[5] *We are poised to remember Earth as the global maritime civilization.*

This recovery of historical taproots excites many people; yet social Darwinism still controls education and the media: We are supposed to believe that archaic people were nonverbal primitives, and that humanity has been always been advancing. How can one appreciate the Lascaux Cave–painters if they are thought of as grunting hairy oafs with clubs who dragged their skin-clad women around by the hair? How can one relate to the indigenous inhabitants of the Americas when they are described as wild hordes of vicious hunters armed with sharp Clovis points, who roared down from Beringia to Tierra del Fuego 11,500 years ago? By being educated with such half-baked ideas, we've nearly lost our ability to correctly reconstruct the past. Meanwhile, as new-paradigm researchers find evidence for highly advanced archaic cultures, more and more people question Darwinian dogma. Why is modern culture so degenerate if we've always been advancing? Casting aside this infantile conditioning, many are going on passionate treasure hunts to get our story back. Even if the new-paradigm searchers sometimes seem like excessive romantics seeking Arthur and the Grail, they are rebooting the hard drive that crashed inside our skulls—the memory records in the right brain. You may feel angry when you realize that fools with superiority complexes who aim to rule the world by controlling access to the past have been leading you around, but it's the truth.

Based on 300 years of scientific research, we now see Earth with fresh eyes. Still, so much of the record of the deep past is lost. Globally mapping the previous world is like working on a 1,000-piece puzzle with only 50 of the pieces, and without a cover that depicts the finished puzzle. To imagine the lost world, we must accurately date, identify, and establish locations for every fragment from the prediluvial world. Plato is the guiding source because he attempted to report the history of his known world. He says that *Atlantis was only one among many* of the leading cultures in a maritime civilization, a clue that takes us beyond focusing only on Atlantis, yet we need to start with it. The Atlanteans probably came through the cataclysm in better condition than land-based cultures because they were seafarers, and I will argue that they had already begun migrating when the worst phase of the cataclysm came in 9500 BC; many of them were in boats just as the myths say. Atlantis was still around and very influential during the early Holocene epoch, since widely separated survival legends report that Atlanteans helped people survive and start over. Regarding this period, Rand and Rose Flem-Ath say, "The Atlanteans now ruled over the ruins of a world humbled by the earth's fearful and widespread desolation."[6] New-paradigm researchers have been working very hard to get information about *hidden data*—artifacts hidden away by old-paradigm archaeologists and anthropologists. For instance, wanting to control the story of the peopling of the Americas, in 1911 the Smithsonian took legal control of all previous evidence that human beings were in the Americas during the Pleistocene epoch—2.4 million to 11,500 years ago by conventional chronology.[7] Allan and Delair's revised chronology (figure 2.5 on p. 53) shortens the Pleistocene to a brief period between the end of the Pliocene epoch and the beginning of the Holocene, which suggests that most of the original people in the Americas perished, and then many new people came in after 9000 BC.

Rand and Rose Flem-Ath argue that the Aymara language of Peru, which is still spoken by 2.5 million descendants, must be a survival from Atlantis. Bolivian mathematician Ivan Guzman Rojas used Aymara as the basic interpretive basis for computer software that translates English simultaneously into other languages. "Aymara is rigorous and simple—which means that its syntactical rules always apply, and can be written out concisely in the sort of algebraic shorthand that computers understand. Indeed, such is its purity that some historians think it did not just evolve like other languages, but was actually constructed from scratch."[8] The Flem-Aths wonder, "Could it have been the survivors of the lost island paradise who gave the Aymara a language so precise, so grammatically pure, that it would become a tool for the most advanced technology of our own century?"[9] Peru and Bolivia are two of the most likely places for such a survival, because incredible cyclopean monuments *13,000 feet above sea level* still exist on the Altiplano, which drastically uplifted only 11,500 years ago.[10] As we have only recently found that Aymara works as a computer language, the value of realizing the levels of our previous attainments is self-explanatory. If the Peruvians derive from Atlantis, what was it like on the original island? Let us take a closer look at Plato's story.

Plato's Description of Atlantis in the *Critias* and the *Timaeus*

The archaeological researcher Mary Settegast says that Plato's story is "our most reliable guide to the Epi-Paleolithic World."[11] Existing in the *Critias* and part of the *Timaeus,* Plato's story is the source for almost all speculations about Atlantis—*Atlantology.* What follows is my own synopsis of Plato's description of Atlantis from the *Critias,* a story that was told to Plato by Critias, who claimed he got it while visiting Sais, Egypt, from Solon, a Greek statesman, in the early sixth century BC.

Fig. 4.1. The Atlantean Seal

The city of Atlantis where Poseidon seeded Cleito was constructed of great concentric circles around a center island. There were two great circles of land around the island, and three great circles of water around the land. The central island had two gushing springs of pure water—one hot and one cold— which were channeled throughout the island for growing abundant produce. The ten children of Poseidon and Cleito lived in districts around the temples in this central complex. The island had its own abundant mineral resources and received many imports as duty. There were plentiful trees and wild animals, and this island in the sun produced domesticated animals, crops, roots, herbs, and drink in rich profusion. This was its natural endowment.

The Atlanteans built temples, palaces, harbors, and docks, and they bridged the great concentric circles of water built by Poseidon by digging a canal 300 feet wide and 100 feet deep from the sea to the outside ring. They made channels through the rings of land at the bridges, which they roofed over. The bridge to the central island led to an exquisite palace, and each successive king added to its beauty, because it was the home of the original Ancestors. The center of the palace was a sacred shrine to Poseidon and

Fig. 4.2. The Sacrifice of the Bull in the Temple of Poseidon

Cleito surrounded by a golden wall, and entry was forbidden. Here there was a temple of Poseidon, which was sided with silver; and the pediments were graced with gold figures—a statue of Poseidon in a chariot drawn by six winged horses. There were other altars inside, and hot and cold springs flowed through fountains into basins and baths, and streams from the springs also flowed through Poseidon's grove of tall trees. The water was channeled to the outer ring islands by means of aqueducts over the bridges. The middle island had a special course for horse racing and barracks for the king's bodyguard. The city was densely built up around a circular wall around the outer ring of the palace, and beyond the city were numerous villages with a wealthy population sprinkled amid rivers, lakes, pastures, and woodlands.

Each of the ten kings of Atlantis had the power in his own region. All ten assembled in the Temple of Poseidon every fifth or sixth year to exchange mutual pledges and deal with mutual interests. Bulls roamed at large in the central palace, and each king entered alone with clubs and nooses to hunt a bull. When a king caught one, he cut the bull's throat over the central pillar, which was engraved with the laws and curses on those who disobeyed the law; the blood flowed over these inscriptions. The kings dropped a clot of blood from each bull they'd slain into a bowl of wine and mixed it. After cleansing the pillar and burning the rest of the blood, they drew wine from the bowl in golden cups, poured a libation over the fire, swore their oaths to the laws and themselves, and drank of this cup. After this they donned their deep-blue ceremonial robes, remained by the fire as it died out, and gave and submitted to judgments. They promised to never make war on each other but come to each other's aid if any one of them might lose his royal power. They would consult each other about daily affairs, and the house of Atlas was leader; but even the king of that house could not put any of his mutual fellows to death without the consent of the majority of ten.*

---

*Plato, *Timaeus and Critias*, 136–44. The *Critias* actually starts out in the *Timaeus*, which is a dialogue about human origins from the cosmic realms. Once humans emerge on Earth; Plato tells the story of Atlantis. The way Plato linked these issues is very similar to how the Egyptians linked Zep Tepi to the Shemsu Hor. This suggests that both concepts represent the same time period more than 11,500 years ago. By analogy, Plato's description of the cosmic time may be right out of the Egyptian temple records.

Prediluvial Cultures

This story of Atlantis is the oldest *historical* description of precatastrophic civilization. Plato repeatedly insisted on its total veracity, and because of his stature as a scholar, there is no reason to assume he made it up. As with the Egyptian records, we need to *seriously* consider all the parts of these ancient sources and cease picking the parts that fit with preconceived notions. Although any academic who takes this story seriously is considered an idiot, many have nonetheless gone on a search for the actual remains of advanced civilizations from more than 12,000 years ago. This is a daunting search because the rising sea levels after the cataclysms totally obliterated the sites of the global maritime ports and cities such as Atlantis. The Flem-Aths argue that the remnants of Poseidon's Island are under the ice of Lesser Antarctica, which could be true based on Hapgood's research of a map that shows ice-free sections of Antarctica—the Piri Re'is Portalon.[12] Getting beyond too much focus on Atlantis, Plato said Atlantis was just one civilization among many 11,500 years ago. Hapgood's *Maps of the Ancient Sea Kings* greatly widens this view to a global maritime civilization, and other scholars who are stretching this view will be discussed.

Prediluvial remains are still being discovered; for example, a major cyclopean monument 150 feet below sea level near Yonaguni Island east of Taiwan is being investigated. Modern marine archaeological surveys are being used in the global search for the seafaring civilizations of more than 12,000 years ago on the continental shelves worldwide. Ocean geologist S. Badrinaryan is responsible for the underwater surveys in the Gulf of Khambat, India, where there is much evidence for many layers of ancient civilizations. Badrinaryan comments that the sea level 20,000 years ago was more than 400 feet below current sea levels, so one place to look for prediluvial civilizations is along the paleochannels of various rivers that flow into the sea. Several major rivers drain into the Gulf of Khambat, and layers of ancient urban sites have been discovered on its paleochannels that are dated to 9500 BC, which got my attention: This is a city that was destroyed during the cataclysm! Even more fascinating is they've found the oldest fired pottery in the world, which has been scientifically dated back to 20,000 to 30,000 years ago. In other words, this site has remnants of pottery from the global maritime civilization![13]

Maps of the Ancient Sea Kings provides ample evidence for a global maritime civilization that was trading all over the world from 17,000 to 6,000 years ago. The fact is, *Atlantis is only one advanced culture among many that existed more than 6,000 years ago.* Earth hosted a global maritime civilization of seacoast cities that are now mostly underwater, and their boats would have rotted because they were wooden. On the land, hunter-gatherers and horticulturists used caves for rituals, such as Lascaux Cave, and we have also found some of their artifacts because their tools and monuments were made of stone. For example, engraved stones were found in 1937 in the La Marche Caves near Lussac-les-Chateaux that depict people from 15,000 years ago wearing boots, pants, shirts, and hats! Some stones show details of men riding horseback and perfectly vested in an altogether modern style.[14] Well, people who wear complex clothing usually live in houses and cities, so these engraved stones have been kept hidden in inaccessible drawers in the museum! When you start to look, signs of the archaic seafaring culture show up everywhere. For example, some of the most amazing artifacts left by the early dynastic Egyptians are boats of "an advanced design capable of riding out the most powerful waves and the worst weather of the open seas" that were buried at Saqqara and the Giza Plateau.[15]

The wall paintings of Akrotiri, a buried city on Santorini Island, depict astonishing fleets of large ships that are very similar to the Egyptian boats.[16] These murals hearken back to the global maritime civilization, even though they were painted around 1600 BC. The great Minoan seafarers plied the waters for thousands of years until the volcano on Santorini erupted and their culture ended. The oldest layers of Minoan sites are at least 7,000 years old, so they flourished for a long time. These murals are precious and were very well preserved by the volcanic ash. The ancient Egyptian boats are really intriguing, because on the Giza Plateau these boats were found resting in their own special stone tombs next to the sides of pyramids, as if they were venerated relics of the seafaring culture or replicas built during the early dynasties.

Plato describes a war between the Atlanteans, Greeks, and Egyptians, who were all sailing the Mediterranean and the Atlantic 11,000 years ago. Plato's war attracts less interest than his description of Atlantis, yet this war sheds light on the origins and politics of the seafarers. Later, Egypt and Greece entered history, but Atlantis did not (except for scattered dwindling colonies), although many indigenous people claim Atlantean descent, such as the Maya. According to Plato, *Atlantis controlled the Magdalenian region* (southwestern Europe). Cultures in the Magdalenian area have other labels, such as the earlier Solutrean and Gravettian phases, but for simplicity's sake, I am using Magdalenian.

Mary Settegast's *Plato Prehistorian* explores this riveting clue in detail, because it is a bridge to cultures that flourished from *30,000 to 11,500 years ago* that have left significant traces. Plato says in the *Timaeus* that the Atlanteans controlled the populations inside Mediterranean Libya up to the borders of Egypt and Europe as far as Tyrrhenia (northern Italy).[17] The famous Magdalenian cave artists of southwestern Europe depict the main elements of Plato's description of Atlantis, such as the key Atlantean animals—bull, horse, and lion. Many have wondered why the Magdalenian artists just disappeared from the face of Earth as if they never existed, just like the fall of Atlantis! *Plato Prehistorian* analyzes the *Timaeus* based on the assumption that it is an accurate description of Mediterranean politics more than 11,000 years ago, which creates a bridge to the mysterious cave painters; it is really the first accurate history of the region.

Atlantis as the Primal Root of the Magdalenian Culture

From 20,000 to 12,000 years ago, southwestern Europe was dominated by the Magdalenian culture. Their remnants have been found in caves on or near rivers that empty into the Atlantic in present-day Spain and France, such as the Lascaux Cave. Deep within these caves are exquisite, world-renowned paintings of bulls and horses—Poseidon's animals—and many have commented on their artistic sophistication and eerie beauty. In popular Greek mythology, Poseidon was the first to tame the horse.

 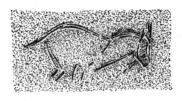 

Fig. 4.3. Paleolithic bridled horses. Adapted from figure 9a of
Settegast's Plato Prehistorian.

More evidence than the engraved stones of Lussac-les Chateaux exists that the Magdalenians tamed horses—for example, 15,000-year-old drawings of horses with bridles found on cave walls. Many archaeologists have concluded that paintings of horses in the caves of St. Michel d'Arudy, Grotte de Marsoulas, and La Marche are wearing harnesses or bridles.[18] The Atlanteans must have had a written language, since Plato said the central pillar was engraved with the laws and curses. The connections between the Magdalenians and the Atlanteans in language, art, and symbolism are major. Anthropologist Richard Rudgley finds many similarities between the Old European script from the Vinca culture (likely derived from the Magdalenians) and Linear A of the Cretans.[19]

Regarding Poseidon's pillar, Settegast compares known Paleolithic signs with early Indus Valley, Greek, and Runic signs and concludes that they all derived from Upper Paleolithic signs. Atlantis may be the inspiration for Magdalenian art, as there was a remarkable regional uniformity in widely separated cave art over a long phase of time. This uniformity has always puzzled scholars. Settegast notes that Magdalenian cave art shows "virtually no regional differentiation," and in southwest Europe "a uniform style is recognizable in the art, and whenever the style changed, it changed everywhere."[20] She suspects "that the original source and conservor of the Magdalenian canon lay elsewhere."[21] There are other Atlantean elements in the caves that are even more spectacular than horse training, linguistic roots, and symbolic derivations; Settegast believes she has actually uncovered the primal/generative ritual source of Atlantis in the famed Lascaux Cave painting of the bird-headed man. Her astonishing interpretation of the Lascaux ritual cave as a root of early Indo-European mythology is presented here in detail because it is a key source for the mysterious primal root.

"First Man and the Primordial Bull" Summarized from *Plato Prehistorian*

The sixteen-foot-deep shaft in Lascaux Cave drops down to a small chamber at the bottom, where there is a six-foot-long painted panel that depicts a bird-headed or masked ithyphallic man suspended at an angle in front of a huge bison. A bird is perched on a pole below the man; the wounded bison hovers above him, and a rhinoceros is behind the man and moving away. Judging by the worn-away condition of the shaft, as well as deposits of bone points and small stone lamps, this was the main ritual cave of Lascaux. Many scholars believe this painting is of the death of the divine twin when the world was created, and Settegast builds on their ideas, since twin kingship is a core archetype in world mythology.

This mythological zone is very rich, so a review of Settegast's thought is needed first. She believes that the Indo-European people remembered a Golden Age when the twins were born. She notes that the main hero/twin kings of Indo-European culture—Yima of Persian history, Yama in the Rig Veda, and Ymir of Scandinavian myth—are all derived from the same Indo-European root, *yemo,* or "twin."[22] When Yima lost his kingly power and glory, it fled from him in the form of a bird, and the ithyphallic man is

Fig. 4.4. First Man and the Primordial Bull

bird-headed and seems to have dropped his bird-topped staff. Also, stories of Yima losing his power are involved with bull sacrifice, the central ritual in the gatherings of the Atlantean kings. An early version of the myth is the story of Gayomart and the Primordial Bull from the Persian Bundahishn, which Settegast examines as the inspiration for the Lascaux painting.[23]

Anthropologist Felicitas Goodman was intrigued by the angle of First Man as well as the odd position of his arms, and she thought it could be a ritual posture. She compares it with a similar dynastic depiction of Osiris with the same angle and arm positions, which depicts Osiris rising toward the heavens (most likely to Orion). Goodman also links this painting to divine-twin mythology. Then by linking the Lascaux painting with dynastic Egypt through posture analysis, Goodman hypothetically spans *12,000 years and links the prediluvial world with dynastic Egypt.* Osiris's twin brother, Seth, dismembered Osiris, and then he was put back together again by Isis so he could procreate and ascend; his son, Horus, is bird-headed. To test this interpretation, Goodman constructed boards to hold students at the same angle (37.5 degrees). She had them assume the same arm postures, she rattled and put them into trance, and they ascended to the sky world![24] I experienced this posture on the boards at the Cuyamungue Institute with Dr. Goodman in 1995, and I ascended right to Orion myself!

Links between dynastic Egypt and the Magdalenian culture are also substantiated by the research of Dr. Stephen Oppenheimer, who has used hemoglobin defects to trace Southeast Asian migratory patterns, which he describes in detail in *Eden in the East: The Drowned Continent of Southeast Asia.* He constructs a link between the universal stories of Southeast Asian twin kingship and the story of Osiris and Seth in the Pyramid Texts, which places the twin myths of Southeast Asian seafaring cultures back more than 5,000 years.[25] Oppenheimer's research highlights the global spread of these cultures on the seas. Meanwhile, orthodoxy still insists nobody sailed the oceans and migrated in boats. Inexplicably, needing to defend the Bering Strait land-bridge hypothesis, which is only part of the story, orthodoxy misses the other half of the story.

Most researchers believe the Indo-Europeans lost their unity and power approximately 11,000 years ago, about the same time as Plato's date for the fall of Atlantis. Regarding the global environment again, in various places the seas rose and/or the land sank—isostasis—approximately 300 feet during the flowering of Magdalenian culture and then approximately 150 feet more during the Early Holocene. The global maritime people would have built their cities on the seacoasts and rivers, just as we still prefer to do today. Now, these areas are hundreds of feet under the sea on the continental shelf as already discussed. How the sea affected these cultures was dramatically emphasized in 1991, when an undisturbed previously inhabited cave from 27,000 to 18,500 years ago—Cosquer Cave—was discovered near Marseille by divers 137 feet below the sea's surface. This 137 foot depth reflects the Holocene rise, and the earlier 300-foot rise would put the cave quite far above the shore.[26] Somebody, either the seafarers or the people who lived on the land, used this cave for rituals.

The Magdalenian cave painters left some stone records of themselves in the caves, yet the ruins of the coastal cities of seafarers lie more deeply submerged on the continental shelves, so everybody thinks the Magdalenians lived in caves! To assist readers in imagining these seacoast cities of more than 12,000 years ago, the illustrator drew an imaginary global maritime city on his rendition of the extended continental shelf 27,000 years ago; Cosquer Cave is beyond the city in the ridge behind the imaginary temple (figure 4.5). Cosquer Cave has paintings from 17,500 to 27,000 years ago, including some beautiful red ochre handprints. Allan and Delair's revised chronology in figure 2.5 (p. 53) makes more sense in light of such vast spans of time; these painters were living during the finishing stages of 29 million years of relatively peaceful evolution.

Returning to the discussion of Lascaux Cave, Settegast believes that the Lascaux ritual painting depicts the mythical or ancestral roots of the original Lascaux group and that it is also a portrayal of one of the mythical twins of Atlantis. She says, "The scene portrayed here may find its closest surviving counterpart in Indo-European cosmogony. The composition in the Lascaux Shaft bears a provocative resemblance to the world-creating death of Gayomart (the Iranian First Man) and the Primordial Bull. . . . Gayomart and the bull lived in a state of divine bliss until the evil principle broke into the world, causing the death of the pair. When the bull died, its marrow flowed forth to create all the nourishing and healing plants; its semen was borne to the moon for purification and thence to the creation of the species of all animals. From Gayomart's body came the metals, from his

Fig. 4.5. Prediluvial global maritime city

own seed, purified in the sun, sprang the ten species of men."[27] Gayomart and the bull have their counterparts in Scandinavian and Vedic mythology, and the Iranian version (the one that is thought to be the original version) is the one that is the most faithful to the Lascaux Shaft. Of course, this indicates that Atlantean influence reached all the way to Scandinavia, which is certainly supported by Hapgood's analysis of the Zeno map.[28] The similarity of the Lascaux Cave posture to the Osiris posture (as compared by Goodman) emphasizes the global nature and great age of this myth. Oppenheimer traces the movement of the story of twin brothers, Kulabob and Manub, from central Southeast Asia to South America more than 5,000 years ago. He believes that this story is the source of the story of Cain and Abel and that the mark of Cain is a common reptilian tattoo that is found in Southeast Asia.[29]

The links between Plato's description of the Atlantean bull ritual, the Lascaux painting, the ascension of Osiris, the originating Iranian creation story, and Southeast Asian mythology are mind-boggling, but there is even more, according to Settegast: The rhinoceros embodies the principle of evil in Eurafrican mythology. This has the elements of the Persian myth of Gayomart in the *Bundahishn,* in which "the bull lived in divine bliss until the evil principle broke into the world, causing the death of the pair."[30] According to mythologist Brian Clark, "Ultrasound technology has revealed that many twin pregnancies result in a single birth, and that one of the twins is either absorbed into the body of the other twin or expelled, unnoticed by the mother, which Clark calls *the vanishing twin syndrome.*"[31] These core twinship myths may even be *biological*! The erect phallus of the man may represent his seed that generated the ten species of humans, and the large bull testicles may represent the flow of the bull's semen that created the plants and animals. Settegast comments, "The slaying of the First Man and the Primordial Bull—the cosmogonic act itself—would have been an eminently appropriate subject for portrayal in the depths of the sanctuary at Lascaux."[32] Human-bison themes have been found at three other Magdalenian sites dating from 19,000 to 14,000 years ago, and Cosquer Cave has a similarly depicted birdman being killed.

Imagine the ancestors of the Indo-Europeans sliding down a rope carrying torches into the depths of Lascaux Cave thousands of years ago to ritualize the slaying of the First Man and the Primordial Bull. Once Goodman discovered that postures took people into specific experiences while in trance, she experimented with them in 1977, and the Lascaux Cave posture caused the group to embark on a spirit journey. She realized that they were rediscovering "a system of signals to the nervous system, a complex strategy capable of shaping the amorphous trance into a religious experience." They had "taken the step from the physical change of the trance to the experience of ecstasy, they had passed from the secular to the sacred."[33] Possibly 17,000 years ago, initiates were taken to see the depiction of the birdman, and perhaps they were taken into the larger area of the cave, they assumed the posture, a rattler or drummer put them into trance, and they took a spirit journey.

These mysterious caves draw us way back in time when life simply sprang forth from the semen of the First Man and the entrails of the Primordial Bull. Since Cosquer Cave exhibits such long time sequences, it seems that *the cataclysmic rift has separated us from direct contact with spirit realms*. Goodman has found a way for modern people to connect with archaic consciousness by assuming the postures while in trance, postures that were used by shamanic cultures for thousands of years. Animals inherit instinctual ways of life in order to function in their habitats; if their habitats are destroyed, they can't live. Velikovsky says that we also inherit racial memory and instinct. There is much evidence that shamanic cultures experience freedom by traveling out of their bodies to access the human spiritual habitat—*fields of energy that function in many dimensions.* If nobody travels there, is this spiritual habitat destroyed? Birdmen may have been depicted all over the world for many thousands of years to remind people they can ascend to the spirits or stars, such as Osiris ascending to Orion.

Alaise as a Magdalenian Travel Center

As we strive to get in touch with the consciousness of people long ago, a sense of their landscape and ways of life really helps, especially with the Magdalenians, since all we have mostly found are their cave remains. It is really hard to think of them as not living in caves, and yet why were they wearing the complex clothing depicted on the La Marche stones? Why were they so fond of the horses that they bridled? This implies mobility and travel. The illustrator helped us imagine a global maritime city by the sea, and the French philologist Xavier Guichard has compiled some truly remarkable and little-known research that may offer more information about the highly developed culture in the Magdalenian region. A philologist studies the origins of geographical place-names. After many years of research, Guichard came to the conclusion that in ancient Europe there were three basic place-names: *Burgus, Antium,* and *Alesia.* Alesia got his attention because it was never given to a town or village founded in historic times, and we even find it in pre-Homeric times as *Eleusis,* which moves us back at least 3,000 years. Regarding its Indo-European linguistic roots, *Ales, Allis,* or *Alles* meant a meeting point to which people traveled, which suggests nomadic travelers. Guichard identified the various forms of *Alesia* by sound, and he found *more than 400* of these towns or villages in France alone, where the name was the most concentrated, as you can see in figures 4.6(a) and 4.6 (b).[34]

Guichard spent the next twenty-five years of his life visiting these

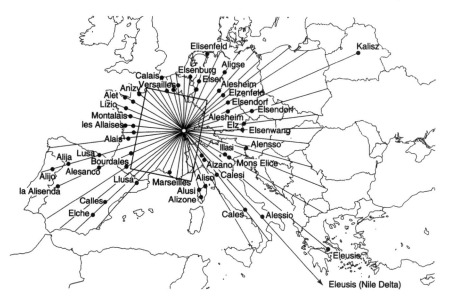

Fig. 4.6a. Alaise locations. From Gooch's Neanderthal Legacy.

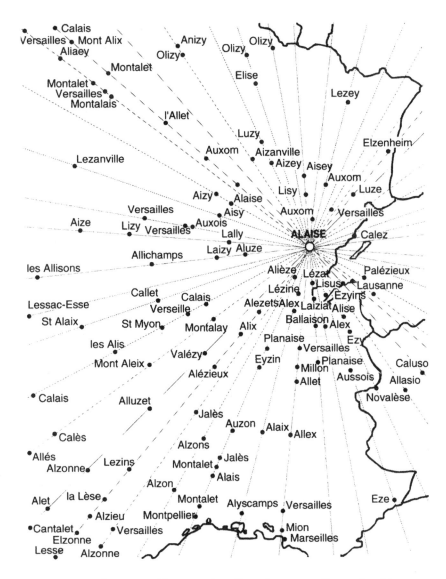

Fig. 4.6b. Inset of figure 4.6a: Alaise locations. From Gooch's
Neaderthal Legacy.

places, and they had two main features: flat areas on hills overlooking rivers, and a manmade well of mineral waters plus available salt. Guichard deduces that these "had all been ancient centers where travelers could stop and drink the life-giving waters."[35] As you can see with Guichard's maps, they appear to be places in a vast geodetic system, and Guichard proposed that the whole of Europe centered on an ancient center called Alaise somewhere between Dijon, France, and Geneva, Switzerland. Analyzing the system, Guichard says this area was divided up by two compass cards, methods used by Greek geographers to mark the meridian and the equinoxes and solstices. This suggests that this system helped Holocene people make sense of the seasons, and it may be only that. Francis Hitching comments that cartographers have found that something is not quite right with Guichard's projections on these maps, and that Guichard may have taken his conclusions too far, even though he had found a central truth.[36]

I mention all this because the Neanderthal researcher Stan Gooch notes that there are twenty-eight radiating lines, which is a sign of Neanderthal and Cro-Magnon moon-based culture, which may mean a *postcataclysmic culture layered this system over Magdalenian sites.* Gooch also notes that the radiating lines are like a spider's web, which is a major Neanderthal archetype associated with the moon.[37] When I look at Guichard's maps, I also see the compass cards, which Jean Richer studied in Greece. Richer found that the early Greek temples and sacred sites are in similar radiating alignments that are evidence of a "cult of a great solar god."[38]

In these maps, I also see a huge nomadic spiral system that centers on Alaise, a system of enchantment of the land and the people as described by Christine Rhone and John Michell in *Twelve-Tribe Nations.*[39] John and I spent many hours talking about enchantment, a very ancient way to harmonize cultures with sound, and John sensed that these kinds of systems based on wheels of twelve go much farther back in time than people think. I discuss geomancy, ley lines, and vortexes in the next chapter, where I initially thought Guichard's research should be. Yet here I tell the story of the prediluvial world. The Magdalenian advance is such a critical part of this story, and there are so many missing links, I've put it here. I think this system could be the remnants of a vast nomadic system from *before* the cataclysm, and then later remnants emphasize the seasons, when the radiating lines were probably reduced from twenty-eight to twelve. I think it reaches far back into the Magdalenian culture and then was continued during the Holocene. The mineral springs and salt, and the locations by rivers suggest an ancient people who used horses to travel

and trade. Could it be a remnant of the land-based system that was organized to supply and link the global maritime civilization? No matter what,
Guichard's research calls for deep study, which will be difficult since only
a few copies of his 558-page book exist in European museums.[40] Armed
with a possible sense of Magdalenian culture on land, we return to Plato's
war to seek more understanding about our loss of primordial memory.

A Three-Part "Fall of Atlantis" Scenario

In Plato's account, the Atlanteans attacked the Athenians, who were allies
of the Egyptians, in 9600 BC, just before the cataclysm. Settegast dates
this war to circa 8500 BC based on uncorrected carbon-14 dating of battle remains.[41] These battle remains could easily be evidence for maritime
raiding and stress among wandering people of the Mediterranean during
a thousand years of resettlement chaos *after* the battle and the cataclysm.
Plato says the war occurred in 9600 BC, and then immediately earthquakes and floods devastated the Greeks. The cataclysm Plato describes
is the same one described in *Cataclysm! Compelling Evidence of a Cosmic
Catastrophe in 9500 BC*. The dates are just too close for it to be otherwise. As already mentioned, marine archaeology off the Gulf of Khambat
supports a huge destruction in 9500 BC.

A proposed pole shift as well as axial tilt and rising seas may have
caused the Atlantean political difficulties. According to Hapgood, from
17,000 to approximately 12,000 years ago, *the magnetic North Pole shifted
from the middle of Hudson Bay in Canada to its present location,* and
Antarctica relocated over the South Pole.[42] Hapgood says, "According to
my interpretation of much radiocarbon and other evidence, a great shift
of the Earth's crust began about 17,000 years ago. It was of course a slow
movement, requiring perhaps as much as 5,000 years for its completion.
North America was shifted southward, and with it the whole western
hemisphere, while the eastern hemisphere was shifted northward. The
effect was to cause the melting of the great ice cap in North America,
while placing Northern Siberia in deep freeze."[43] Hapgood's mechanism is
a gradual crustal shift, whereas in *Cataclysm!* Allan and Delair propose an

instantaneous shift in 9500 BC. J. B. Delair helped me clarify this issue in a letter dated August 3, 1999, in which he says that during a conversation he had with Hapgood about this in London a few years before he died, Hapgood admitted the crust would not slip as a single unit over 5,000 years as described above. Yet the movement of the magnetic pole would have created dramatic temperature changes at and near the poles.

The Flem-Aths are in agreement with Hapgood that a crustal displacement occurred, but they feel it was more sudden and was triggered by astronomical cycles. Regarding crustal shifting and astronomical theory, the Flem-Aths say, "We suggest that if the shape of the Earth's orbit deviates from a perfect circle by more than 1 percent, the gravitational influence of the sun increases because its path is narrower at points. The sun exercises more pull upon the planet and its massive ice sheets. Their ponderous weight alternately pushes and pulls against the crust and this immense pressure, combined with the greater incline in the Earth's tilt and the sun's increased gravitational pull, forces the crust to shift."[44]

Desmond Lee, who translated the *Timaeus* and the *Critias,* commented, "The idea of a lost world or continent is an invitation to let the imagination run riot."[45] Atlantis has driven thousands of researchers crazy, but now we have enough scientific and archaeological data to begin to clarify the real story. The main issues are: (1) If Plato's island sank, *where* is it now? (2) Is Plato's date of 9600 BC correct? And, (3) if Atlantis is the originating culture for many world cultures, how did it pass down its knowledge? These questions won't go away even though orthodoxy continues to reject the probable existence of the global maritime civilization and continues to debunk anybody who talks about Atlantis. What follows is my own highly speculative scenario of the lost island, Atlantis. I incorporate the Flem-Ath Antarctica hypothesis—the lost city of Atlantis is under the ice of Lesser Antarctica—because their case is excellent.

According to conventional science, Antarctica and northern Europe were getting colder and freezing up 17,000 to 11,500 years ago, and North America was warming as the polar ice melted. Cambridge geologist Tjeerd H. Van Andel says the end of the glacial maximum 18,000 to 12,000 years ago was totally atypical of previous glacial phases and that ice cores indicate a sharp cold phase 12,500 years ago (Younger Dryas) that caused very rapid climate changes.[46]

Most habitation sites were destroyed 11,500 years ago, so I can only speculate on what people were doing in this environment. Yet we have enough data to float some working images: Because of climate change and rising seas, approximately 17,000 to 15,000 years ago people began moving from one place to another. Because of rising water and intensifying cold, between 14,000 and 12,000 years ago the Atlantean kings in Poseidon's city on Lesser Antarctica would have been forced to move. Various early legends say that they arrived at islands in the Atlantic that were accessible to the Straits of Gibraltar. Plato says these islands were Atlantean colonies or trading partners for thousands of years. The secondary location in the Atlantic is probably Plato's island (or islands) that sank beneath the mud. The Atlanteans would have needed easy trading access to the Mediterranean colonies, such as the Magdalenians. Secondary locations could have been the landmass that encompassed all the Cape Verde, Canary, Madeira, and Azores Islands, as well as the mysterious equatorial island ("93") that can still be seen in the Piri Re'is map, which is at least 8,000 years old according to Hapgood. He points out that the Neolithic Subpluvial period, approximately 10,000 to 6,000 years ago, was a very rainy period, and then notes that the Piri Re'is map reflects this period or even an earlier time.[47] The Atlanteans might have been in the Caribbean, the Bimini region, Central America, or much of the whole region. Andrew Collins proposes that the Bahamian and Caribbean archipelagos and Cuba were the landmasses that were sunk by a "comet impact in the West Atlantic Basin at the end of the Pleistocene epoch."[48]

The migrating Atlanteans may have first gone to the southern end of South America and into Brazil. The Monte Verde site in Chile and the most recent archaeological finds in Brazil are demolishing the old-paradigm "peopling-of-the-Americas," which hypothesizes that Mongoloid people wandered across Beringia—the land bridge between Russia and Alaska— approximately 11,500 years ago and then migrated into the Americas in only four hundred years, a patently absurd idea. Recently, archaeologist Thomas Dillehay's Monte Verde site has furnished incontrovertible evidence for human habitation in southern Chile 12,500 years ago, which certainly gets our attention because the site is close to Lesser Antarctica.[49]

So who were they? The Brazilian anthropologist Walter Neves discovered the skull of a young woman, "Luzia," who wandered the south-central savannah of Brazil 11,500 years ago and had Negroid rather than Mongoloid features. According to Neves, "Luzia belonged to a nomadic people who began arriving in the New World as early as 15,000 years ago."[50] The discoveries in Brazil are the basis of a 1999 BBC documentary called *Ancient Voices*. It posits that the first settlers in the New World were from Australia, because skulls in Brazil thought to be 12,000 years old match those of Australians living about *60,000 years ago*. Artifacts from northeastern Brazil indicate human habitation as long as 50,000 years ago. Neves also measured hundreds of skulls that are between 7,000 and 9,000 years old, and these skulls go from exclusively Australian to Mongoloid.[51]

In other words, *South America must have been already populated before 11,500 years ago, and then was repopulated after the devastation by people coming down from Central and North America*. Rising seas were inundating the Asian continental shelves, so Far Eastern seafarers traveled east to South America, west to India, and even to the Fertile Crescent. Because Antarctica is close to Australia and southern Chile, the Monte Verde site may be part of the massive migrations thousands of years ago.[52] The theory that Atlantis was once located on Lesser Antarctica helps explain the great age of the Australian aboriginal culture and the likelihood of a similar situation in Brazil. Again, the remnants are few because almost everything in under the sea.

Without extensive archaeological investigations on Lesser Antarctica, it is impossible to prove it was the location of Poseidon's Island. Hapgood reports that Ross Sea cores on Antarctica show it was ice-free from 15,000 to 6,000 years ago.[53] Plato's report of the island that sank could also be one of the secondary locations that sank 11,500 years ago. To me, it's most probable that the early fall of Atlantis occurred in two main phases: (1) migrations out of Antarctica 15,000 to 12,500 years ago, and (2) the sinking of secondary sites 11,500 years ago during the cataclysm. Cultures around the world would have been exceedingly challenged by the Atlantean dispersal to warmer Atlantic islands before the disaster. There is much evidence in legends that the secondary Atlantean colonies may have sunk in the crustal shifting, which may be why other locations, such as the Caribbean region, are remembered as sunken parts of Atlantis. One thing is very likely: In regions like the Caribbean, Sundaland in the Far East, the Mediterranean, the coasts of India, Egypt (buried because the Nile moved), and Lake Tritonis in Africa, seafaring people were very active in the latter days before the cataclysm and during the Early Holocene. (See appendices B and C for more detail on these global changes.)

The third phase of Atlantis is the early Holocene around 9000 BC, when cross-cultural legends report that Atlanteans provided assistance amid rising seas and continual crustal adjustments. Many regions were plagued with more volcanoes, earthquakes, and floods, which subsequently created confusion about the 9500 BC disaster. For example, the Far East, North America, and the Black Sea regions experienced crustal uplifting or subsidence, flooded continental shelves, and flooded lakes for thousands of years. Examining the demise of Atlantis as one player in the midst of the global maritime cultures offers the best scenario. For example, Plato's war suggests that the Atlanteans pressured other surviving cultures: They attacked the Athenians because they wanted to occupy the Mediterranean. This is a riveting clue because before 10,500 BC the Mediterranean Sea was much smaller. Around 12,000 years ago, many rivers drained into the Mediterranean depression, and then it probably filled up after the cataclysm.[54]

Looking at things from the vantage point of the Egyptians and Athenians, *suddenly the Atlanteans just showed up ready for war,* exactly as Plato said. If we use our modern experience, this makes a lot of sense: Wars happen when cultures are stressed by climate change, seismic activity, and migrations. Plato's war was going on almost exactly when the cataclysm happened, which probably ended the war. Putting it all together, this war is a sad story of the Atlanteans seeking new territory, and eventually losing the battle. I believe that this war and its lingering mythology is the genesis of many modern problems, such as global war, excessive economic and political control tendencies, wandering peoples, and obsession with scarcity. The Atlantean attack on the Mediterranean world may be why the New World Order seems to emulate Atlantis. There are persistent rumors of Elite secret power bases on Antarctica, so perhaps the New World Order has already found Poseidon's Island.

Allan and Delair's revised chronology really straightens out the historical emergence of human cultures after the cataclysm; there is a literal before-and-after point when the prediluvial world ended. This explains the latest archaeological digs in Brazil, and it may assist in the reappraisals of cultural dispersals, such as Oppenheimer's excellent Sundaland hypothesis. By using 9500 BC as a dividing line, we begin to make sense of dispersal patterns, resettlement, and the rebuilding of cultures. The facts are, an advanced global civilization ended abruptly 11,500 years ago, and then people began again in the early Holocene amid a field of chaotic Earth changes that did not settle down until 6,000 years ago. Faulty sequencing scrambles our brains because *time relates events*. Using Allan and Delair's chronology, the Pleistocene is a cataclysmic division between the Holocene epoch and the Pliocene and Miocene epochs that explains why archaic humans seem to be merely stone cultures—little else survived the destruction. Judging by new Brazilian, Australian, and Asian timelines, the global maritime civilization may have achieved *50,000 years* of human evolution when the cataclysm occurred, which is verified by the Egyptian temple records. The Vela supernova event that caused the cataclysm was a rare event in Earth's history; normally Earth changes are not so dire.

The Goddesses Neith and Athena

Returning to Plato's description of Atlantis, male kingship, control, and bull sacrifice were the basis of the politics, society, and rituals, and these elements still exist today. Plato said that the original Athenians were a wise and judicious people, great seafarers who venerated the goddess. The Egyptians of Plato's time said that they shared their ancestral records with the Greeks because both venerated the same goddess of wisdom—Neith in Egypt and Athena in Athens.[55] According to the description of Atlantis in the beginning of this chapter, the Atlanteans were the descendants of the sea god Poseidon and the Earth-born woman Cleito, who bore Poseidon five sets of male twins. Like a queen bee, Cleito was kept in the center of the Atlantean complex, and all power emitted from that center.

Cleito was grabbed and raped by Poseidon, and the Atlanteans discuss no goddess of wisdom. The Egyptian and Greek pantheons have *balanced* proportions of male and female deities. Archaeologist Marija Gimbutas points out that when archaic cultures worshiped the goddess, they lived in peace for thousands of years.[56] The Egyptians said that they shared their knowledge with the Greeks in 600 BC because the Greeks lost their records during recurrent catastrophes; they needed these records so that they could recover their memories.[57] In the *Dawn of Astronomy,* J. Norman Lockyer identifies Neith, or Nit, and Athena as goddesses of the Pleiades, and in both cultures, major temples were dedicated to them, such as the Parthenon in Greece.[58] This is why I asked the illustrator to include a replica of the Parthenon in his imaginary prediluvial city. These goddesses

Fig. 4.7. Neith and Athena

were equated with wisdom and good memory, and later you will see that they are very archaic and hearken back to the time before the axis tilted. The Pleiades were known as the Seven Sisters in early North America, as well as Siberia and Australia; this common heritage suggests they were venerated as long as 40,000 years ago.[59] We must remember our records, which is why the goddess must be venerated: *She is the protector of wisdom and memory.*

By contrast, the Atlantean culture venerated Poseidon, who used an Earth-born woman as a birthing machine for the five sets of twin kings. Then the sons claimed the right to take what they wanted and eliminate anyone who got in their way. They went to war against their neighbors, but the early Greeks and the Egyptians won that battle. After the cataclysm, the Greeks, Egyptians, and Atlanteans re-created their civilizations during the Age of Cancer—8800 to 6640 BC—which I think of as the *first complete precessional age.* This was the time of the goddess, because Cancer rules the moon, which is a profound source of wisdom. The Greeks and Egyptians highly valued the arts of the goddess—wisdom, cosmology, healing, and divination—which, as you will see in chapter 7, are the *forbidden* arts of Christianity.[60] The Atlanteans invented trade, mapmaking, weights and measures, autocracy, ritual power-bonding, and the birthing of sons to colonize the planet. Both approaches are essential cultural ways, and when the planet is balanced, both gods and goddesses influence humanity. We must learn to live again by the magical and initiatic arts of the goddess, or the New World Order will totally control the world. Each one of us has the ability to use these powers by working with nature. How? There is an ancient science called geomancy—Earth divination— that is being recovered now that cosmic energy is flowing into our solar system. In the next chapter, we will explore ways to work with these powers to reattain harmony with Earth.

5 GEOMANCY AND PRIMORDIAL MEMORY

The Goddess in all her manifestations was a symbol of the unity of all life in Nature. Her power was in water and stone, in tomb and cave, in animals and birds, in snakes and fish, hills, trees, and flowers. Hence the holistic and mythopoetic perceptions of the sacredness and mystery of all there is on Earth.

MARIJA GIMBUTAS[1]

Geomancy and Sacred Sites

Geomancy is the study of Earth's energy and how humans interact with its subtle but measurable forces; it is a science for living harmoniously with Earth. Vestiges of this science can be found in megalithic sites all over the world, because long ago archaic people used geomancy to detect Earth energy. They located their sacred sites where contact with the divine is especially available. English sacred-sites researcher John Michell says we cannot penetrate the megalithic world until we see that their stone monuments are "the instruments of their science."[2] I experience megalithic standing stones, ancient springs and water temples, barrows, dolmens, straight tracks, and gigantic geometrical forms as old treasure maps to other times and dimensions. Sacred sites and temples create a form that draws specific energies to their locations. During the past two hundred years, people have begun to study these markings and monuments, which exhibit similar patterns around the world. They were planned and measured by similar systems, and local legends often say giants built them.[3] Geomancy has established that megalithic and cyclopean structures often mark *vortexes,* or places where powerful telluric or inner Earth forces circulate that respond to cosmic cycles. But nobody really knows why these structures were built.

In modern times, geomancers often use *dowsing* to determine where the energies flow at sacred sites because it detects electromagnetic forces that lead to vortexes, places where these forces intersect and become spirals.[4] Holding two metal rods that respond to the connection between the energy in their bodies and water and minerals in the earth, dowsers follow the electromagnetic forces by taking the direction the rods point to. The places where water flows and where minerals lie indicate where subtle energy exists at sacred sites, and dowsing detects these unusual Earth energies. Many books detail the *construction* of sacred sites. Here I highlight the *forces* available in these places, because geomancy often adds insight to the astronomical, archaeological, and mythological data of sites. Before studying the archaeological and mythological data for a sacred site, I usually go there and tune into the feeling of the site for days, because this is how I get the deepest insight. Often these places have unusual telluric forces and alignments to the stars, moon, and sun; also a lost Earth technology was used to enhance these forces. Some researchers have even discovered linkages between the sites and the originating myths of the people who inhabited the land where they are located.

For some mysterious reason, accessing telluric and stellar forces was very important to our ancestors, and their sacred sites were often technologically advanced in this regard. They created things we can barely imagine building today, and now we are in the early stages of comprehending what our ancestors were really doing in these places.[5] For example, the inventor John A. Burke and the naturalist Kaj Halberg have given solid evidence that ancient megaliths were built to amplify naturally occurring electromagnetic fields, which the ancients used to enhance their seeds in order to improve agriculture.[6] Just like the data convergence in the Earth sciences, sacred-sites research has also matured. Geomancers have uncovered a global network of sacred sites, and now many writers are homing in on exactly what people might have been doing there. Also, sacred sites can often be used to trace the wanderings of cultural groups, because each culture has specific geomantic laws they superimpose on their new temples.

Old-paradigm archaeologists and historians rarely consider the possibility that these sites were constructed by advanced scientific skills. Meanwhile, archaeoastronomy has successfully argued that archaic people created a monumental global work of art. For me, megalithic or Holocene science was obviously very advanced but *radically* different from modern science. Also, precataclysmic cyclopean technology differs radically from the megalithic, and then *both* technologies differ radically from modern science. Often when modern science "discovers" a new technology, we can suddenly see that archaic people had already been using it. For example, sonics—sound technology—was probably used to levitate huge stones, as is discussed later. The public is very curious about standing stones that weigh tons and also unusual Earth energies, so the popular media exploits this interest by offering programs about the *ancient mysteries*. Millions have heard that ancient sacred sites are astronomically aligned and located in places known to access potent Earth forces. Many people who visit these sites find they can feel subtle energetic differentials in these sacred places, causing them to feel time warps, déjà vu, and the presence of nearly visible entities. Visiting these places sometimes activates very deep and dark emotions, which can disturb unresolved emotional conflicts, such as catastrophobia. This is because the forces of the dark and the light intersect in places where the geomantic energy is strong, and people report a wide range of emotional responses to this.

Fig. 5.1. Callanish stone circle

According to geomancy, lines of energy—*leys*—run everywhere beneath Earth's surface, and sacred sites were built and rebuilt where they intersect. These crossings create channels or conduits of energy that draw water, which is why dowsers can detect them. John Michell notes, "All megalithic sites, every stone, mound, and earthwork, are located over or beside a buried spring or well or at the junction of an underground stream."[7] Built above these energy streams, the sites were designed to enhance them, generating strong electromagnetic fields that we can feel, especially because we are mostly water ourselves. Sacred sites are located all over Earth as a patterned global network of electromagnetic fields. Within this mysterious network, electromagnetic energy flows more strongly during equinoxes, solstices, and new and full moons (especially during eclipses); scientific tests have detected enhanced electromagnetic fields during such times. Yet on ordinary days, often there is little energy.[8]

This mapping of *Earth's circulatory system* exists all over the planet, and archaic people put stupendous effort into building it. Geomancers, archaeoastronomers, and new-paradigm researchers are studying this system, even if archaeologists and scientists ignore their findings. I think it is perilous to ignore the implications of this system because these enhanced electromagnetic fields can improve our health, which surely was the same for people thousands of years ago. Like those who go to spas today, people went to sacred temples during important times of the year to enhance their health and well-being. Alternative or complementary medicine is based on enhancing the bioelectric fields of our bodies, which closely reflects the ancient beliefs; humans may need to experience vortexes and leys. This special energy flow attracted people to sacred places for rituals and festivals during special times, and this created community.[9] *Living harmoniously with Earth was their religion; vital living was their prayer.* I use the word *prayer* because I will never forget the time when I was walking with my husband among the gigantic megalithic standing stones of Avebury Circle muttering, "Why did they build these?" He replied, "This is their cathedral." I opened this chapter with a quote about the goddess because I have always felt that Avebury Circle and Silbury Hill are temples of the Earth Goddess. Michael Dames says this in *The Silbury Treasure: The*

Great Goddess Rediscovered.[10] The latest new thoughts about Avebury come from new-paradigm writer Ralph Ellis; he successfully argues that *Avebury Circle, seen from above, is a representation of Earth floating in space!*[11]

Sacred Sites, the Ether, and Time Discontinuities

Successive cultures built their sacred sites on older remains; thus, like the myths, sacred sites are layers of time. For example, when the Roman Catholic Church dominated Europe during the Dark Ages, they located their churches right on top of megalithic power places, many of which were on top of Paleolithic sites. In a letter in AD 601, Pope Gregory I urged St. Augustine to seek out pagan temples, purify them, and convert them to Catholic churches. Regarding the intentions of these early church builders, John Michell says, "The first missionaries founded their churches at those places where the celestial forces asserted their strongest and most beneficial influence, proving thereby to the local population their knowledge of these forces and their ability to maintain the fertility and prosperity of the district by their invocation."[12] Once the church took control of these venerated sites, the local people were gradually blocked from creating their own ceremonies there and eventually were denigrated by being called pagans and witches if they did so.

Once the Age of Science began, the Roman Catholic Church ended the ceremonies based on the natural cycles. The people could not feel the rejuvenating energy anymore, they lost the connection with the ancestors they venerated in these places, and the church decreed that a priest was required as an intercessor. Cruelly evicted from their sacred sites, the people have been progressively disconnected from Earth, while large control systems, such as the Vatican, use the available energy of these sites as power plants for their own programs. As already described, the Aymara culture on the Altiplano of Peru and Bolivia may have retained prediluvial knowledge, and its last lineage fell during historical times. After the Spanish conquistadors finished slaughtering the people, they sent in the Jesuits with their training manual, *The Extirpation of Idolatry.* Upon entering a village, the Jesuits got the lineage *waka* and destroyed it, and they destroyed or defaced the *pacarina.* The *waka* is the holder of the ancestral knowledge, and the *pacarina* is its place of emergence.[13] No matter what anybody does, the power of Earth energy still exists in these places, and it is heightened when people go there and meditate.

Victorian scientists called this special Earth energy the *ether,* and John Michell says the ether is "a manifestation of the relationship between space and time."[14] We are evolving by a *new time factor since 9500 BC,* and sacred sites are refuge zones, just as they were in the past, especially during times of rapid change. In general, ancient sacred calendars, such as the Mayan calendars, are based on planetary and star cycles, which often are the same cycles that sacred sites are aligned with. The calendars were studied and stored within sacred sites, and these sites encourage us in our evolution. The planetary and star cycles documented in the calendars indicate *when* these sites are "active" or have more ether, such as during equinoxes and solstices. I have taught students how to tune in to the ether at sacred sites in Egypt, Greece, England, Indonesia, Mexico, and the Americas. Together, during carefully selected times, we've felt the past, present, and future merge when the ether has come into ceremonies at these sites. Often, we were seized by spontaneous recall of past and future events as our ancestors came to us. Once at Malia, on Crete, the alternate reality that interfaces with Malia suddenly superimposed itself on the site, and I was able to watch the original teachers teaching children in the temple. It is interesting, regarding this book, that these teachers were using a form of psychoanalysis to purge fear of Earth changes from the minds of very small children. The original builders of these sites constructed them so visitors would always experience these connections during active cycles. Once a person visits on a pilgrimage, they are a living part of the temple for the rest of their lives. *Sacred sites are libraries of time and dimensional breakthrough zones.*

We exist in linear space and time, and it seems like that's all there is until we find ourselves in a simultaneous-reality experience. We have entered the *vertical axis* of consciousness, where there are many dimensions, some solid, some not. This is not as esoteric as it may sound. For example, advanced mathematics is based on proofs of many other dimensions and time zones. People get Ph.D.s and awards for these proofs, yet, I ask, how does the existence of these other dimensions affect us? Shamans travel into the Underworld or Upperworld by journeying up or down the sacred tree, which is a *vertical axis*. Anthropology describes these kinds of shamanic journeys, and according to consciousness research, these dimensions can be *experienced* by anyone who develops the paranormal skills to access these other realities. Any one of us can be sensitized to the ether where the intersection with space and time exists. In my case, I have fun traveling around in these realms, and then I dedicate my research time to finding credible sources for what I've already found. I write about these possibilities because Western society is dangerously out of touch with the vertical axis, the Tree of Life, the access to other worlds; ordinary reality seems boring. I much prefer indigenous life, because in our expanded world, we live in normal space and time while totally in touch with other realms. Judging by how indigenous people and their sacred sites have been treated for the past 2,000 years, the bored Western mind plans to end this opportunity. Mathematicians and physicists concoct formulas and conduct experiments that *prove* other dimensions exist, and even they become mystics when they discover the vertical axis accidentally during their calculations. Most of us can't understand their equations, yet we can easily discover the vertical axis by going to sacred sites and just feeling it. The point is, tuning in multidimensionally is fun, very informative, and even necessary for life and creativity. Why *not* just assume these nonphysical and nonlinear worlds are real and then contact them?

Sacred Sites as Energetic Safety Zones

Many people return to the great sacred sites during equinoxes and solstices, and energy is building in these places during the Galactic Winter Solstice: 1987–2012. The ancients created these places with time-release art forms that are enlivened by human interaction during special times. Sacred sites and the areas near them are *energetic safety zones* during the most intense phases of the galactic alignments. Archaeologists have rebuilt many crumbling sacred sites during the past 100 years, and then the people who visit them experience spirits, time discontinuities, visions, spontaneous recall of past lives, and feelings of connection with the original builders. What is going on? I can personally report that the more people visit these places, the more the mysteries deepen for them, unless they travel like common tourists. Sacred-site quests are creating a new global mythology, because in these places *another world opens that is enfolded right in the middle of mundane existence.* Earth is the divine planet because so many realities coalesce on Earth and move through the Milky Way galaxy to connect with the stars.

Without sacred places that focalize subtle forces, we are stuck in linear space and time like butterflies on pins in glass cases while the galaxy sparkles with the lights of billions of stars. The people who first constructed the temples knew or felt how Earth's energy works according to specific laws. Later, based on what the ancients had already discovered, church builders constructed steeples, naves, high ceilings, symbols, windows, and altars to enhance these forces. Like modern archaeologists, they participated in maintaining the geomantic system, yet their purpose was to control the world by drawing energy-starved people into the churches. When I was a very small girl, I used to steal into the Catholic cathedral next door to my house because there was so much energy in the sanctuary. As an adult, I discovered it was built right on top of a great Native American sacred site, which made me acutely sensitive to Earth energy.[15]

According to geomancy, the vortexes form a global network of enhanced electromagnetic fields, and major stone complexes often mark these zones. Prediluvial cultures probably first enhanced these places, but their work has been mostly destroyed. Megalithic standing stones frequently mark the sacred sites of lost cultures. Roman roads were built on megalithic roadbeds that may overlay Paleolithic roads, which marked ley lines. This is why I think the Alaise sites discovered by Guichard may go back before the Holocene. John Michell says, "The Romans were not particularly surprised to find so many stretches of straight track in Britain, for they came across them in every country they invaded."[16]

What did these original builders know? Most importantly, what if we *need* to enhance this global system again for our health, well-being, and planetary viability? As already discussed, the legends of various cultures are connected to their sacred sites. Many new-paradigm researchers are building connections between the sites and related literature that universally tell of past catastrophes and the later reemergence of the people. It is awesome to visit the sacred places of mythic cultures that were destroyed by "monsters in the sky" that brought floods, hurricanes, volcanoes, and earthquakes. Similar myths, such as the Enuma Elish (Sumer), the Popul Vuh (Maya), the Mahabharata (India), and the Flood story in Genesis are the stories of these times. As a result of the catastrophic data convergence, we now know that these great records describe real events and when they occurred. This makes the great disasters intensely *real*. For example, the Mahabharata actually describes the destruction of Harappa and other sites on the Saraswati Plateau of India about 4,000 years ago.[17] *A new global myth is emerging, and, as always, the sacred will be the inspiration.*

Everything that has ever happened on Earth is available to us now by going on the quest, the awakening. All of us can open our memories over great spans of time just by following our passion. By going on the trail of your personal mythos, you awaken archaic memory that activates dormant parts of your brain. We go directly into the Egyptian initiatic library in this chapter, because the Egyptian mysteries are still relevant today. Our sense of self comes out of our conceptions of those who walked before us: Think of yourself as having evolved from apes and rushing madly on to computer man; then imagine your ancestors as members of a global maritime civilization that was using mysterious technologies that were in resonance with Earth. Often I wonder if we are becoming global again because technology is linking us by frequency waves. Considering Calleman's analysis of the Mayan Calendar, (while I work on this revision) it is Day Seven of the Eighth Underworld, the Galactic (AD 1999–2011).

The Galactic Underworld is a 13-year period of evolving technology that is bringing us into oneness as a species. Day Seven in 2011 is technology's *fruition*. This morning, February 11, 2011, Egypt was liberated from thirty years of despotism under Hosni Mubarek because the revolutionaries organized and directed their liberation with computers! So did Tunisia a few weeks ago. This chapter has much detailed

Egyptology because Egypt is the center of Earth's landmasses; *Egypt guides Earth awakenings.* We have arrived at a truly amazing moment: Secret temples can be visited, previously hidden sacred texts can be read, and now light frequencies are linking us together. As you will see in detail in this book, we are allowed to see secret texts and enter temples that only the selected few were once allowed to enter.

As archaeologists dig up and reconstruct villages and temples that were described in mythology thousands of years ago, scholars craft a new timeline. By this collective effort, we are redefining ourselves as a species. Those who are blocked by unresolved trauma from past cataclysms find the past elusive; their curiosity is dulled by free-floating anxiety. However, calendars and signs in the sky say that now is the time to create an entirely new future based on the correct reconstruction of the past. Our experiences during the cataclysms boil within our cells. This is why scientists have done everything possible to push the date of the ultimate horror as far back in time as possible. Regarding *Mapping the Mind,* scientists are forced to be very left-brained, and so they easily suppress the right-brain fears. Until recently, popular cataclysmic analysis focused on the extinction of the dinosaurs 63 million years ago, caused by an asteroid that plunged into the Gulf of Mexico, and children were scared half to death by the film *Jurassic Park,* which was marketed to them through McDonald's. Even new-paradigm researchers seem to go to great lengths to avoid the memory. For example, the astronomer Tom Van Flandern bases his "exploding planet theory" on the origins of comets 3.2 million years ago, and he pays little attention to the termination of the Pleistocene.[18] Meanwhile, the extermination of the dinosaurs and the exploding planet are both too far back in time to be the cataclysm that is recorded in global mythology.

Axial Tilt Theory

The most significant change in human cultures at the beginning of the Holocene was the adoption of agriculture, which I've already suggested was forced on cultures by the new seasons and the destroyed landscape.

Before the cataclysm, people were much freer as hunters and foragers. Suddenly everybody had to work all the time, and it is unlikely that they would have chosen this without necessity.[19] Seeds were sacred to these early farmers, and they would have always carried them with them. Consider the earliest pharaonic cartouche, the Sedge and the Bee, which has never been deciphered. To me this represents seed and pollination as the basis of pharaonic power, the organizing power of agriculture. Pharaonic Egypt, by the yearly flow of the Nile, is a model of a theocratic system created around agriculture. The 9500 BC cataclysm explains many of the truly bizarre elements in the wild creation stories in mythology that are consistent around the world. Egyptian mythology and mystery plays evidence many signs of a recent axial tilt and related disruptions in the sky. For example, the story of the dismemberment of Osiris by his brother, Seth; the search for his body parts by Isis; and the battle between Horus and Seth in which Horus loses his eye and Seth loses his testicles—all read like an *anatomy of the cataclysm.*

There is much evidence for the cataclysm in the Egyptian records, because the myths are very astrophysical. These records survived due to the favorable Egyptian climate and the powerful and long-lived temple tradition. As already discussed in chapter 3, there are multilayered human cultures throughout the past 40,000 years along the Nile, and the First Time, Zep Tepi, represents the period *before* the cataclysm. Dynastic

*Fig. 5.2. The Sedge
and the Bee*

Egypt based its temple technology totally on the mythical First Time, a record they preserved in stone. The great wisdom teachings from before the cataclysm are the foundational unifying source of dynastic Egypt; therefore, *the dynastic records propel us right back to before the disaster.* Dynastic power—divine kingship—was derived from the sages, the primordial Shemsu Hor. Yet during the pharaonic period there were significant changes, because *the world had changed.* The dynastic Egyptians were adamant that Zep Tepi was eternal, timeless, and harmonious, but they adopted systems that were obsessed with duality, time, and seasonality! The very conception of the two kingdoms—Upper and Lower Egypt—is profoundly dualistic, so something really had changed. I believe it was the division of the Earth (Geb) and the sky (Nut) caused by axial tilt (see figure 5.4 on p. 135). Axial tilt split the woman as sky from the man as Earth, as Earth discovered a new relationship with the sun.

Egyptologist Jeremy Naydler says, "Egypt is an image of heaven, or so to speak more exactly, in Egypt all the operations of the powers which rule and are active in heaven have been transferred to a lower place. Even more than that, if the whole truth be told, our land is the temple of the entire cosmos."[20] Many have been very drawn to studying the Egyptian records because they find profound resonance in them with the needs of the modern world. The dynastic foundational ceremonies were devoted to reconciling axial tilt so that the land by the Nile could find a new relationship with the cosmos. *They found new ways to bring heaven into Earth.* Of course, ceremonies and sacred texts are always devoted to reconciling the sacred and the profane. However, the cataclysm introduced a more radical level of disorder that threatened to cut off access to the divine. We are still working out this crisis, and Egyptian sacred science offers deep understanding. Earth's geology as well as its climate was radically altered, and the dynastic Egyptians *took action to reestablish divine order—Maat—in the world.* They maintained Maat for thousands of years, and they recorded exactly how they did it. I will use the term *Maat* for their world in which earthly order was continually created by divine manifestation. The sacred was experienced in ordinary reality by participating in mystery plays that anchored the altered sky in the mundane world; the key was to mark the cardinal directions to strike the *new order of time.*

Some find it very difficult to enter the Egyptian mind because we exist in complete disorder with no cosmological sensitivity. Reestablishing a vertical axis was the method the Egyptians used to maintain Maat by divine kingship, which involved balancing chaotic elements with harmonic processes. For example, they adopted the goddess of chaos born in the cataclysm—Sekhmet—and the god of chaos—Seth—as representatives of the principles of cosmic order. In so doing, they helped their people live harmoniously with Earth, because disasters are part of human experience. They believed that personal alchemical transmutation causes heaven to descend to Earth, so they precipitated the divine into everyday life on the Nile by means of yearly ceremonies. The Egyptian records describe exactly how they did this year after year. Knowing that the cataclysm caused the initial disharmony, they worked with these gods, or *neter*s, to reweave the dimensions. Their records are the most complete and accurate ancient source on how axial tilt altered life for human societies 11,500 years ago. The pharaoh or king is the exemplar of cosmic principles, and all Egyptians were encouraged to aspire to personal transmutation. If many individuals achieved spiritual consciousness, the whole field of Egypt would be transfigured. The pharaoh is the exemplar because societies deteriorate when their leaders are immoral and unethical.

Old-paradigm Egyptology is a compendium of guesswork by scholars who are the first to admit they can't understand what the ancient Egyptians were doing. Scholars have built upon an edifice of the erroneous initial conclusions by archaeologists more than a hundred years ago, who were often little better than pirates instructed to fill museums with their loot. As soon as the hieroglyphs were deciphered and Egyptologists thought they could read the inscriptions on the walls of the tombs and temples, their monotheistic prejudices made it nearly impossible for them to correctly interpret what they read. And they interpreted the sites by a faulty timeline.

Meanwhile, new-paradigm researchers have been correcting the monotheistic bias and the faulty timeline, and recently enough texts have been more correctly translated, making it possible to enter the ancient Egyptian mind. We begin by listening to them first. The early dynastic Egyptians insisted that their culture was totally derived from a much older First Time, and there is no reason not to believe them. They retained their records in rituals and mystery plays, so we explore the most important ceremonies that are depicted in detail in reliefs and recorded in documents.

The Mystery Plays in the Temples

In the dramas in the temples, actors in many dimensions play out their relationships with the cosmos. The pharaoh is always there in the center linking heaven and Earth in correspondence with the *dynastic cosmogenesis:* the unification of Upper and Lower Egypt by the divine kingship of the pharaoh or Horus king. The pharaoh or king was the mediator between the world of the people and the gods who lived in the temples. Zep Tepi was alive in the temples, and events that happened on Earth also occurred in the spiritual world. This is the same as John Michell's argument that the ether is a manifestation of space and time; that is, this precipitation of time into the temple is totally multidimensional.[21] This is what it means to *contemplate,* to be one within the temple. Priests and priestesses cared for the homes of the gods, but the king and the royal family were the mediators. The common people were never allowed into the interiors of the temples where the mystery plays were portrayed in sacred art, and so it is amazing that we can see this art and be in these rooms, which is like being in heaven. All Egyptians believed that what went on in the temple created their world on the Nile, and sometimes they observed processions outside the temple. For example, at certain times of the year, the gods would come out of the temples carried by the priests. *For the ancient Egyptians, the physical world emerged out of the spiritual landscape, and the divine landscape was continually painted during temple ceremonies and public festivals.* If these scenes were *not* painted in ceremonies, how were the gods to know how the humans chose to live? In other words, those who served in the temple talked to the gods expressing their intentions for a good life. Although the people never entered the inner sanctums of the temples, they lived every day knowing that the god lived in the *naos,* or central heart of the temple.

Priests made daily offerings to the gods whose dramas and lives were portrayed on the walls, which often show the gods being blessed by the pharaoh. These scenes were eternal and active in other dimensions where the gods actually lived. If the king blessed a god or neter—divine energy form— the neter had a job to do for the king, such as making sure the people were fed by blessing the sun and calling for rain. In the new dynastic reality, the sun was taking a new journey on the horizon, which was utterly fascinating and fearsome. What if the sun didn't stop at the Tropic of Cancer or Capricorn one day and kept on going north or south? To deal with that problem, they located one of the most ancient temples, the Temple of Khnum, at Aswan. There the Nile emerges from the heart of Africa through the First Cataract right on the Tropic of Cancer, where the sun stopped and turned at the summer solstice and the measurement of the Inundation began. The Nabta Playa site is also located on the Tropic of Cancer, about sixty miles

Fig. 5.3. Everyday life by the Nile

west of Aswan. This suggests it may be a precursor site of the Temple of Khnum.[22] The sun needed solar barques, called boats-of-the-sky, to carry it, and sometimes humans had to persuade the sun to maintain its journey by sacrifices and agreements.[23] People needed to become the sun to know it, and then the plants would thrive.

The temples were constructed of stone, and the reliefs were cut in granite walls, making them eternal, just like the nonphysical worlds and the gods. Also, stone resonates to sound and vibration, and stone with high quartz content was often chosen. Meanwhile, all the people, including the royal family, lived in mud-brick homes because the gods had originally made them out of the Nile mud, like the first man in Genesis, who was made of clay. We can see by their pictorial renditions that the Egyptians were profoundly grounded in mundane life by the Nile. Remember, as you consider this exquisite relief, they believed life would continue to be this way if they depicted it artistically. Because the people lived in the land of the gods, *Khemet,* minute pictures of their daily lives were depicted in stone on the walls of the tombs and temples, even though nothing is left of their houses and villages. Life by the Nile would continue as long as it was continually drawn on the walls. If you ever go to Egypt, you will know this is true, even in spite of the Aswan Dam, which has stopped the flow of the yearly Inundation.

The theological reliefs are pictorial and highly symbolic, and fragments of the myths from sacred texts are carefully placed in the art. Similar texts were used and reused for different scenes to invoke energy from other dimensions, bringing the sacred into this dimension. Now that many of these sacred texts have been translated, whole scenes come alive; the intuitive mind comprehends symbols and mythological scenes. Like a painting being painted, a whole worldview becomes visible, and possibly this waking-up could even change the modern world.

I was reminded of this possibility when the Eyptian people liberated themselves from Hosni Mubarek's rule on February 11, 2011. Assuming that the gods actually do exist in another reality, what happens to a person who goes to Egypt now and contemplates these sacred scenes? For example, Barack Obama visited Egypt and the sacred sites in June of 2009 and he seemed to be very moved by the reliefs. I have been staring at these walls and meditating with them in books since I was five years old, and I have taught in the temples many times with my Egyptian master teacher, Abdel Hakim. He used to read some of the text for me, and now most of these texts are available in good translations. Like an ancient face lying on the bottom of a muddy stream that becomes visible when the silt clears, the new and emerging translations are giving me new sight. But still most of my understanding is intuitive. Who were these people on the Nile who believed the divine lived in their world because they maintained a living relationship with it?

The Emergence of the Primeval Mound and the Divine Cow

When the Nile receded at the end of the Neolithic Subpluvial, a time of abundant rain about 6,000 years ago, the river cut a new channel, vast lakes dried up, and new shorelines formed. Long before this time, the creator, Atum, came out of the Primeval Mound and begat Shu (air) and Tefnut (water), who begat Geb and Nut. Then Geb lay on the ground and became the god of Earth, and Nut made her body into a canopy of stars over Geb and became the sky (fire). When the mounds and shores emerged again, Geb and Nut begat Osiris, Isis, Seth, and Nepthtys. Before the birth of the four children, who symbolize among many things the four directions, the earlier divine parents ruled Earth during the First Time. After the cataclysm, Osiris and Seth carried on a great battle over their sister, Isis. Seth dismembered his brother, Osiris, and eventually Osiris's son Horus avenged his father by battling Seth. Osiris became a transfigured green god who carried the life force of the annual Inundation, while Seth carried the dry and hot energy of the desert. As previously mentioned, this myth is actually astronomical and describes elements of the cataclysms. After the disorder, Osiris arose again, since when seeds germinate, life returns with the sun.

Before the Aswan Dam was built, annually the Nile made layer after layer of mud. When the waters receded, Osiris emerged on the Mound of

Fig. 5.4. Geb and Nut

Creation, the agricultural god awakened by the sun. The elderly people in Egypt still remember when the Nile rose and flowed with mud before the Aswan Dam was built. Sometimes great Inundations forced them to move out of their mud houses, and the Nile sometimes flowed into subsidiary channels that fertilized distant fields. The people know that the records of their ancestors lie deep in the mud or out in the red desert, the home of the fire element. The key pharaonic ceremonies, festivals, mystery plays, and sacred texts come alive in Maat, when the Primeval Mound rises out of the waters. And Isis eternally returns to search for Osiris so that she can birth Horus. The sun, or Re, as viewed from the river, which lies north and south, mysteriously moved north and south on the eastern and western horizons. Yet during Zep Tepi, the sun rose and set at the same place on the horizon all year, and the stars rose and set nightly in the same locations. Once Egyptian culture emerged again on the Nile, around 4000 BC, a potent new cosmology was born: Khemet, the black Earth, reentered the universe and sent waves of intentions to the heavens. Sacred temples were built for the gods to live in, and new ceremonies were needed because the relationship with the cosmos had changed. Geb and Nut's four children— Osiris, Isis, Seth, and Nepthtys—created new sacred space by representing the four cardinal directions.

Once the waters receded, nearly all the temples from the First Time were buried deep in the mud and sand. Archaic elements carried forth in dynastic ceremonies indicate that the sages possessed the records of Zep Tepi, so they venerated the few temples that miraculously survived the cataclysm, such as the Osireion and the Valley Temple of the Sphinx. Seti I aligned the temple's heart, the *naos,* of Ammon with the naos of the Osireion. He designed his temple by following the records of the First Time, as you will see when we examine the Standard of Abydos. Just as people today venerate old sites that are found when we build something new, Seti discovered and restored the Osireion.[24] The reliefs and geometry of Abydos Temple show that it was a re-creation of Zep Tepi, and it is one of the most potent geomantic places on Earth. *Seti I resurrected Zep Tepi:* Seti I embodied Seth, who dismembered Osiris, so his temple resolves conflicts between the dark and light. Life in Khemet resolved dualities in the past by creating unity in the current world, so when the dynastic Egyptians reanimated an Elder, such as Seti I, all the potency of Zep Tepi manifested. Sages appear when the homes of the gods are maintained, because they can communicate with Elders in the sacred places. Like sowing a field with grain, all they had to do was link heaven and Earth with their minds and hearts by stating their intentions to the gods, and the sacred precipitated into the world.

Dynastic Egyptians remembered the cataclysm, which is obvious by their obsession with the dismemberment of Osiris. There is a less well known and very archaic myth from the New Kingdom, "The Book of the Cow of Heaven," which processes the emotional conflicts brought on by the trauma.[25] The eruption of Thera on Santorini devastated the

Fig. 5.5. Watering Osiris, who grows corn in his body

whole Mediterranean world circa 1600 BC. This wreaked havoc in Egypt, especially in the delta region, and this myth emerged at this time. It was used to help people understand why yet another disaster had come about, and it also explores whether human behavior causes Earth changes. Before the New Kingdom, there are few signs of preoccupation with this kind of human guilt, which is always a symptom of unresolved trauma.

Let us consider this story: *Long ago when the gods lived on Earth . . .* The sun god Re called the gods together for advice because the human race was plotting against him and fleeing to the desert. The gods told Re to destroy the human race by sending out "the Eye of Re," as if Re could separate an aspect of himself to be used as a weapon. Instead Re sent the Eye out as Hathor, the divine cow, to slay the people in the desert. Normally Hathor is the goddess of beauty who suckles the pharaoh, so in this action, Sekhmet—the goddess who rages against humans whenever they need a lesson—came into being as an aspect of Hathor to do the deed. She was ready to destroy the world again (cataclysmic repeat), but Re relented. He got Sekhmet drunk to stop her raging and restored peace, but Sekhmet remained as the goddess who would destroy the people again if they did not respect the sun god. In the last part of the myth, Re became weary of governing society, so he withdrew into the sky and charged the other gods with the rule of heaven and Earth. Before ascending to the sky, Re created cyclical time, precession.

The Book of the Cow of Heaven emerged in 1500 BC, yet it has extremely archaic aspects. This is why I suggest it processes the originating cataclysm that was reignited by Thera's eruption. Re's dramatic withdrawal to the sky is a significant loss of power—the alteration of the sun's path in the sky.[26] This is fascinating because then human power could increase with the advent of precession. Certainly, Sekhmet became prominent during a very troubled time in Egypt, which is dramatically described in the Papyrus of Ipuwer, a lament of cataclysmic destruction, which sounds very much like the plagues of Egypt in the Bible.[27] During the New Kingdom, there was great destabilization in the Mediterranean region caused by Santorini's eruption that resurrected the unresolved trauma from the cataclysm that ended Zep Tepi.

The Battle of Horus and Seth

How to deal with chaos is a very active theme in Egyptian theology. Menes, the First Dynasty Pharaoh, instituted divine kingship circa 3200 BC. Thereafter the pharaoh was the divine incarnated son, Horus, who held Egypt in Maat. From then on, every time a king died, the possibility of chaos returned. Therefore, in the succession rites, the dead pharaoh had to became Osiris at the exact moment when the successor became the Horus King. The dead king had to be passed into the new pharaoh, who in turn helped him become Osiris. Both these vital passages required a great amount of energy, so the ceremonies were based on the most foundational myth of Egypt—the great battle between Horus and Seth—the cosmological cataclysmic myth. The formation of the political order came with Menes, the first dynasty king. Menes is named after the ithyphallic god Min, who embodies the sexual powers of the pharaoh. Menes assumes the Horus form as one who battles chaos and establishes divine kingship, the continuous introduction of the divine plane into everyday Egyptian life. We must understand the politics and theology of Menes to see how these aspects of kingship by the pharaoh were played out in the various mystery plays.

Once a new unity of Upper and Lower Egypt was accomplished, duality, chaos, and disorder were banished. *Order was held in place by continually repeating the original formula:* the institution of the dual monarchy of Osiris and Horus. In *Kingship and the Gods,* Egyptologist Henri Frankfort describes how Egyptian theological beliefs were the foundation of politics and were reenacted in the mystery plays.[28] Kingship is a *living force* that did not exist before Menes, who put together an institution that acquired "transcendent significance for the Egyptians. . . . He imparted to it a form harmonizing so perfectly with the Egyptian mentality as to appear both inevitable and perennial. . . . This extraordinary conception expressed in political form the deeply rooted Egyptian tendency to understand the world as pairs of contrasts balanced in unchanging equilibrium."[29] This living force came into Egypt *exactly* at the beginning of the Sixth Underworld of the Mayan Calendar, when it also emerged in Sumeria and many other places on the planet. In Egypt, this yin/yang sense of the world was represented by Horus and Seth, as north and south, or as the east and west banks of the Nile. The Egyptians believed that any totality was composed of opposites, a condition that recognizes that things operate in a spectrum from dark to light, negative to positive, or black to white, which is so perfectly expressed by the classic yin/yang symbol. The Egyptians held a wide spectrum of dark and light, while Judeo-Christian theology tends to be very judgmental of the dark side. Judeo-Christian writers in Egyptology tend to characterize Seth as evil and Horus as good because they suppress their own dark sides, the Sethian forces. However, the ancient Egyptians always balanced the dark and light as a way to deal with the evil in the world.

Frankfort says regarding the First Dynasty of Menes, "A state dualistically conceived must have appeared to the Egyptians the manifestation of the order of creation in human society," and he notes that "the dual monarchy had no historical foundation," that it was a "totality as an equilibrium of opposites."[30] This enabled them to create a new political order in a world altered by the changing sky, when the equilibrium of opposites brought in divine forces. This was carried out because they believed that right order and divine connection prevent chaos; Sekhmet would not rage again. Assessing the spiritual significance of Menes's achievement, Frankfort says, "A historical innovation of such importance could be only the unfolding of a preordained order, the manifestation of what had always been potentially present."[31] The dynastic Egyptians exactly followed the ceremonial practices created by Menes for more than 3,000 years. (See appendix A.)

These ceremonial practices are the most complete example of the Sixth Underworld's creation of kingly and state power that exists, and they also contain many elements from archaic prehistory. They actually record human adjustment to seasonality and agriculture by delegating power to kings and priests, and they shed light on the kingship ideal that played out during 5,125 years of history. In them, we can see elements that deal with axial tilt and the desire for order instead of chaos. We begin with the intriguing Mystery Play of the Succession.

The Mystery Play of the Succession

The Mystery Play of the Succession was carried out so that the new pharaoh could become the Horus King exactly when his predecessor became Osiris in the Underworld. The funeral of the old pharaoh and a preliminary coronation of the new pharaoh had already occurred, and the succession was performed during a time that had cosmic significance. It was performed up and down the Nile to bond the people to their new king and to assure them of the eternal life of the old king. During this ceremony, the pharaoh assumed power over the annual flooding of the Nile and the harvest by assuming the seed potency of Osiris, and he restored harmony between the cosmos and society by becoming the new Horus. Each action in this play could not be altered without dire consequences, because it was a formula for the simultaneous assumption of power and the transfiguration of the mummified king.

After the initial opening scenes, the king becomes Horus by taking his Eye, which opens the mythological level. In the myth, Horus grows up and takes back his Eye after avenging the death of his father, Osiris. The Eye of Horus has the power to revive Osiris, so the new king assists his predecessor to become Osiris.[32] The next scene is the threshing of the grain, because agriculture is the basis of the king's power, and then the Djed Pillar is erected. You will recall from chapter 3 that the tilting Djed Pillar may represent the time the axis tilted and the world fell into chaos. Whenever it is erected to a perpendicular position, cosmic imbalance is being corrected by human actions. By erecting the pillar during his succession ceremony, the king demonstrates that he will maintain the land in harmony, and the vertical axis to the sky is reinstated. Then the Djed Pillar tilts, and a mock battle is fought in which Geb, the Earth god, resolves the discord in the heavens.[33] The essence of kingship is revealed: *Kingship holds chaos in abeyance while order in the political realm brings Maat.* The products of Egypt—furniture, food, jewelry, and clothes— are brought and named "the Eye of Horus," and then the climax occurs. Standard-bearers come in carrying powerful fetishes of the Shemsu Hor, and mysterious Spirit Seekers (shamans) go around them and make the king *both* Horus and Seth.[34] The king will embody chaos within order, and as Frankfort explains, "The duality of kingship represents conflicting powers in equilibrium."[35] The gold crown is brought in, sacrifices from the two regions are carried out, the crown is put on the king's head, and the king's first act is to distribute bounty to the people, showing that he will be beneficent. This ceremony demonstrates that the king has assumed power over the forces of chaos.

Finally it is time for the transfiguration of the previous king, now that Egypt is safe from chaos. This timing is very interesting: It shows that the people believed that their political order could prevent future chaos because Osiris is a potent metaphor for the cataclysm itself. In cosmology, Osiris is the planet and its moon that orbited between Mars and Jupiter, Tiamat and Kingu in the Enuma Elish, where the asteroid belt still is composed of parts of this destroyed planet. In European culture, this disturbing memory is remembered as Humpty Dumpty, who fell off the wall and couldn't put himself back together again. Do you remember hearing this little rhyme when you were a child? Even the king's men couldn't put Humpty Dumpty back together again, yet the ancient Egyptians have more insight: Osiris is transfigured since he died in the cataclysm, and he returns eternally to bring order to the dynasties. *The dual monarchy of Menes was used to resolve catastrophobia.* The previous king is now the living Osiris, and next in the play Horus embraces Osiris as if the new king also can even travel in the Underworld! This is accomplished by means of an archaic reed bib worn on the front and back of the king—the *Qeni*—which is imbued with the immortal essence of Osiris.[36] At this moment, the divine power of kingship is transferred to the new king while the previous king is supported in his transition to the hereafter by the vital force of his son. The pharaonic transfer is complete again. Frankfort notes that the Qeni hearkens back to the times of the oldest shrines in Egypt when the Nile Valley was swampland before the end of the Subpluvial.[37]

This power transfer is exceedingly archaic and imbued with cataclysmic memory: Osiris represents those who died on the Nile thousands of years before Menes. What was new with Menes was the full and longlasting integration of all the shrines on the Nile into a unified system of controlled agriculture. The king is responsible for agriculture and water management, because the sudden arrival of seasons necessitated planting and storage. The emergence of the Primeval Mound called for management of the volume of the Inundation by opening and closing canals and overflow lakes, by means of the dike system managed by nilometers that measured the flow. Please consider how life constantly changed and was rebalanced before the Aswan Dam, which is strangling modern Egypt. It encourages overpopulation because it allows people to settle on the land that would normally flood during the Inundation, the flood that brought fertile alluvial soil for Egyptian agriculture. Next we will look into the ceremony that *renewed* the powers of the king.

The Heb Sed Ceremony

There is a literal obsession with seasonal solar cycles in the Heb Sed ceremony, which was held for the pharaoh whenever he was losing his powers. When he was in his power, the Nile did not flood excessively or dry up catastrophically, and the grain fed the people and many refugees who came to the Nile for food. No matter what, this ceremony—the Jubilee—was performed after the pharaoh's first twenty-nine to thirty years, which is the exact cycle of Saturn around the sun, and then every three years thereafter.[38] He requested it whenever he felt his personal or political power waning, and it renewed the faith of the people in their leader, although it was quite arduous. The oldest cycles observed in the ceremonies were lunar, which were always a critical part of the Egyptian sense of time. The solar cycles were obsessed with the journey of the sun rising in the east and setting in the west and its journey on the horizon. At summer solstice, the sun attained zenith position over Aswan, where the Temple of Isis was built on a mound above the cataracts. Isis is the mother goddess who generates all life, and her energy came from the sun's zenith over the place where the Nile flowed in. Before the tilt, the sun was always above the equator, and Khemet was in a perennial warm springtime, the First Time. Before axial tilt, the climate in Egypt was ideal.

The Heb Sed festival expresses pharaonic intentions to gain the powers of seasonality, whereas the Succession is more about the *transfer* of power. The Heb Sed reveals how *the king holds power within the four cardinal directions, the new field of Khemet.* As we look into it, remember that indigenous people today still locate themselves by the four directions as a way to center and ground power, and to bring the sacred into the profane. Everything changed on Earth when the sun began to rise and set in moving locations. The ecstatically free, exceedingly psychic, and simple life of the Nile foragers had to be surrendered to agriculture. A well-documented site on the Anatolia Plateau offers insight about this moment. The settlers of Abu Hureya on the Euphrates River adopted farming about 8000 BC after previously being hunter-gatherers. Suddenly their previously well-formed skeletons, according to Brian Fagan, "show clear signs of malformation resulting from long hours spent on their knees grinding grain."[39] The dynastic Egyptians *had* to farm. This necessitated a central power, the pharaoh as Saturn who rules the principle of necessity. If the pharaoh ruled for twenty-nine to thirty years, one Saturn cycle, he *became* Saturn or Father Time.

The Heb Sed began with the building of a special festival hall with a throne, a court, and a palace made of reeds to symbolize archaic times. Once complete, the structures were purified, and barges with statues of gods arrived from the Nile. The king would meet with their officials, signifying the reception of the divine plane. Also present were the Great Ones of Upper and Lower Egypt, who had been at the king's Succession. All divine and regional powers participated, including representatives of the people from every social level of every section of Egypt. This connected the whole country. The festival opened with a procession of all the gods and people presided over by Sekhat-Hor, another form of the cow goddess who suckled the king. Then there were days of blessing and visiting shrines and more processions, and all the power fetishes from modern and ancient times were blessed. Frankfort's detailed text catalogs many wonderful archaic elements that prove that this ceremony is already very ancient.[40]

Finally it was time for the pharaoh to do the "dedication of the field," a section of the courtyard made into a fourfold course set out to the cardinal directions, which represented Egypt as a whole. This empowers him as one who *controls the directions.* He crosses the directions by fast long-stride steps as if he is flying, first as ruler of Lower Egypt with the Red Crown, then of Upper Egypt with the White Crown and carrying a shepherd's crook and flail. The flail held by the flying king caught my eye because the angle is exactly 23.5 degrees, as we've already seen with the tilting Djed Pillar. He leaves the crook and flail in the palace and picks up a house document called the "will," the "Secret of the Two Partners"— Horus and Seth—again reconciling the two. The Edfu Texts say about the king: "He runs crossing the ocean and the four sides of Heaven, going as far as the rays of the sun disk, passing over the earth, giving the field to its mistress."[41] This action is cosmic and obsessed with the four directions. As king of Lower Egypt, he is carried by the Great Ones of Upper and Lower Egypt in a boxlike litter as two officials from ancestral cities stand on either side of the king and sing an antiphonal hymn. Then they change places and sing from before and behind the king, so that each has spoken to the directions. This is repeated until each man has sung to each direction, and then it is time to do the same action, but for Lower Egypt. Ultimately, the king is carried in a basket to the chapel of Horus of Edfu. There a priest gives him a bow and arrows, which he shoots to each of the four directions, after which he goes to the chapel of Seth of Kom Ombo

Fig. 5.6. The Heb Sed ceremony

and shoots four times again. This ceremony reaches deeply back into Zep Tepi, before seasonality, when the king's greatest power was as a hunter! Finally, he is enthroned four times, once to each of the directions, upon a throne ornamented with twelve lion heads (the constellations on the ecliptic), and he pays homage to the royal Ancestors, the Shemsu Hor.

The Standard of Abydos

We return to Seti I's temple at Abydos to place the two great mystery plays into context. The Standard of Abydos is illustrated because it is an important model of the four cardinal directions and the vertical axis. It was carried in the Procession of Osiris, which was a yearly festival at Abydos, a favorite procession for the people. Osiris was the most popular god because he emerged out of the primeval waters when time began.

Dismembered by his brother, Seth, still Osiris fathered Horus, the king. Osiris is a powerful symbol for sexual potency, death, continuity, dismemberment, and rebirth. He kept the hearts of the people alive in life, and when they contemplated their inevitable demise, they believed Osiris would lead them beyond death into heaven. The Standard of Abydos is an *ideal model for the vertical axis of consciousness,* and it was located in Abydos Temple, the funereal and ascension center of Khemet. With Abydos as the vertical axis ascension center on the Nile, it becomes easier to see that the main pyramids, especially at Giza, are scientific devices, whereas Abydos is theological. Now that we have seen how the pharaoh took and held his power by the mystery plays, we must understand more about Abydos, the central location of the journey to the sky. Let us consider this mysterious Standard, which is depicted in the Cult Chamber of Osiris at Abydos Temple.[42]

Ta Wer is the original name for Abydos, which means "Mound of Creation," on which Osiris emerged after the cataclysm. This fetish represents the rebirth of Osiris because the round object on the top, divided by four levels (like the Djed Pillar), represents the head of Osiris, which was buried at Abydos.[43] The long pole represents the vertical axis that connects Earth and sky, and it emerges through a platform at midlevel (Earth), which has figures and two cobras aligned probably to the equator, and four

Anubi to symbolize the four directions. The whole device is locked in place by standards holding up lions on higher platforms that wear the headdress of the invisible god, Amun. The lions are the double lions of the ecliptic, Aker. The pole itself seems to be actively birthing the head of Osiris out of the Earth dimension, which is the platform with the figures supporting it by the directions. Researcher Alan Alford says about Utterance 356 of the Pyramid Texts, "This passage explicitly states that Seth was buried *beneath* Osiris at Abydos." Alford suggests that Seth is the pillar itself.[44] Noting that some texts say Osiris passed through Abydos during his transfiguration, Alford sees this passage as from the interior of Earth, passing vertically up through Abydos (probably the Osireion) and to the sky.[45] The idea that the vertical axis is the Sethian force itself is profoundly transformative, because it explains why spiritual seekers usually have an encounter with the dark forces every time they move deeper into the initiatic quest.

This Standard was carried yearly at Abydos among the people, and

Fig. 5.7. The Standard of Abydos

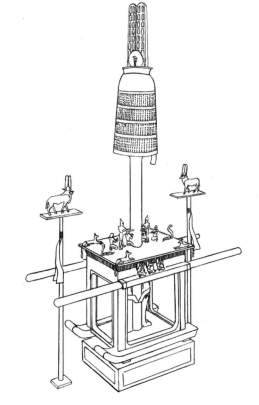

it helped them understand their life on Earth by the four directions, and then their ascent on the vertical axis of consciousness. This Standard is an exquisite rendition of birth, mortality, and transfiguration for every human being. It explains why anybody, including Osiris, would want to incarnate. Jeremy Naydler says about the current loss of this sense of the vertical axis, "The decline of this mode of experiencing the world, which led to objects becoming increasingly opaque and incapable of transmitting any transcendent value, lies behind the development of the secular, materialistic worldview of modern times."[46]

The basic premise of this chapter is that *the dynastic revival was based on the culture of the First Time that existed before the cataclysm,* which must have been extremely advanced given the complexity of the dynastic model. As we can see by looking into two mystery plays and the Standard of Abydos, when dynastic Egypt was conceived it was obsessed with the cycles of the sun, with the four directions, and with managing agriculture. Osiris brought agriculture to Egypt as the green god, fecundating Khemet from the Underworld. Every pharaoh became Osiris after death, yet while alive, the pharaoh was the Horus King. Osiris was the most popular god of the common people. Abydos contains the richest early predynastic sites as well as the Osireion from before the cataclysm. It is no accident that Seth was the inspiration for naming the great New Kingdom Pharaoh Set I, who had the artistic and theological brilliance to restore the Osireion and construct a new temple to access the vertical axis. Abydos Temple is one of the most multidimensional places on Earth.

We leave the mysterious land of Khemet for now because it is time to explore other cultures that existed from 9000 to 4000 BC, when there are few available sites in Egypt during the Blank.

6 ÇATAL HÜYÜK AND NOAH'S FLOOD

Whatever other hand than mine
Gave these young Gods fullness, all their gifts?
Like forms
Of phantom-dreams, throughout their life's whole
*   length*
They muddled all at random, did not know
Houses of brick that catch the sunlight's warmth,
Nor yet the works of carpentry. They dwelt
In hollowed holes, like swarms of tiny ants,
In sunless depths of caverns; and they had
No certain signs of winter, nor of spring
Flower-laden, nor of summer with her fruits . . .
Until I showed the rising of the stars,
And settings hard to recognize. And I
Found Number for them, chief devise of all,
Groupings of letter, Memory's handmaid that,
And mother of the Muses. And I first
Bound in the yoke wild steeds, submissive made
To the collar or men's limbs, that so
They might in man's place bear his greatest toils.

AESCHYLUS, *PROMETHEUS BOUND*

The Wanderers after the Cataclysm

To ascertain where the advanced cultures on Earth went after the cataclysm, we need to identify their basic characteristics: The survivors were global seafarers and astronomers, who sailed away to find new homes. They were great temple-builders as well as magicians, since this was required to build cyclopean monuments. Based on what the dynastic Egyptians said about their ancestors, the Shemsu Hor, they believed in various forms of divine kingship, priestly orders, and goddess worship. Once they found a viable home, they would have attempted, at all costs, to reestablish their civilizations. Logically, unusually advanced cities and villages from 9000 to 6000 BC are the new homes of the survivors who landed in boats, crawled out of caves, and came down from high mountains. This happened all over the planet. Appendix C shows how Earth changes correlate with the emergence of Holocene cultures. Here I focus on the Middle East because it is the location of the greatest number of advanced archaeological sites from 11,500 years ago. There is an identifiable progression in cultures from 9600 to 3000 BC based on the examination of sites by archaeologists, climatologists, and ecologists during the last 100 years. The mythology and sacred texts of Eastern and Western civilization emerge from this period, so these sites hold great memory resonance for all, and new discoveries are very exciting. For people of the Middle East, these discoveries are a renaissance.

After the cataclysm, culture flowered again in the Middle East during the Early Holocene (see figure 2.5 on p. 53), when the rising seas and Earth changes erased many of the activities of many early people all over the planet. This is why Plato's works are so important to us now, and apparently that is exactly what he intended. Plato cataloged the main cultural prototypes in the Mediterranean region—the Atlanteans, Magdalenians, Athenians, and Egyptians—so we will begin by looking for what happened to them after 9500 BC. The Atlanteans are mentioned in the early records of many world civilizations, yet they did not establish another homeland that came down through history. The Atlanteans may have had colonies in the Americas, since the Maya claim descent from them. They could have gone to what is now known as Tibet, archaic India, even China, but this is beyond the scope of this text. The Atlanteans are essentially precataclysmic, yet there are many reports of postcataclysmic Atlantean colonies; their cultural imprint is still potent in many places, as if they are a lost dream. I have more than 100 books on Atlantis, and I remember reading somewhere that at least 5,000 books on Atlantis have been published. Many archaic myths refer to them, and Aymara may actually be their language; in that sense, one could say Peru and Bolivia are their homeland. The Altiplano has cyclopean structures that are as compelling as the Valley Temple on the Giza Plateau.

The Magdalenians and other artistic cave cultures disappeared as distinct cultures 12,000 years ago, and many scholars think they are probably the precursors of the Azilian culture.[1] Recalling the Magdalenian ritual cave of Lascaux, I've already discussed in chapter 4 how the story of the First Man and the Primordial Bull continued on in Indo-European mythology, which helps us trace the wandering people. To simplify, Plato's archaic Athenians are the ancestors of the Greeks; the Shemsu Hor are the ancestors of the dynastic Egyptians; and now we look at how the culture of Çatal Hüyük passed to the Minoans. The Egyptians reemerged on the Nile, first as the Gerzean and Nagada cultures, and then by predynastic times they evidenced signs of descent from the Shemsu Hor. Both the Minoans and early Egyptians are derived from cultures that established early civilizations soon after 9500 BC. Both were great seafarers, so next

Fig. 6.1. Bulls' heads of the Tomb of Uadji

we seek their original ancestors. Archaeology and climate research indicates that the Fertile Crescent, Anatolia, and Iran were quite hospitable, which is confirmed by the advanced sites from circa 9500 BC in this region.

Evidence for a close relationship between the Minoans and the Egyptians is on the walls of the Fifth Dynasty Pyramid of Unas at Saqqara in Egypt. We see beautiful Minoan geometrical designs and the double ax (labrys) incised and painted with red carnelian and blue lapis lazuli on the walls behind the sarcophagus in the chamber where the Pyramid Texts were inscribed circa 2500 BC. One might assume that this means that Unas married a Minoan queen, but everything on the walls of the Pyramid of Unas is an archaic record of a time Unas wished to commemorate—Zep Tepi. As you will later see in detail, the double ax is the symbol for the Age of Gemini—6640 to 4480 BC. Thus, it is most likely Unas meant to indicate that the Pyramid Texts were cataloged during the Age of Gemini. Many researchers have concluded that Çatal Hüyük was the seed culture of the Minoans, which means Çatal Hüyük is an ideal place to look for evidence of an *archaic Minoan/Egyptian connection*. The *pre*dynastic 6,000-year-old tombs at Saqqara provide strong evidence for an Egyptian connection to Çatal Hüyük. For example, the Tomb of Uadji has raised bull reliefs that are *exactly* the same artistic style as the bulls' heads of Çatal Hüyük, as in figure. 6.1.[2]

The boats buried near the pyramids at Abydos and Giza closely resemble the great Minoan flotilla depicted on the walls of Akrotiri on Thera, reliefs that were well preserved by volcanic ash during Thera's eruption. The reliefs of Akrotiri are a *time capsule of the seafaring Mediterranean world,* the Holocene remnants of the global maritime civilization. During the Fifth and Sixth Dynasties in Egypt, Minoan culture was at its peak. Pyramids were even built in the Peloponnese that have recently been dated to this time, when there was major pyramid building in Egypt.[3] *The Minoans and the dynastic Egyptians are the direct descendants of Holocene seafaring cultures, who derived from wandering survivors after the cataclysm.* Remember, Plato said that the Athenians led the Egyptians in the war against the Atlanteans. However, later history reveals that the Egyptians were able to retain their cultural hegemony more successfully than the

Athenians/Greeks, who were constantly challenged by more frequent and intense Earth changes because of unstable faulting in their region. The Egyptians often assisted the Greeks in their travails because the Nile was more stable.

In his examination of the Edfu Building Texts, Andrew Collins argues that after leaving Egypt circa 9500 BC, remnants of the Egyptian Elder Culture (his term) sailed to the Levant and built Nevali Çori in southeastern Turkey, an astronomical temple of the Age of Cancer. Collins dates Nevali Çori to 9000 BC by star alignments to Cetus and Eridanus, and the site has been carbon dated back to 8000 BC.[4] Advanced early Anatolian sites that date back as far as 9600 BC, such as Göbekli Tepe and Nevali Çori, create a context for Çatal Hüyük as a later development. The evidence for advanced cultures in this region is accumulating, and there has to be an explanation for such advanced early development at these sites, which I will consider in detail later in this chapter.

The builders of Çatal Hüyük are probably derived from Nevali Çori, Göbekli Tepe, and other early sites in the region, since Nevali Çori and

Fig. 6.2. Nevali Çori courtyard. Illustrated from the photograph in Collins's Gods of Eden.

Göbekli Tepe date to right after the cataclysm. Remember, Çatal Hüyük has elements that suggest cultural links between the Egyptians and the Minoans. Collins notes that the Edfu Texts say that the Egyptian Elders report that they sailed away and lived in exile for thousands of years, so they are the most likely genesis of early Holocene cultures in this area. Collins also argues that they may be the ones who inspired the later Mesopotamian pantheon.[5] We are suggesting that the Elder Culture settled in many places in Anatolia and the Levant right after the cataclysm. Then they built Nabta Playa, and then once the Nile was habitable, they returned to Khemet. That is, the Egyptian Elders inspired many of the Mesopotamian elements while they were in the region. This is important because many scholars see the similarities between early Mesopotamia and Egyptian art, such as Walter Emery and Henri Frankfort, as though the early Egyptians got their styles from the Sumerians. Yet Collins and I believe the Mesopotamians were inspired by the Elder Culture.

The Egyptians retained their records in the Edfu Texts of the time of blackness and chaos before their ancestors crossed the sea to repopulate the Nile at *"the beginning of time."*[6] As was discussed and illustrated in chapter 3, there are many Egyptian elements in the early cultures west of the Nile in the Libyan Desert, such as the Tassili n'Ajjer after 9000 BC, which suggests that some Egyptian clans fled out into the desert. It is almost certain that the pharaonic Red Crown is the royal symbol of the people who fled to the desert, and the White Crown represents the seafarers and those who went to the Levant and Anatolia. These clans reunited as the Double Crown for the unification that occurred right at the opening of the Sixth Underworld, the National Underworld.

Let us summarize the cataclysmic dispersals before going into more detail: A few thousand years before the cataclysm, the Atlanteans moved out of Antarctica and resettled on a large island outside the Straits of Gibraltar, from which they exerted pressure on the Mediterranean cultures. Around 9600 BC the Atlanteans attacked the Athenians, who led the Magdelenians and the Egyptians into battle against them. The Athenians won just when the global maritime world was engulfed in the great disaster, as Plato reported. After this, coming off mountains and out of caves and landing in boats, the seeds of the cyclopean Elder Culture spawned new cultures circa 9500 BC, just before the Age of Cancer began. This was a time of constant global climatic upheaval, and the sites that survived are very informative.

Archaic Mediterranean Archaeological Sites

Climatologists have profiled global climate during the past 20,000 years, which totally revises prehistory. This *settlement archaeology*—the study of entire regions—puts individual sites into context.[7] Ecologists and geologists team up with archaeologists and anthropologists and invent new fields, such as *geoarchaeology*.[8] Climate and Earth changes in a given region often indicate where there must be archaic sites that are underwater or buried in ash or mud. When they are found, the logical deduction is that they are *the sites of the precursor cultures of the great civilizations that we once thought "just appeared."* The Aegean Sea rose 300–450 feet from 16,000 BC to 7000 BC (or the land sank), and the coastlines were inundated so that seacoast cities that did exist are deeply underwater. To repeat for the last time, in the global maritime culture, almost everybody lived by the sea. *Any* remains in the region from before 12,000 years ago prove that people had once lived there.

Settegast argues that the discovery of an inhabited cave in the Peloponnese in the 1960s—Franchthi Cave—provides the "evidence of an established tradition of seafaring in the Late Paleolithic Aegean."[9] Until Franchthi Cave was found, it was assumed that *nobody ever lived in the whole region before 6000 BC.*[10] Just like the Magdalenian caves, the Franchthi Cave site offers little information about the true level of attainment of the Greeks 12,000 years ago. It is a peripheral, marginal, or ritual site that does not reflect the true level of Late Paleolithic Greek culture. Then there are no sites from 9000 to 6000 BC, very much like the Blank in Egypt, which reminds us of the magnitude of the earth changes, especially the steadily rising seas.[11] Confirming the long relationship between the Minoans and the Egyptians, the Egyptians said to the Greeks in Plato's day, "You are left, as with little islands, with

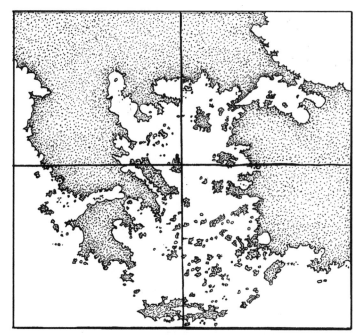

The Ibn ben Zara Map, Aegean

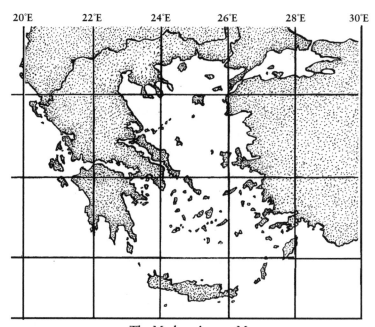

The Modern Aegean Map

Fig. 6.3. The Ibn ben Zara map (top) and the modern Aegean map (bottom)

something rather like the skeleton of a body wasted by disease; the rich, soft soil has all run away leaving the land nothing but skin and bone."[12] Compare the Ibn ben Zara map of the Aegean, which is thousands of years old according to Hapgood, with the modern map of the Aegean, and it is obvious why advanced sites must be a few hundred feet under the sea.

Well, nearby Palestine, Syria, and Anatolia are on higher plateaus, where there *are* advanced sites from 11,500 to 7,000 years ago. Archaeologists have found the remnants of the early movement and settlement of postcataclysmic cultures, but they have not yet agreed upon the patterns or sources of these cultures. The richness of these sites exists because this area did not succumb to the rising seas, and they are probably representative of what is underwater on the ancient shores of the Aegean and the whole Mediterranean region. The Natufian culture was extensive throughout the eastern end of the Mediterranean, where there was a "virtual explosion of arts, crafts, and technologies."[13] Suddenly there was advanced ancestor worship and wonderful art, as well as elements that are very Atlantean, such as veneration of the bull. Regarding these sites, a few archaeologists cited by Settegast have said, "The Natufian impulse was already old at the moment of its appearance in this land which formerly knew no art, or at least no imperishable art, of any kind."[14] These "already old" cultures didn't just come out of thin air; they are the creations of refugees from destroyed cities who started anew. According to Mary Settegast, refugees of the *Timaeus* probably founded the very early East Anatolian site, Çayönü.[15] In the middle of these cultural advances, a great flood caused by the Aegean Sea flowing into the Black Sea 7,600 years ago created another great wave of change. Eminent scientists William Ryan and Walter Pitman make a powerful case in *Noah's Flood* for the impact of this event triggered by the rising seas.[16] The story of the Black Sea Flood is a graphic example of cataclysmic cultural dispersal that puts sites in the whole region into context. The next section is my summary of Ryan and Pitman's hypothesis.

Noah's Flood and the Rising Seas

The story begins 20,000 years ago, when the seas were 400 feet lower than they are today. Northern European ice sheets were melting, and water raced into the Black Sea, which was an ice lake. The glaciers melted as the earth sprang up once the heavy weight of the ice lifted. The burgeoning lake found an outlet through the Sea of Marmara, through the North Anatolian fault, and into the Aegean Sea. Then 12,500 years ago cold returned during the Younger Dryas, and the glaciers sucked up the water in the Black Sea, which became an isolated lake. The old outlet, the Salkarya Channel, filled up with debris and formed a huge earthen dam. New river valleys cut down to the edge of the retreating lake, and people came there to escape the desiccation in their own regions. They began early farming in the rich deltas of fecund silt. The shrunken Black Sea was an oasis in a desiccated world for 1,000 years, when there is much evidence of struggle and near-starvation all over the region. Then 11,400 years ago, the people who were left moved away and settled elsewhere to farm.

From 11,400 to 8,200 years ago, people lived in villages such as Çatal Hüyük and Çayönü, and they farmed all over the Near East. The Mediterranean rose a few hundred feet, yet still the dam in the Salkarya Channel cut off the Black Sea. In 6200 BC, cold and dryness returned again. The people abandoned their villages, such as Çatal Hüyük, and some

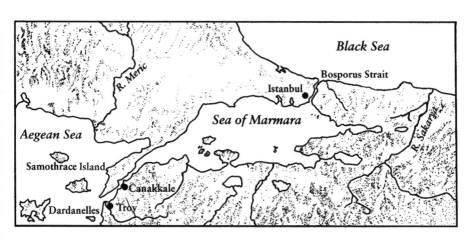

Fig. 6.4. The Sea of Marmara and the Black Sea

returned to the shores of the Black Sea to farm in the river valleys and deltas. The climate warmed again in 5800 BC, when many of the abandoned villages on the Anatolian Plateau were reoccupied. By 5600 BC, the Aegean Sea had risen so high that it was poised to breach the dam that kept the seawater from the Black Sea. First the winds and tides caused periodic incursions, until finally the water began to cut a river across the slope and down to the old channel toward the lake. Within days the small river became a torrent carrying tons of debris and mud. It cut into the bedrock, gouged a 475-foot-deep flume, and two hundred times the amount of water that flows over Niagara Falls rushed in daily. The rising water swallowed the shores, and the flood continued long after the people had fled. After two years the Black Sea had risen 330 feet, so the freshwater lake became a salt sea. Dense Aegean saltwater still flows through the bottom of the Bosporus into the Black Sea, whereas fresh water flows on top in the opposite direction.

Ryan and Pitman argue that the farmers of the Vinca culture, who hastily abandoned the shores of the Black Sea, took their culture with them and seeded many cultures: west to the Balkans and all the way to Paris; north to the Dnieper River in Russia; by water into the Aegean and Ionian Seas; east to the Caspian Sea; and south to the Fertile Crescent, where they seeded the 'Ubaid culture, the precursors of the Sumerians.[17] Sumerian legends are the basis of the Flood stories and the story of Noah's Ark in Judeo-Christian traditions, which is why Ryan and Pitman title their book *Noah's Flood.* The Black Sea Flood is a great example of how later cataclysms got mixed up with the earlier ones, which then triggered more collective fear. In general, science has ignored the Black Sea Flood hypothesis, which is just another example of their own inner blockage around remembering great disasters. Many new theories are coming forth regarding the ancestors of the Sumerians, the 'Ubaids, which of course raise new questions about the Flood legends in the Bible. Stephen Oppenheimer's *Eden in the East* posits that the sailors from Sundaland seeded the 'Ubaid culture, whereas *Gods of Eden* by Collins presents evidence that the 'Ubaids are from the Neolithic village of Jarmo in Iraqi Kurdistan.[18] Major revisions are happening in ancient history, which I will discuss more in subsequent chapters. Here we need more information about climate and Earth changes in the Middle East.

Crustal Shifting in the Cradle of Civilization

Çatal Hüyük in present-day Turkey is a precursor site to Minoan sites such as Knossos, Malia, and Akrotiri that were destroyed during the eruption of the volcano on Thera dated to 1626 BC.[19] Terror from this cataclysm in the Aegean is buried in the Western psyche because repeat cataclysms occurred within historical times in the "Cradle of Civilization." Figure 6.5 depicts Knossos just before Thera exploded.

The courtyard of Knossos, where the central ritual was bull dancing, was exquisitely decorated with hundreds of raised bullhorns. Knossos revered the goddess, and palace life and the mystery plays, including bull dancing, continued right up to when Thera erupted. The seafaring Minoan culture was mostly destroyed in the fire, ash, and great tsunami. The warlike Mycenaeans conquered its feeble remnants, which was the end of the last great goddess culture. For the Minoans and the Mycenaeans, and for people all the way to the coast of India, this collapse was a repeat of two previous cataclysms 11,500 and 7,600 years ago.

Fig. 6.5. Knossos Palace on Crete

Fig. 6.6. Three ladies of Knossos Palace

These great Earth changes in the Mediterranean 3,600 years ago ended a beautiful culture that was the final repository of thousands of years of exquisite art, theater, nature, beauty, and architecture. We know a lot about them because their palaces and cities were buried in volcanic ash, so they've enabled us to view the last intact goddess cultures. *The goddess was responsible for the pacification of Earth,* so, when the Earth quaked and fumed, she lost her power. In Egypt, we see a similar outcome: When the eastern Aegean exploded, Sekhmet as the raging goddess of fire and destruction prevailed over Hathor, the goddess of beauty, harmony, and music. The Egyptians became warlike for the first time, which was their eventual demise. Before this disruption, Egypt was a defensive country. Hapgood says before we got the exact date (1626 BC) of Thera's explosion, "A worldwide geological upheaval took place around 1400 B.C., and there was the *final* readjustment of the Earth's outer shell to its new position after its last displacement."[20] The Aegean basin subsided when Thera erupted, and Crete was devastated when the Minoan palaces were buried in ash. There were massive earthquakes in Egypt, where many of the temples, including Karnak, were severely damaged. Whole islands in the western Mediterranean sank, and the Caspian Sea, where the Russians have since found a sunken city, subsided. Nearby in India, the Saraswati River region uplifted, destroying the Vedic culture, which is described in the Mahabharata.[21]

According to the seismologist A. G. Galanopoulos, Santorini's volcanic core collapsed and formed a deep caldera, which sucked in billions of gallons of seawater and generated a tsunami that was *300 to 600 feet high.*[22] The great wave moved out from Thera into the Aegean to the distant Mediterranean shores, where it crashed over the Cycladic Islands and Crete. Oceanographic engineer James Mavor puts it simply: "The eruption and collapse of Thera (Santorini) is the greatest natural catastrophe that has occurred in historical times."[23] The Aegean region and the entire Near East were thrown back into a regression. Western civilization emerged eight centuries later in Athens with little memory of the recent cataclysm. Just as the people in the late Roman Empire did not know about Pompeii, the early Greeks did not know about the Minoan palaces on Crete or the cities on Thera. The Minoan culture was so totally devastated that its scripts are still only partially deciphered. Until 100 years ago, people believed Greek was the first language in the region.

Regarding the background of modern Western civilization as it is taught in schools, the Classical Greeks "just appeared" in Athens 2,800 years ago. A few hundred years later, Alexander the Great spread the Greek ideal all over the Cradle of Civilization. It became the credo of the Roman Empire, and this *Greco-Roman ideal* is the basis of Western education. However, our real past is so much older, richer, more evocative, and more feminine. Our memories of thousands of years of life, art, and rituals in happy cultures were buried under volcanic ash until very recently. The day Thera exploded, our forebears who sailed the Aegean from 9000 to 1600 BC were forgotten. As the Egyptians said to the Greeks, "You are all young in mind, you have no belief rooted in old tradition and no knowledge hoary with age. . . . Writing and the other necessities of civilization have only just been developed when the periodic scourge of the deluge descends, and spares none but the unlettered and uncultured, so that you have to begin again like children."[24]

J. B. Delair says that *most of the Holocene terrestrial disturbances were aftermaths of the crustal disturbances generated 11,500 years ago.*[25] Appendix B covers this aspect of Delair's work in detail, and I argue that we must begin to understand how much Earth changed so recently. We, like the Greeks 2,500 years ago, are like little children who have forgotten the past. As difficult as it is to live after the war-ravaged twentieth century, *Earth changes have been steadily diminishing compared to the recent past.* Now we must heal the emotional response patterns caused by them, such as constant warfare. The Age of Aries was an age of war and aggression, when the goddess was forgotten. Now we will go deeply into the lost culture of the goddess to awaken our latent creativity, because memories of this blessed way of life have the potential to terminate violence and warfare. Why do I say that? Well, if we add the time acceleration hypothesis to this equation, we can see that the rejuvenation of our inner feminine is what can free us to embark on a new evolutionary path. According to Carl Calleman, the Eighth Underworld—AD 1999–2011—is an accelerated force that is processing all the events and traumas of the last 5,125 years, when civilization became the basis of life. Civilization created wars between cultures, and so our next step is the reemergence of the feminine, the creatrix of art and beauty over 102,000 years, the Fifth Underworld.

Çatal Hüyük and the Precession of the Equinoxes

Mary Settegast says, "The range and beauty of these Neolithic settlers will not be fully appreciated until we come to the well-preserved site of Çatal Hüyük in the late seventh millennium."[26] Its discoverer, James Mellaart of the Institute of Archaeology at the University of London, was amazed by

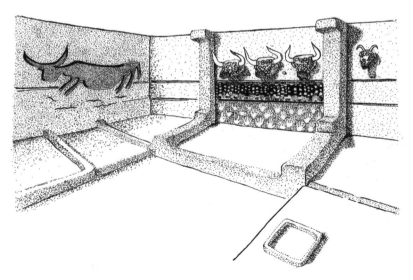

Fig. 6.7. Çatal Hüyük Bull Shrine

its similarity to Minoan sites, as are most people who compare them.[27] His discovery shocked archaeology in the 1960s, because then it was believed that the first urban communities arose circa 3500 BC.

Çatal Hüyük was an advanced urban farming culture that existed *thousands of years before it was thought possible.* It destroys the prevailing timeline of Mediterranean and Near Eastern archaeology. Archaeologists and historians recognized the distinctive shift into city culture triggered by the advent of the Sixth Underworld. I point this out because the early cities like Çatal Hüyük feel very different than Sixth Underworld male-dominant city cultures, such as Sumeria. Mellaart was able to excavate only 4 percent of Çatal Hüyük before his funds were cut off, and excavations have been resumed only recently. Çatal Hüyük is replete with complex plaster shrines of bulls' heads and leopard sculptures; wall paintings; iron and copper beads; clay stamp seals; greenstone axes; obsidian spearpoints; white marble sculptures (which resemble Bronze Age Cycladic sculpture); and extraordinary murals that seem to be calendars, as well as murals depicting hunting scenes, figures, and landscapes.[28] To emphasize the sophistication

Fig. 6.8. Goddess giving birth on the Double Leopard Throne

of this site, which is more than 9,000 years old, many illustrations are given here. Unexcavated levels still lie below.

Mellaart says, "The archaeological, anthropological, and artistic record of Çatal Hüyük is strongly suggestive of an important heritage from the Upper Paleolithic."[29] This means it was built by survivors of the cataclysm. The main mound goes back thousands of years before the culture of its top layer, which was mysteriously deserted in 6200 BC. Then there is a gap from 6200 to 5800 BC, when the people may have gone back to the shores of the Black Sea because there was a severe cold period during that time.[30] Thus, the top layers are time capsules from 6200 BC, the early stages of the Age of Gemini. The bull cult was very prominent, suggesting Atlantean influence, and veneration of the birthing goddess is also very evident, which suggests that the people retained symbols from the Age of Cancer. A clay figurine of a mother giving birth while sitting on a *double leopard throne* was found in a grain bin, as if she was there to enhance the harvest. This may suggest the end of the Age of Leo moving into Cancer. Çatal Hüyük was a key ritual center during the Age of Cancer—8800 to 6640 BC—when agriculture developed.

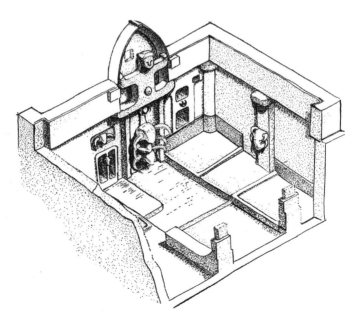

Fig. 6.9. Goddess giving birth to a ram above the Three Bull Heads Shrine

Collins argues they were practicing *vulture shamanism.*[31] This idea really resonates with the Age of Cancer, which was deeply involved with the Underworld. The rooms were filled with numerous ritual heirlooms of families, birthing women, and embracing couples, and even a goddess giving birth to a ram above three bulls' heads. The lower layers of Çatal Hüyük take us deeply into the Age of Cancer, the deep core that reunites us with the goddess. According to Calleman, this period was during the maturation of the Fifth Underworld, the 102,000-year-long Edenic phase when we were very much in tune with nature. In that sense, Çatal Hüyük is really not like a city; it is more like a nest in the Earth, as are many other Fifth Underworld remains.

Some murals exhibit very primal geometrical symbolism, exquisite metamorphic paintings, and animal, human, and landscape art. There are some strange murals with netlike patterns that are astronomical. Two murals to be discussed here describe time and cycles, as other researchers have also suggested. For example, in figure 6.10, note the prominent double ax on the left of the mural, which was later a symbol of Knossos. Hertha von Dechend "proposed that the double-axe was actually associated with the Precession of the Equinoxes."[32] *This is the oldest known representation of the double ax on Earth.* Along with sacred twinship, the double ax is a key symbol for the Age of Gemini because it expresses duality, and it is also an ideal symbol for axial tilt. The fact that this mural was painted during early Gemini suggests that tracking precession may have become an important activity during this age, especially since Mercury, the planet that influences mental comprehension, according to astrology, rules the Age of Gemini. Once precession was noticed, marking the shifts between

*Fig. 6.10. Wheeled cross mural. Adapted from figure 112 of
Settegast's* Plato Prehistorian.

the ages would have been important. It makes sense that an early ritual center like Çatal Hüyük would have been used to study this great change in the sky. I propose *Çatal Hüyük is a library of precessional information from the Age of Gemini.* This is extremely important because it suggests that this site was active when the new religion of this period—Zervanism or Magism—was founded, a religion obsessed with cosmic time cycles.[33]

Analyzing the mural, the double ax on the left signals that the Age of Gemini has arrived. In the center of the mural, note the distinctive "wheeled cross," which is a wheel of time spinning as a four-directional, nearly equal-armed cross with arms ending as Poseidon's trident. When J. B. Delair commented on the manuscript for this book in January 2000 regarding my thoughts on this wheeled cross, he noted that the trident was a specially made weapon for Marduk by Ea that was used to dismantle/divert Phaeton. Thus, its presence in this mural definitely suggests they knew that precession emerged out of the cataclysm, since Marduk has become Phaeton in the Babylonian legends. As with Hamlet's mill, this wheeled cross—which Marija Gimbutas finds in later Greco-Balkan pottery to be "symbolic of the perpetual renewal of the cosmic cycle"—is the central image of moving time here.[34]

To me, it looks as if Poseidon's trident is "clicking" time into place on the next wheel, which is divided into eight sections by the central cross, a very simple and graphic portrayal of cyclical time. There are also four divided wedges representing the two ages between the fixed cross, making the total of twelve Great Ages. The large wedges in the second wheel could be the four fixed ages—Taurus, Leo, Scorpio, and Aquarius—and the smaller paired wedges would be the cardinal and mutable Great Ages. I propose *the second wheel is the circle of the twelve Great Ages and the first wheel is clicking in the Age of Gemini.* Next, to the right, there is a bull's head with wavy lines, which suggest energy flow, or maybe water for the demise of Atlantis. Possibly they wanted to point out that the Age of Taurus follows the Age of Gemini and will be very energized because it is a fixed age.

The symbols in this mural are *very* specific and shout, "This is where we are now!" The most intriguing element is right above the place where Poseidon's wheeled cross is clicking in the Age of Gemini by the wedge that represents both Gemini and Cancer. Notice the little human figures flying into the wheel that *may depict the ancestors of Çatal Hüyük returning from the shores of the Black Sea.* Maybe these are ritual postures. These ideas may seem far-fetched, but archaic people were very deliberate in their art; they only included elements that informed them and depicted their own stories. *Incorrect symbolism misrepresented the cosmos and the gods; it could bring evil or chaos into the world.* This mural is very intentional, and anthropologists have already suggested what some of the basic elements mean. We will probably never know what murals like this mean exactly, but they stimulate our imaginations and draw us back in time. This wheeled cross of Poseidon's trident is one of the oldest ones in existence, and it is certainly a very potent symbol for the perpetual return of cosmic cycles and possibly even the return from the Black Sea.

The mural in figure 6.11 is much more complicated than the wheeled cross, so we need more background on these murals. First of all, they were painted and then quickly erased by a layer of white paint after they were used, which is why we can see them today. Modern Tibetan monks and the Déné (Navaho) make very complex sand paintings that depict patterns of cosmic harmony. They align with the harmony they've created in the moment, and then they destroy the design by remixing all the grains. These are intensely sacred rituals because they believe they are directing the world with them. Once the designs are created, it would be destructive to fix them in time, because they were created to influence events on Earth for a specific time. This probably is much the same as the thought behind the Çatal Hüyük murals, since they painted them and then painted over them until it was time to create another one. The Tibetan and Déné cosmograms are cosmic instructions in time, and these murals certainly seem to depict cosmic time cycles. Anthropologist Brian Fagan comments, "Clearly, these wall paintings had a profound transitory significance, perhaps as an element in powerful ritual performances that unfolded in the shrine."[35] Of course, no one realized that archaeologists would remove the paint and expose the murals. I propose that *the murals are ritual art instructions that depict time cycles.*

I think the second mural is also precessional, and what it may represent is incredible. One's first impression is that this mural is *very* deliberate.

Settegast argues that this mural suggests that Zervanism was practiced at Çatal Hüyük.[36] Zervanism is the religion of the Magi that conceived of time as infinite, as eternity. When we factor in the wider context for the region in light of Ryan and Pitman's *Noah's Flood,* the Magi may have been the astronomer-priests of cosmological science for the whole region at this time. Just as the people who lived long ago on the shores of the Black Sea may have developed agriculture, they could also have experienced a cosmological breakthrough. *Hamlet's Mill* refers to the Age of Gemini as Time Zero, because it was when the constellations Gemini and Sagittarius rose during the equinoxes.[37] That is, as Gemini and Sagittarius rose, the edge of the galaxy was visible as a vertical backdrop. As for the age and nature of religions in this region, the Indian-Iranian prophet Zarathustra (also known as Zoroaster) was a *reformer* of Zervanism. This makes his time later, and he already goes back thousands of years. Aristotle said the time of Zarathustra was 6350 BC. Zarathustra *abolished* the worship of time or fate, which was the basis of Zervanism, and so Zervanism is much older. Çatal Hüyük must be a Magian or Zervanian sacred site.[38]

For the Magi, time was "zodiacally conceived," and Settegast believes that the text printed above figure 6.11 represents the Zervanite or Iranian Magite view of celestial influence on earthly events.[39] This mural is approximately *8,700 years old,* yet the text above the mural was written only 1,000 years ago, and they are clearly connected. We can associate this text with this much more ancient mural because the written forms of ancient wisdom are derived from the old oral traditions, which always reach way back in time. This text is from the Bundahishn, which has many elements that easily could be 8,700 years old or more. As we view the exactly dated mural in light of this text (assuming time was zodiacally conceived), the twelve hands above are the twelve signs and the seven hands below are the seven planets, which are connected by netlike patterns. According to Settegast, "The netlike pattern of weaving between these rows of seven and twelve hands at Çatal Hüyük is itself a traditional symbol for the connections between the heavenly bodies."[40] These murals, taken together, strongly suggest that Çatal Hüyük was a major astronomical temple during the Age of Gemini that was devoted to studying planetary and precessional star cycles.

I think this mural traces the planetary influences during the Great Ages, and the netlike lines probably represent planetary orbits. Allow me to interpret it going right to left, as the Great Ages move in reverse order. The Age of Gemini is the first black hand above with very complicated nets for planetary movements occurring during Gemini. The second of the twelve hands above is the Age of Cancer, where new patterns are indicated, and the circular design may represent a simple hearth or early round houses when the first people settled here. Next, *three pyramids* back to Leo with a zigzag lightning bolt, odd hut or cavelike dwelling, and that could be Giza Plateau! Then right in mid-Leo, there is a huge dichotomy that represents a discontinuity in 9500 BC, chaos indicated by isolated squiggles between two upper hands. A god of destruction at this time was Teshub (who is later Zeus), and his symbol is the lightning bolt, so this hints at great destruction, possibly violent weather occurring during the Age of Cancer. As we move further back in time, the mural depicts earlier ages—such as Virgo, Libra, and Scorpio—because the people at this time would have thought of the zodiacal ages going back forever in time. Their portrayal of these ages before the dichotomy is radically different than the ages of Leo through Gemini, and the patterns are significantly more orderly, which may reflect the time of Paradise. Going back to the Age of Gemini, we see that there is a black rendering of a bull's thigh, which represented the stars around the North Pole in early cultures, such as Egypt. The netting going further back is more geometrical and orderly, *perhaps portraying a time before the axis tilted.*

The mural makers may have retained records of the patterns in the

"All welfare and adversity that come to man and the other creatures come through the seven and the twelve . . . for the twelve signs of the zodiac and the seven planets rule the fate of the world and direct it." —*Bundahishn*

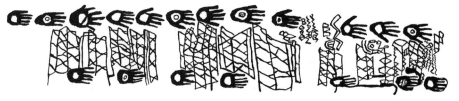

Fig. 6.11. Twelve hands above and seven below. Adapted from figure 119 of Settegast's Plato Prehistorian.

sky before the seasons began, and the order and clarity of the patterns before the dichotomy may depict the Golden Age. I propose that this mural attempts to show 26,000 years of time based on the mural maker's current understanding of the Great Ages, and it shows radical astronomical differences in the planetary orbits before and after the axis tilted. *The change in the night sky would have been their central story,* and they would have painted murals to comprehend these patterns. We are so lucky to be able to consider these ideas, even though it is difficult to understand the archaic mind. The more we realize how the Great Ages have literally been mutating the human brain, the more it is logical that the people would have created paintings such as this one to depict the long cycles of time. It is *we* who have forgotten until very recently how important this information is. This mural may map planetary patterns and the Great Ages as the astronomers of Çatal Hüyük understood them.

The only way we can penetrate archaic memory banks is by freeing our imaginations. No one will ever be able to prove what the ritual cave of Lascaux or the murals at Çatal Hüyük mean; however, we can hope that we will be able to read more and more things into these ancient records as we learn more about the people who lived there. Regarding the hands used to depict the Seven and Twelve, the Magdalenians frequently used red ochre hand impressions in their cave art. They are virtually ubiquitous, and I've seen them in Hopi kivas. I've always felt like they did this to reach through time to us as if they could touch us. Perhaps, but maybe hand symbols are used to depict time cycles? As we have better information on specific sites, then it may be possible to connect ancient cultures to each other and decode such symbolism. Plato has been our guide for what the world was like thousands of years ago, so I complete this chapter by exploring another mystery that comes to us from Plato. The *Timaeus* opens with the Atlantis myth, describing a society that still existed in the days of the ancient Athenians, yet this section is only six paragraphs long. Then the *Timaeus* goes on with *sixty more* paragraphs that describe the manifestation of the physical world after the mythical time. Few people have paid any attention to Plato's odd and arcane description of the manifestation of the material world; however, because it follows his description of Atlantis (which is later completed in the

Critias), I think it is worth considering. As you will see, it actually says a lot about human consciousness during the Age of Cancer—8800 to 6640 BC.

The Earliest Writing and the Platonic Solids

The most challenging part of my education with my grandfather was his insistence that I study the *Timaeus* when I was eight years old and report back to him on my understanding of it. Well, I was fascinated by the story of Atlantis, but Plato's writing about the physical world coming from the world of forms frankly made my head hurt! Finally, I see the importance of the rest of the *Timaeus*. A group of research chemists have discovered how to create newly structured molecules based on the Platonic solids: They've made new molecules—such as octanitrocubane or ONC, which may end up being the basis of a cancer cure—that are the most powerful nonnuclear explosives ever found and that are expanding the horizons of organic chemistry.[41] As for the Platonic solids, Plato says that the four elementary constituents are earth (cube), air (octahedron), fire (tetrahedron), and water (icosahedron), and the dodecahedron symbolize the universe. *These chemists have discovered a new chemistry by studying Plato and following his forms!*

The next connection to the world of forms is Near Eastern clay tokens that are found in almost all sites from 8000 to 6000 BC in Iraq, Iran, Syria, Turkey, and Israel. These clay objects hardened by fire are well-made miniature cones, spheres, disks, tetrahedrons, cylinders, and other geometrical shapes, some of which are Platonic solids.[42] They were a system of counting or early writing that enabled people to bridge different

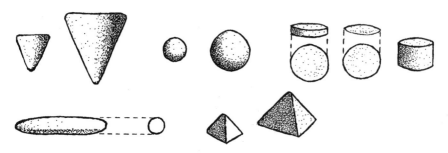

Fig. 6.12. Near Eastern clay tokens. Adapted from figure 11 of Rudgley's The Lost Civilization of the Stone Age.

languages, and being so portable, they are universal and were well developed by 8000 BC. If they had existed before the cataclysm, they would have been found in the caves and other sites, where prediluvial bones with notations have been found. I've already noted in chapter 4 that there is much evidence for writing systems before the cataclysm, and I think these tokens are evidence for entirely new levels of abstract thought.

Plato's essential doctrine—the material realm precipitates out of abstract forms—goes even further back in time. The anthropologist Richard Rudgley has a fantastic chapter in *The Lost Civilizations of the Stone Age* titled "Paleoscience."[43] Among many amazing finds, a million years ago our Acheulian ancestors in Europe, Asia, and Africa exhibited a remarkable degree of uniformity in crafting their hand axes. It is always possible to recognize their hand axes because the chipping and napping are so much the same that one craftsman could have made them all. Of course, that is impossible, and so the logical deduction is that this uniformity is the result of some form of social knowledge that enabled them to have an *image of the tool* in their minds. Rudgley says that the "origins of aspects of mathematical knowledge may be traced back to the time of the hand axes."[44] He believes we can't understand the human story without taking into account the innovations and developments that occurred in the Stone Age. According to Calleman, the Fourth Underworld is 2 million years long, and the midpoint and apex is 1 million years ago, exactly when the Acheulian hand axes appeared everywhere, a global synthesis of human minds guiding their hands.

Regarding the mysterious Neolithic tokens, I think they are advanced tools of the Fifth Underworld that kept alive the critical human knowledge—*matter precipitates out of abstract form*—which is obviously what mattered to Plato. Of all the things my grandfather stressed, he said that this is the most important idea, and now I see why. Once we realize that *our thoughts create our tools,* such as the Acheulian axe makers and the Neolithic makers of Platonic solids, we might be able to imagine how our ancestors created the Great Pyramid. Allan and Delair have proposed that the cataclysm interrupted 29 million years of evolution, and all that remains now are stone remnants that survived the destruction. The next chapter supports this long evolution by means of evidence in stone.

7 THE FALLEN ANGELS AND THE STONES OF ICA

What womb brings forth the ice,
who gives birth to the frost of heaven,
when the waters grow hard as stone
and the surface of the deep congeals?

Can you fasten the harness of the Pleiades
or untie Orion's bands?

Can you guide the Crown season by season
and show the Bear and its cubs the way to go?

JOB 38:29–32[1]

Draco and the Great Bear

The constellations that travel around the North Celestial Axis—the *circumpolar constellations*—are a great clock that ancient traditions say reads the rise and fall of humanity. The great macrobiologist Michio Kushi says, "The circumpolar stars, as a whole tell a story, the voyage of human civilizations through the stages of the 26,000-year cycle. The ancients used the patterns of the stars in the night sky as we use printed books, movies, or television—as a medium for preserving and conveying information."[2] According to Kushi, we are ending a time of war and struggle and beginning the time of Paradise.

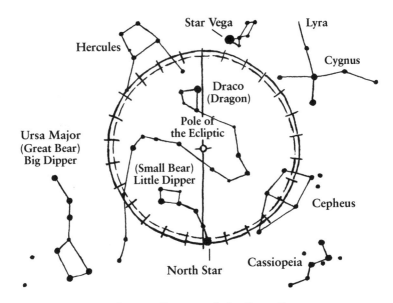

Fig. 7.1. Draco and the Great Bear

He describes the period we've been in for the last 10,000 years as a time of a wilderness coming to Earth, when we were heavily influenced by the constellation Draco—the Dragon, or the Serpent of the biblical tradition—when we were expelled from the Garden of Eden.[3] Negative vibrations have been devouring us, and we've almost lost our way because our thinking has become more and more deluded. Now, as we come to the end of this time, we see the fruits of our destruction, and we want to change. During this time of darkness, we consolidated our efforts by creating institutions just to survive, and we also have become very solid and materialistic. The time has come to break down these patterns and become less dense, which will enable us *to use the full powers of thought in the material world.*

The previous chapter ends with a bold concept: Matter precipitates out of abstract form by our thoughts; more simply put, our ideas create the things that appear in our material world. Of course, there are many other orders of creation, such as minerals, plants, and animals. During the Eighth Underworld—1999 to 2011—we've become creatures who e-mail each other and interact less and less in person; yet who wants this? Many religions seek an ultimate solution, but this fading desire is based on old systems used for 5,125 years that are collapsing. To foster this process, time speeds up as old ways of life just disappear. Amid this high velocity, deep archetypal forces are activating within people that could become emotional whirlwinds that feed on negative thoughts. Such calamities can be avoided by processing our shadows or dark sides to avoid being caught in the vortexes of the collapsing old systems. The time-acceleration hypothesis says we are approaching an evolutionary peak, not just an end of old ways. The most important theme in this book is that many people believe the world is soon coming to an end, yet they are probably wrong. They pray for an apocalypse to escape the troubling images that fester in their minds, which could bring about the end for many people. However, it will not be the end of nature.

Most people are not aware that the shadows they struggle with come from inner confusion caused by the false story of the past; people feel guilty about something they can't even describe. *These painful shadows were born during the horrific survival times following the chaotic Earth changes.* We must open the curtain on this period, since cataclysmic myths are always paired with stories of humans who disobeyed God and *caused* the great disaster in 9500 BC. This idea of a wrathful god and humanity's Original Sin is driving the human species straight toward destruction. For instance, in Genesis 6:1–12, the sons of God came down and seduced the daughters of men, giants were born from them, and evil came into the world. This caused God to send a great flood, Noah's Flood, but Noah, his family, and the species *survived*. According to early sources of this story in the Bible, after the Flood humans wandered around Earth in a daze among serpentine giants and great bird-gods, who taught humanity the arts of civilization. From this moment on, we've been cast as mixed beings of heaven and Earth—*the children of the Fallen Angels.* These stories are the source of intensely shadowed and separated parts of our psyches that are all mixed up with cataclysmic memories. Surely, we are more than fallen sinners who can never recover from the trauma lurking back in the mists of time?

During the time of Paradise before the cataclysm, Kushi describes the "whole planet united in a time of peace, creativity, and harmony by the descending (centripetal) energy which formed the galaxy, the solar system, and this earth."[4] Kushi said back in the 1970s that the time of Paradise opens with the current solstice alignments when Earth's axis points directly through the Milky Way, when we receive an "enormous flow of galactic current."[5] The mass of stars in that plane "shed their influence directly down through the central, vertical (north-south) energy channel both of the planet and also of humanity as well as all other life forms on earth. Not only is the human brain more active during this period, all botanical sources of our food are much more vigorous, requiring hardly any cultivation."[6] The previous time of Paradise Kushi describes may have lasted at least 30 million years, while the last 11,500 years have been a time of struggle, with the serpent Draco writhing in the northern polar sky.

Kushi describes a *vibrational world* in which the creation of realities by thought requires the reception of energy throughout the whole body, not just thinking in the head. I started this chapter with our exciting future because the deeply suppressed material in this chapter will be horrific and shocking for many readers. We are conditioned to avoid unpleasant ideas that force us to face inner darkness because if we face ourselves, nobody can control us. As Paradise comes again to Earth, our bodies need fine-tuning to receive these subtle frequencies. Subtle glands that access very high frequencies, such as the hypothalamus and thymus, are activating now, and if we have massive emotional blocks, our physical bodies can't handle the secretions of these glands.[7] The global recovery of archaic memories is causing a mind-bending spiritual crisis that is reaching its apotheosis due to time acceleration. It is so important to realize that time acceleration is causing old *ways* to end, not our planet. Of course, many people cling to the old ways.

As people look deep within and face their hidden violence and heartlessness, personal boundaries dissolve and connection with nature intensifies exponentially. People sense that their own inner anger and fear is related to the pain in the world, so they *feel* Rwanda, Bosnia, Iraq, Afghanistan, Libya, and Egypt, which opens their hearts. Remarkably, each time a person lets go of his or her need to be separate from the whole, deeply honest encounters with the self cause miracles to happen: Suddenly disasters in politics, such as potentially terrible violence in Tahrir Square in Cairo, just don't happen. This is because *nature reformulates her fields in resonance with the human heart when we intentionally align ourselves with others.* Nature devolves into separation and chaos when evil people project their lies and hatred into the collective mind. Regardless of this temporary mental lock, the divine is enfolded in the mundane world; it responds to love and our personal quests, birthing waves of grace in the material world—miracles. Here we remember the unrecognized dreams, loves, and magical powers of the people lost in the cataclysm when our cosmic dream was shattered. We sing the forgotten songs of the ancient ones.

The Collective Nightmare of the Global Elite

Moving out of our personal realms, which we so carefully construct around ourselves to feel safe, we now explore the current group mentality, where there is a collective madness building in the realm of emotions and archetypes. The truth is we live in a world that is controlled by covert Elite groups that are strangling the human heart. These Elite members come out of the old wealthy families who supply individuals for the important positions in politics, religion, medicine, banking, and business. This is not news; however, *how* they use their power is not well understood: They use the forbidden arts of the Fallen Angels—creation by thought, astrology, natural healing, and alchemy—while simultaneously debunking these arts so no one else will be able to use these powers or be able to see what they are actually doing. For instance, the Elite created a mass trauma event on September 11, 2001, then labeled it "9/11" to hook people into the emergency code number: 9-1-1. They often use number magic or sound coding in names—such as Obama, when everybody is supposed to worry about Osama—to plant fear and confuse the people. Those outside the Elite cannot see that they do things like this because the Elite wear suits and red ties while smiling benignly on television. Meanwhile, for the public, any contact with these arts is a total embarrassment, like hanging out a shingle advertising that one is a palm reader. Thus, ordinary people are robbed of the use of magical skills, while the Elite runs rampant using the manipulation of occult forces in their secret cabals. As Andrew Collins says, "Initiates and secret societies preserved, revered, even celebrated the forbidden knowledge that our most distant ancestors had gained their inspiration and wisdom, not from God or from the experiences of life, but from a forgotten race remembered by us today only as fallen angels, demons, devils, giants and evil spirits."[8]

This program can be observed by watching the behavior of the Elite over great spans of time. As we've already seen, the Elite have continually stolen the knowledge of sacred cultures and either destroyed it on the spot or stored it for reference in hidden places, such as the Vatican Library, archaeological museums, the Smithsonian, and private collections. By using ancient calendars, totemic artifacts, bones, and divination systems, they've worked together in secret to control the world for thousands of years.[9] (See this and other endnotes for good books about the Global Elite.) To control the world, the Elite need the forbidden arts, but *why?* Because when the planet is functional and healthy, people live in small bioregions and know how to use these forces to live in harmony with the land and maintain their freedom; they can't be controlled. By taking the sacred sites and magical powers from the people, the Elite extend these forces throughout their own interlocked systems for control and personal gain. At this point, we live in an era when they plan to call in their chips, since they know the time of Paradise is coming. Remember, the conquistadors with their priests stole the calendars of the Maya.

In *From the Ashes of Angels,* Andrew Collins tells the story of the angels in Christian, Hebrew, Iranian, and various Middle Eastern scriptures, who interbred with the women of Earth thousands of years ago. Their children are the *Nephilim,* the basis of the Elite bloodlines. He also describes the angels teaching the forbidden arts and sciences to humanity during the crucial survival times as *physical beings who walked among us.*[10] Later, Christianity conspired with the aristocracy to eliminate the evidence for the corporeal nature of the angels, and this evil alliance continues today. When the Europeans colonized the Americas, the Inquisition had already stripped the forbidden arts from the common people of Europe. The conquerors of the Americas were trained to look for any traces of the forbidden knowledge, and then the priests swept in right behind the legions and destroyed or gathered it for future reference, and they built churches on the original sacred sites. Those who survived the genocide mostly forgot the real story of the ancient times.

In the eighteenth century, when archaeologists and geologists dug up mammoth and dinosaur bones, the public was consumed with curiosity about these amazing finds, which directly contradicted current science dictated by theologians. Quickly, the Elite set up university and museum systems to control and manage the finds; they were to be investigated by chosen archaeologists, curators, and professors, who were instructed to select only certain parts of the data. The selected data was used to construct a mythology that supports the Elite—social Darwinism—based on the premise that humanity is always evolving from primitive to more advanced levels, which blocks the recognition of prediluvial civilization. Elite science retards human memory recall, which is why the new-paradigm movement attacks social Darwinism. No wonder the stories of the Fallen Angels were covered up! *The Elite assumed the power of the angels themselves, a Faustian pact of major proportion and consequence.* But finally and unavoidably, the evidence for previously advanced cultures is flooding in, and our deepest memories are beginning to awaken.

Underground Cities and the Survival Times

Revised construction dates for the Sphinx, Valley Temple, and the Osireion; evidence of advanced machine tooling in Egypt; and the written records of Egypt all support the existence of a highly advanced culture in Egypt before 12,000 years ago. Heavy rain and flooding forced the Elders—the Shemsu Hor—to sail away in great boats to seek safety, whereas others migrated west into Libya. The Edfu Building Texts that were cataloged during dynastic Egyptian times record this primary exodus, and evidence has now been discovered for where they went:[11] Around 12,000 years ago, somebody built thirty-six underground cities in the center of the old Turkish kingdom, Cappadocia, which *200,000 people* could have inhabited comfortably. The largest one, Derinkuyu, covers two-and-a-half square miles; only eight levels have been thoroughly explored out of twenty known to exist; and just this one complex could have adequately housed around

20,000 people. It has complex four-inch-diameter ventilation shafts that go down more than 200 feet into the various levels, which would have required metal-tipped drills. Tunnels linking one city to another have been found.[12] Collins comments that these troglodytic people "were hiding not from people, but from the forces of nature."[13]

Regarding such forces of nature, there was a global magnetic reversal called the Gothenburg Flip that occurred between 13,750 and 12,350 years ago, which most likely triggered the Younger Dryas, a short ice age from approximately 12,500 to 11,500 years ago.[14] Those days would have been dark and damp; people would have longed for light, but at least they could survive. The lowest and oldest levels have higher ceilings than the upper levels, which suggests the lowest levels were, as Collins puts it, "designed to suit a tall race of people."[15] Stone tools used to carve them out that date to the end of the Paleolithic Era were found nearby. I wonder how long these people had to live underground?

Regional myths tell stories of Ishtar, Inanna, and Persephone descending into the house of darkness, which could be Derinkuyu or nearby Çatal Hüyük, where all entrances are down through the roofs and there are no windows. There are countless ancient stories about people going underground during Earth changes. Çatal Hüyük excavator James Mellaart notes that murals in levels above the unexcavated lower levels have paintings of archaic reed structures, the regional ancestral houses of 11,000 years ago.[16] These are very much like the structures that were built for the pharaoh's Heb Sed ceremony, to honor the life ways of the ancestors, the Shemsu Hor (see chapter 5). As Andrew Collins reports, "The epoch surrounding the climatic and geological upheavals that accompanied the last Ice Age is the only time when humanity has spent long periods of time hiding away from the outside world."[17] Further, he surmises that the Elder Culture went to Derinkuyu around 12,000 years ago during the climatic upheavals.[18]

I think heavy rains afflicted the Nile during the Younger Dryas after the Gothenburg Flip, when there was a drop in Earth's magnetic field that increased tectonic activity and climatic variation. The Shemsu Hor might have built the lower levels of Derinkuyu around 13,000 years ago. According to Allan and Delair, before the cataclysm, the Anatolian Plateau was on the northern edge of a vast continent from northwest Africa to Asia Minor (the Aegean continent or Tyrrhenia), and north of it was a vast lake, which can be seen in figure 2.4 (p. 51), the tentative map of the prediluvial world.[19] With no Mediterranean Sea in the way of getting to the Anatolian Plateau, and with the Nile Basin flooding, the Nilotic people could have moved north to the high plateau. The Egyptian Elders may have built the lower levels of these cities during this phase to have a place to move their people, since the Younger Dryas was a mini–ice age. It was a good choice, because tufa stone deposited there by two nearby volcanoes is hundreds of feet deep. The Elder Culture could have survived the cold underground for a considerable time at Derinkuyu. I propose the early dynastic journey through the underworld, which is described in the *Twelve Hours of the Duat,* an ancient Eguptian sacred text, is a distant memory of this terrible time. *The more that prediluvial geography and weather changes are taken into account, the more mythology makes sense.*

Archaic Middle Eastern mythology has stories of two main cataclysms—the end of the Pleistocene epoch in 9500 BC and the Black Sea Flood in 5600 BC. In the Bible, Noah was instructed to build an ark because a flood was coming, which probably is a memory of the 5600 BC Black Sea Flood, since Noah had time to prepare. The Persian text, the Zend Avesta, contains stories that may go back more than 12,000 years. For example, the flood hero Yima was instructed by Ahura Mazda to build a *var*—a "subterranean fortress or city," the underground cities![20] Yima was told to build the var to survive amid horrible cold, which in fact prevailed in this region during the Younger Dryas. It is common knowledge that there are great tunnels and caverns under the Giza Plateau, and my teacher, Abdel Hakim, told me in 1996 that he walked in them when he was a child. In his latest book, *Beneath the Pyramids,* Andrew Collins reports on his explorations of the great tunnels and caverns under the Giza Plateau.[21] Lynn Picknett and Clive Prince describe extensive covert testing and explorations seeking the locations of these tunnels under the Giza Plateau.[22] Many people report exploring huge caves in the mountains in Peru, and there are huge underground caverns right under the Dome of the Rock in Jerusalem. Modern Jews and Arabs may battle over the entrances to the caves because they believe the end times are coming soon and the caves are a refuge.[23]

Underground cities probably helped people survive 14,000 to 11,000 years ago. The story of Noah's Ark most likely refers to boats that were used to survive the Black Sea Flood, since people had time to prepare by building the ark and collecting the animals and plants while the Black Sea rose gradually over two years. Archaic legends are later compilations of stories from many different times that got jumbled together in the oral tradition, and often the bards carefully memorized stories that they didn't understand anymore. Then early scribes listened to the bards and carefully copied stories that didn't make sense to them either. Both the bards and the early scribes attempted to faithfully transmit these stories, the sacred records of their ancestors. Now, in today's age of science with detailed knowledge about climate and Earth changes, it is possible to better determine which event a story is describing. In summary of the Elder Culture: The Egyptian Elders built underground cities for survival during the Younger Dryas and occupied them. Once the cataclysm spent its fury, the rivers drained, fertile soil was again deposited, and Earth could be settled again. They moved out of the underground cities and first settled in nearby Asia Minor in Kurdistan and founded many sites, such as Nevali Çori, Göbekli Tepe, and Çatal Hüyük. Then we see them emerge in mythology.

Archaic Sacred Texts and Zarathustra

The Fallen Angels of Christianity and the Watchers in the Book of Enoch are found in much earlier Iranian and Indian sources, which Collins traces in detail. Names for the archangels confirm "the powerful relationship between Judaism and the Indo-Iranian myths found in both the *Zend Avesta* and the *Rig Veda*."[24] He argues that the "source material for the fall of the Watchers really had come from the rich mythology of Iran."[25] According to historians, the Iranian hero Zarathustra lived circa 600 BC. However, this line of prophets goes back much earlier, as already discussed in chapter 6. The Magi worshiped the oldest Indo-Iranian deities, the ahuras—shining gods who bask in heavenly realms—and the daevas—ahuras who fell and became Earth-bound devils, or Fallen Angels.[26] This fall occurred *before* Zarathustra, who reportedly slayed the daevas because they were sexually involved with Earth women, which is classic behavior by the Fallen Angels.[27]

The Persian *Bundahishn* tells the story of a pure couple who were seduced by Angra Mainyu (by the daevas in another source), a serpent with two feet, and the couple ended up worshiping their seducer. From then on their descendants are tainted and could only be forgiven by Mithra, a Persian god we will hear much about in the next chapter. I hardly need mention that this legend of the fall and the need for salvation while a serpent is involved is obviously similar to the story of Adam and Eve in Genesis.[28] Zarathustra preached against the daevas, whereas the Magian priests followed the dualistic doctrine of both kinds of deities. Zarathustra preached that only Ahura Mazda should be worshiped, so he accused the Magi of worshiping "the Lie."[29] That is, *Zarathustra stifled further discussions about angels being involved with humans,* but these juicy stories persisted in folktales and literature. For example, the Iranian Book of Kings, the Shahnameh, has many wild tales of daevas who could take physical form and "lie with mortal women to produce offspring with physical characteristics that matched, almost exactly, the progeny of the Watchers in the Hebraic tradition."[30] These angels are the same as the Watchers in the Book of Enoch, a major Judeo-Christian source that was not included in the Bible and was totally suppressed by the early church. One of the main characters in the Shahnameh is Kiyumars, who is Gayomar in the Zend Avesta, the same "First Man" as in chapter 4. These stories all interlock, and if Settegast is correct that this myth is depicted in Lascaux Cave, then *these are fragments of a prediluvial creation myth that survived the cataclysm.* The only way to determine the earliest source is to examine them by the known characteristics of different time periods.

The Watchers, the Nephilim, and the Fallen Angels

Who were these Watchers, and what were their physical characteristics? The angels in the Book of Enoch, the Elohim (who are also in the Bible), were tall with fair skin and thick, white wool-like hair. They shined like the sun, and their eyes burned into one's soul. People were afraid to look at them because their faces were like snakes or vipers.[31] The Book of Enoch, which is extremely ancient, was unavailable to Christians in the West until a copy turned up and it was translated into English in the early nineteenth century. In the mid-twentieth century, the Nag Hammadi library and the Essene Scrolls were found, which contain much information about the Watchers, as well as other texts that were kept out of the Bible. The Essene Scrolls are still only partially translated because orthodox Jewish and Christian theologians have conspired to keep them hidden. The Nag Hammadi library has been translated, yet most theologians can't make sense of it because it is filled with weird and archaic material.[32] Both sets of texts are loaded with graphic and odd stories about the same angels and Watchers we find in the Book of Enoch and in Persian and Indian literature; it is no longer possible to keep hiding these strange beings. When Christianity strengthened its grip in the fourth century, the Essene Scrolls were hidden in desert caves near Jerusalem; the Nag Hammadi scrolls were hidden in Egypt; and then eventually the early church fathers banned the Book of Enoch as well as other apocryphal books that tell about the Fallen Angels. No wonder: These books report that *the source of evil in the world is these angels, not the sins of Adam and Eve,* the central doctrine of Roman Catholicism.

The Book of Enoch was left out of the Bible, while other books that contained stories of Fallen Angels were severely edited. The fact is, these recently discovered early sources are *more genuine* sources for early Christian beliefs than the Bible. These finds expose the extent of the fourth-century biblical "doctoring"; that is, *they reveal what desperately needed to be hidden* if the rising church was to be in control. These texts reveal the real truth about the Gnostics, who were banished as heretics by the early church. The Gnostics taught that the Genesis story of Eve being tempted by the Serpent is actually a garbled account of viperlike Watchers luring human females that is reported in the Book of Enoch and other Jewish legends. In the Book of Enoch, two hundred Watchers led by Shemyaza descended from the mountains of northern Palestine to mingle with humanity and sample the delights of women. The women gave birth to creatures called

Nephilim—fallen ones—giants who sinned against animals, devoured the locals and each other, and drank blood.[33] Before they went on their rampages, they taught the secrets of heaven, such as metalsmithing, geography, healing, astronomy, and architecture.[34]

The Bible is very confusing and contradictory about God bringing on the Flood to rid Earth of these fallen creatures. Meanwhile, the Book of Enoch describes angels begging God to not destroy them, and there is much evidence that some members of the fallen race—the Nephilim—actually survived these horrific times.[35] The most clear evidence in the Bible for the existence of these Watchers is in their Nephilim children—the Anakim, Emim, Rephaim, and Zuzim—who were giants wandering around Canaan when Abraham and the Jews arrived circa 1800 BC. There are reports of battles with giants in the Bible, such as David and Goliath, and Joshua sending out a spy, Caleb, to murder the giants in their chief city, Hebron.[36] As I have observed the hideous genocide and purposeless wars during the twentieth century, I have come to believe there is only one possible source for Elite cruelty; they are the descendents of the Fallen Angels.

According to Roman Catholic doctrine, Eve's sin was that she ate fruit offered to her by the Serpent, and thereby got the "forbidden knowledge." Because she disobeyed God, her progeny is doomed to misery, suffering, and an evil nature; just by being born, humans are sinners. According to salvation theology, the church must cleanse this sin soon after birth by baptism, and if one obeys the will of God, as interpreted by the Roman Church, they will be saved. As for Eve, St. Augustine put the blame on her and called it Original Sin, which makes her a temptress of the Serpent. Meanwhile, *stories of the Fallen Angels suggest that Eve's progeny are the children of the Watchers.*[37] The name Eve in Hebrew means "snake," and in some Jewish accounts, Eve is the "ancestral mother of the Nephilim," the gods who came down to Earth.[38]

When the early church formulated the canon in the early fourth century, the common people knew all about these legends. The problem was that people who followed the Book of Enoch often became Manicheans or Gnostics, just as did St. Augustine when he was young. The early church fathers believed that these old tales were directly in the way of their plans to control the human path to salvation, so they developed campaigns against *heresy*—thinking differently. They got rid of anything that was in the way of their plans: The Alexandrian Library was burned, the church persecuted many early Christians, and Satan was selected as the root of evil in the world. *The church's core creation doctrine was and is based on a sinful primordial mother, Eve.* Therefore, devotion was shifted to Mary, the mother of Jesus. Meanwhile, Mary Magdalen, a priestess who was probably the wife or consort of Jesus and was certainly one of the early disciples, became the whore: Christianity is founded on the hatred of women—*misogyny*.[39] Once the Bible canon and the priests were organized, the Roman Catholic Church moved out with the army of Christ, slaughtered the Gnostics, and gained territory by building its churches on the ancient sacred sites. The Vatican Library and inner church cabals continuously destroyed or hid the records of conquered cultures.

Some writers argue that the Watchers and the Nephilim were extraterrestrials that came down to Earth to control and assist humanity after the Flood—the ancient astronaut hypothesis. Collins and I suggest a much more reasonable explanation, one that naturally emerges by staying in the context of the terrible conditions humanity had to bear during this time. The Watchers sound very much like stronger humans and masters of great shamanic skills who intervened to help save totally destitute survivors.[40] The archaic sacred texts and the Bible contain survival stories of daughters bearing children by their own fathers, sisters bearing children by brothers, and fathers being asked by Yahweh to sacrifice their sons. This was a terrible time when people were unable to produce enough children to keep themselves from dying out, a time of great starvation. The horrible stories of sacrificing children may be about Nephilim children born to distraught mothers and fathers, as you will see next in the story of the birth of Zal. Stories of giants devouring people and themselves reflect times of mind-boggling chaos, when races of people who were larger or somehow more powerful mixed with desperate survivors. Can any one of us judge people who live in times when people have to survive at all costs? So, why is the Elite—the potent brew of priests and kings—so determined to cover up these stories? Maybe they can't face their own shadows. In other words, I think the Elite's real problem is unprocessed emotional conflict, not the addictive bloodline that they seem to be so proud of.

Vulture Shamanism and the Birth of Zal

Where did the angels, Watchers, and giants come from? Kiyumars, the hero of the Shahnameh, goes back to the earliest times in Iran because he is the same as Gayomar, the hero of the Zend Avesta. A text in the Shahnameh, the "Birth of Zal," is a fascinating and very archaic story of the founding of a line of Iranian kings. The legendary Kiyumars worked metal tools and weapons, irrigated the land, and founded agriculture, the same skills as the advanced people who appeared after the cataclysm, and as the Fallen Angels. Here is the story of Zal from the Shahnameh, which is a condensation of the tale as told by Andrew Collins.[41]

In these days long ago, a king named Sam married a beautiful lady, who gave birth to a boy who was tall and shining with white hair and skin. His mother named him Zal, which means one who is aged. Sam was horrified because he thought Zal was the son of a daeva, Magi, or demon, so he left Zal on the side of a mountain to be devoured by beasts and birds of prey. The mountain where Zal was left was the legendary home of the Simurgh, some kind of noble female vulture or mythical bird. When the Simurgh saw the infant Zal lying exposed to the elements, instead of eating the baby or feeding it to her young, she put Zal in her nest. Her baby birds were also kind and loving to Zal, who grew up to be a fine young man. Sam assumed Zal was dead, but one day he dreamed his son was still alive, so he prayed to the great god Ahura Mazda for his son's return. The Simurgh heard his prayer and knew she must return him. Zal was unhappy because not only had the mysterious bird protected him, it had also taught him many ancient secrets, including the language and wisdom of his own country.[42] The Simurgh gave Zal one of her wing feathers, so she could appear if ever he needed her. Zal married a foreign priestess, Rudabeh, who was a descendent of a serpent king and was much taller than Zal. She was white as ivory with a face like Paradise. When Zal's queen was ready to give birth the first time, she was

Fig. 7.2. Vulture shaman

unable to deliver and was in grave danger. With his feather, Zal called in the Simurgh. She came and gave his wife a drug to free her from pain and anxiety, and she used a seer who recited incantations to lion-boy while he was drawn out by cesarean section.* His mother named him Rustam. She was given another drug that instantly restored her health, and the shining boy became the legendary hero of Iran.

Collins notes that "the account of the Birth of Zal was almost identical to the miraculous birth of Noah presented in the Book of Enoch," and Zal was married to Rudabeh because "they each bore very specific qualities that were deemed necessary to perpetuate the existing line of divine kings."[43] Because this story is very archaic, and Iranian mythology influenced the later Judaic tradition, there was a much older primary source for both stories.[44] Collins explores the possibility that the Simurgh preserves the story of "a much earlier shamanistic culture" that practiced vulture shamanism, which uses birds as carriers of the soul after death.[45] The First Man of Lascaux Cave is bird-headed, and he has a bird on his staff, which he has dropped. Regarding the birth of Zal, his marriage is arranged with another Watcher, he becomes the legendary hero of Iran, and the central player is the Simurgh. Collins argues that the Simurgh was one of many shamans who wore vulture feathers, and I totally agree with him, since this form of shamanism is still being practiced today. Vulture shamanism would have been critically important for burial needs after the cataclysm, as well

---

*Collins, *From the Ashes of Angels,* 115. Where I use the word *seer* for clairvoyant, in his text, Collins uses *hypnotist.*

as an ideal shamanic practice for traveling to the Otherworld. Collins asks whether "the Watchers actually were distorted memories of a shamanistic culture that had once inhabited a mountainous region, perhaps in Iran, and possessed a knowledge of science and technology well beyond that of the less evolved races of the Near East?"[46] I have no doubt this is true, because many weird archaic tales make sense only by viewing them as shamanic. Let us imagine this:

Imagine being in a family living in the lower levels of Derinkuyu. The cataclysm is over, and still there are constant small to large Earth movements. Way above on the surface, the winds are fierce amid numbing cold. It's the warm time of the year when there are a few months to plant, harvest, and hunt; it is your turn to venture out with a small group to obtain food. You go to the surface through tunnels and emerge and trudge along, staying close to surface caves for safety. The cloudy sky is darkened by circles of vultures watching to see whether your group is bringing out a body for excarnation. Not long ago, the land was littered with the bodies of animals and people, and the vultures multiplied to cleanse it. If vultures had not consumed the carrion, the people would have died of disease, and so you learned to respect the vulture for cleansing the bodies of your loved ones. Birth and death were intertwined, and the vulture was the great mother who fostered life by honoring death; she didn't attack healthy animals and people. After she cleansed the dead bodies, their spirits ascended through the higher realms of heaven and returned to the stars. Sometimes she went with you on a flying journey to the spirit land to teach you that death was not to be feared. Still, you feared the vulture, which could strip your body clean in an hour; she rules death and shamanic dismemberment.

Bird shamans are also found in Sumerian and Babylonian sources, such as the fabulous winged birdmen of Mesopotamia, the Annunaki, sons of heaven and Earth, who were also called shining serpents.[47] The Kharsag Tablets are the oldest Sumerian texts that describe a cataclysm, probably the Black Sea Flood. Christopher O'Brien and Barbara Joy O'Brien, the scholars who translated the tablets, say the flood caused a dispersal that resulted in the foundation of the Mesopotamian city-states, which is in agreement with *Noah's Flood*.[48] According to Collins, the dispersal occurred around 5500 BC, but he argues that the original homeland was Kurdistan. Between 9500 and 8000 BC, Kurdistan "produced some of the first known examples of animal domestication, metallurgy, painted pottery, proto-agriculture, trade, urbanization and written language."[49] Turkish scholar Mehrdad Izady says Kurdistan "went through an unexplained stage of accelerated technological evolution, prompted by yet uncertain forces."[50] Collins proposes the Watchers caused this acceleration based on finds in Shanidar Cave in Kurdistan, which has sixteen levels and was occupied for 100,000 years. A section of the site dated to 8870 BC contains a deposit of "mostly articulated wings of at least seventeen birds, including vultures." The on-site archaeologist concluded that they are wings used by bird shamans, and she linked them with vulture shamanism practiced at Çatal Hüyük, where "a human figure dressed in a vulture skin" is depicted.[51]

Are the Watchers derived from an Egyptian Elder Culture that survived by living underground at Derinkuyu? Andrew Collins argues that Nevali Çori was an Elder Culture religious center that was built when the climate improved in the Middle East.[52] The Blank phase on the Nile suggests that many of the people lived away from the Nile for 5,000 years and then returned when it was possible to establish their culture again. Figure 7.3 depicts a painting on a prehistoric vase from at least 5000 BC from the

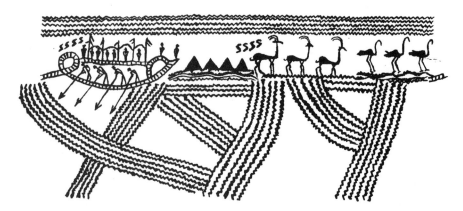

Fig. 7.3. Decoration on a prehistoric Egyptian vase from
Lamy's Egyptian Mysteries

Delta region of northern Egypt.[53] These vases are similar to painted pottery from Elam in southeastern Iraq, which points to the time when the Elder Culture left the sites in the Middle East, then dispersed after the Black Sea Flood and returned to the Nile. It shows people taking boats on the Nile all the way to the headwaters of Lake Victoria. The conventional belief is that the four triangles are African mountains. I think they are pyramids, which has obvious implications regarding Giza Plateau. I will discuss these implications at the end of this chapter when we look at some global maps with pyramids. As we've already seen, Çatal Hüyük has much affinity with the Minoans, who share attributes with early dynastic Egypt, as in the reliefs in the Pyramid of Unas. More answers about these early massive waves of cultural dispersal come out when we return to the global seafaring civilization that was breaking down in 10,500 BC. It was nearly destroyed in 9500 BC, so there must be other places where people went underground. Next we will consider evidence from the Altiplano of Peru and Bolivia, where the most complete library of a prediluvial culture was found in 1961.

The Mysterious Stone Library of Ica

In 1961, a cache of engraved stones was found near the Nasca Plain in Peru, when a flood of the Ica River exposed a cave that contained tens of thousands of the engraved stones. In the region where they were found, small and large bones of prehistoric animals have been found on or near the desert surface. The stones are a complete library of the astronomy, geography, medicine, and way of life of a remote humanity that *cataloged the fauna and flora of the Cenozoic era*—60 million years ago to now. Soon after the discovery, some of the stones were brought to the distinguished Dr. Javier Darquea Cabrera, who was eminently qualified to evaluate them, as he was a physician, medical professor, founder and director of Casa de la Cultura of Ica, and a biology and anthropology professor at Gonzaga University in Ica.[54] After repeatedly attempting to get Peruvian and foreign archaeologists and anthropologists to examine the stones to no avail, Cabrera investigated the nearby area in the Ocucaje Desert where they'd come from. There he found a full paleontological measure of fossils of fauna and flora of the Cenozoic era in sedimentary rock a mile from where the cache was found. The strata contain *Triceratops* bones, and a complete skeleton of a phitosaur, a reptile similar to today's crocodile.[55] J. B. Delair and E. F. Oppé report on various researchers who have found jumbled remains of Pleistocene animals and humans around the Altiplano, and *some of the human skeletons are of gigantic size,* suggesting the Giants and the Watchers.[56] Immediately, Dr. Cabrera presented his findings in a lecture for an international academic conference in 1985, and he was totally ignored.

The cache was found by *huaqueros,* local indigenous people who search for artifacts to sell, and this find was a gold mine for them. The local people were also fascinated with them, and they thought they were relics of their most distant ancestors, so they began making their own versions, which distorted the credibility of Dr. Cabrera. The Peruvian establishment embarked upon an ambitious debunking program by setting up the local peasants as the makers. Dr. Cabrera pointed out that the local peasants would have to be biology professors, surgeons, and master astronomers to craft these bizarre stones, and that at first they sold them for much less money than they'd need to charge if they actually had carved them.[57] Cabrera submitted thirty-three stones to a mining laboratory to analyze the nature of the stone and the antiquity of the engravings. Geologist Eric Wolf reports that the stones were shaped by water in the rivers, and they are andesites—igneous rocks with chemical components that have been mechanically subjected to great pressure, which increased their compactness and specific weight. They are almost as hard as quartz, yet they have the perfect surface for carving, because a fine patina of natural oxidation coated them over time. There is no irregular wear on the incisions, and there is a uniform patina over the carving, which *proves they are very old.*[58] The baffling, gigantic interlocking stones of Tiahuanaco are also andesites.[59]

Other engineers who tested the stones agreed with Eric Wolf. They added that the andesites are from lava flows of the Mesozoic, which opened around 185 million years ago and was terminated by cataclysms around 60 million years ago, after which the Cenozoic began. In 1966, archaeologist Alejandro Pezzia Assereto of the Patronatio Nacional de

Archaeologia del Peru was present when one of the same engraved stones was discovered in a pre-Inca grave.[60] This establishes that these stones are at least 2,000 years old, but they are certainly much older, and the pre-Inca culture frequently buried ancestral power objects in their tombs. The content depicted on the stones indicates that they are ancient, and the area where they were found has massive and chaotic deposits of pre-Pleistocene fauna and flora that perished by geological upheavals of inconceivable violence and extent.[61] The Ica Stones are ancient; they cannot possibly be fakes, and I believe they are one of the *most important archaeological discoveries of all time* because they may be a pre-cataclysmic evolutionary record. According to Carl Calleman, the Mayan Calendar is a record of 16.4 billion years, and we have to wonder how the Maya got that information.[62] The engraved Stones of Ica substantiate vast ranges of ancestral knowledge; they are a huge threat to the archaeological establishment. The attempt to destroy the Stones of Ica may be one of the most heinous Elite actions of all.

The Peruvian establishment forced the local huaqueros to declare publicly that they'd made them all. They agreed to lie because they traffic in archaeological objects, which is a sticky trade.[63] The stones are extremely detailed and specific, and it is not difficult to differentiate the fakes from the real ones. Fortunately, once Cabrera realized his find was being debunked, he bought every ancient engraved stone he could get his hands on. He dedicated his life to studying them and getting the world to pay attention, and then he died in 2001. He is the direct descendant of the Spaniard who founded Ica in 1563, and the world is very lucky he cared. He exhibited 5,000 of the stones at the Casa de Cultura to awaken interest, again to little avail. Unfortunately, a great earthquake flattened Ica in August 2007, but the stones survived because they are carved on andesite.

Dr. Cabrera was an academic biologist and anthropologist, so his dating of the stones and his subsequent interpretation were based on the conventional geologic column and Darwinian evolutionary models. The stones depict the fauna and flora of the Cenozoic era, which made Cabrera think humans have been around for that long. I think they are the work of advanced humans before the cataclysm, the *advanced arts of a very ancient civilization.* The lack of interest in them on the part of archaeologists, anthropologists, and biologists is truly shocking. Dr. Cabrera, himself confounded by the stones and the great span of time involved, concluded that the people who carved them must have been a highly advanced race from a planet in the Pleiades, which didn't help his cause. He concludes that they were advanced teachers of the indigenous Peruvians that left for their planet before or during a great cataclysm.[64]

We can seek answers about who they were without resorting to the ancient astronaut hypothesis. I have noticed that people who have not experienced shamanic flight often conclude that fantastic dismemberment or flight images must be signs of spacemen. Although I differ with this idea, the person who knew the most about these stones was Dr. Cabrera, who studied them for more than forty years. I have not examined them in person; however, Dr. Cabrera carefully photographed and diagrammed them so that others could consider them. Guy Berthault's suggested revision of the geologic column, Allan and Delair's revised chronology for the Miocene and Pliocene epochs, and Calleman's Mayan Calendar hypothesis lead to other possibilities for dating this cache. Based on the revised chronology and the Mayan Calendar, *these stones may depict a people at the peak of their evolution circa 25,000 to 13,000 years ago who were masters of the classic forbidden arts.*

I think the Ica astronomers at some point must have realized a cataclysm was coming because of unusual changes going on around 14,000 years ago. As you will see in a moment, stones that depict Earth and its systems support this idea. The stones may have been used for teaching purposes for thousands of years, so they buried them in a safe place. They might have hoped that they could find them after the Earth settled down. The whole region has huge caves in tufa rock, which were ideal for underground cave shelters, just like Derinkuyu in Turkey. However, unlike the Anatolian Plateau, where Derinkuyu is located, the Altiplano uplifted thousands of feet during the cataclysm. Some caves there have some of the most astonishing Late Pleistocene deposits—drift—that contain Miocene/Pliocene deposits, which suggests that hardly anything survived in this location.[65]

These stone carvers were not primitive, as can be seen by the information on the stones, and they would have known that stone was the only medium that could survive. I strongly suspect the archaic Icans were the same predi-luvial culture as the Tiahuanicans, because they both used andesite as their chosen medium, which is very hard to cut. In both cases their remains are so advanced that they are totally baffling. We will examine an astronomi-cal stone and two global maps of Earth as it probably was at least 12,000 years ago.

Ancient Astronomers Study the Sky and Global Maritime Maps

The stone shown in figure 7.4 has three lateral triangle faces that depict astronomers searching the sky with telescopes, and its triangular superior face is a zodiac encircled by a cometlike object with a long tail. By studying 12,000 stones, Cabrera deciphered their symbolic language, which he called "glyptolithics." Glyptolithics is too complex to describe here, but my analy-sis has to be partially based on Cabrera's linguistic decipherment. Readers will not be surprised to hear that Cabrera's books are not available, so we've illustrated three of the stones for this discussion. (Fortunately, since the earlier version of this book, subsequent researchers have contributed much information about these stones on the Internet, so just Google "Stones of Ica.") In the top of the first stone, Cabrera sees a thirteen-constellational zodiac, adding the Pleiades to the current twelve constellations based on the glyptolithic symbols for planets and stars. Cabrera says a "comet" coming between Sirius and Regulus in the Leo constellation and traveling out the opposite direction through the Pleiades constellation during a solar eclipse is being observed with *telescopes*.[66] When the comet "passed close to the Earth," he wrote, "it had picked up human life and taken it to the con-stellation of the Pleiades."[67] Cabrera believed this was a glyptolithic man facing an imminent cataclysm on Earth, who returned to the Pleiades. We have to respect this possibility, because so many indigenous people around the world claim Pleiadian origins. Richard Rudgley notes that the com-mon heritage from the Pleiades is so widespread that it dates back more

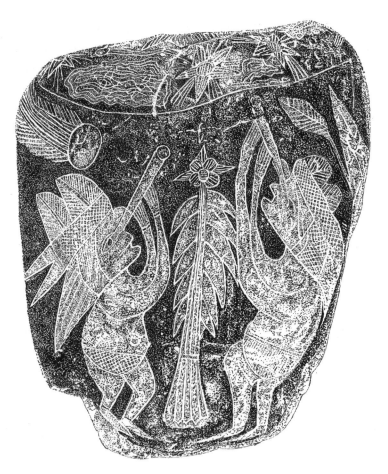

Fig. 7.4. Three views of Phaeton on an Ica Stone. Adapted from the cover and illustration pages 41–49 of Cabrera's The Message of the Engraved Stones of Ica.

than 40,000 years.[68] However, according to my training, these Pleiadian connections are not physical; they are in another dimension. Dr. Cabrera had many discussions about his interpretation with astronomers in Paris who agreed that this stone depicts truly astonishing levels of astronomical knowledge regardless of where this astronomer is from.[69]

Could this stone be a depiction of the supernova fragments (Phaeton) moving through space toward our solar system? If so, did the people carve it in haste just before they were overwhelmed by Earth changes? They could have detected the astronomically near Vela supernova, which exploded around 14,000 years ago, and then they could have seen the fragments approaching this solar system, which would have taken from a few hundred years to a thousand years to traverse interstellar space to the edges of the solar system.[70] Next—as a chill creeps up my back—I remember that Allan and Delair say that the persistent connection between the Pleiades and ancient cataclysms exists because it "is an indication of the celestial direction from which Phaeton arrived—*from that of the Pleiades and Orion*" [italics mine].[71] Based on records kept by Arab and Coptic historians regarding the Leo constellation, Andrew Collins says they concluded that the great event took place during the Age of Leo, which fits with Plato's date and Allan and Delair's conclusions.[72] *This stone may depict Phaeton coming to Earth from Orion and the Pleiades during the Age of Leo.* I realize there is confusion about whether Phaeton is coming in or leaving by the Pleiades, and there is room for interpretation, yet all these elements cannot be just coincidental. *The importance of this ancient stone is incredible.*

Dr. Cabrera had two stones (it may be one stone with a carving on each side) that are "story" maps of the world—that is, they contain information about the quality of civilization on various continents. These stones, by the way, are usually around a foot in diameter. Some of Hapgood's maps depict the seafaring world during the Early Holocene epoch, when the prediluvial seafarers would have really needed global maps. The Ica Stones accurately depict fauna and flora going back 60 million years, and these two maps may depict the prediluvial world sometime within this time frame. Regarding the first stone, Dr. Cabrera believed that it is a map of glyptolithic man's home planet in the Pleiades, and I respectfully disagree. I think it depicts Earth during some phase of the Pliocene or Miocene epochs—from 29 million years ago to about 20,000 years ago—because the proportion of land to sea is great (which is also the case in Allan and Delair's tentative reconstruction of the prediluvial world in figure 2.4, p. 51). The upper Ica Stone map shows the Western Hemisphere with North America above and South America below and Mu and Atlantis to the sides. Above, there is a corresponding letter-coded drawing of the landmasses depicted on the stone. Similarly, below, we have the second map of the Eastern Hemisphere

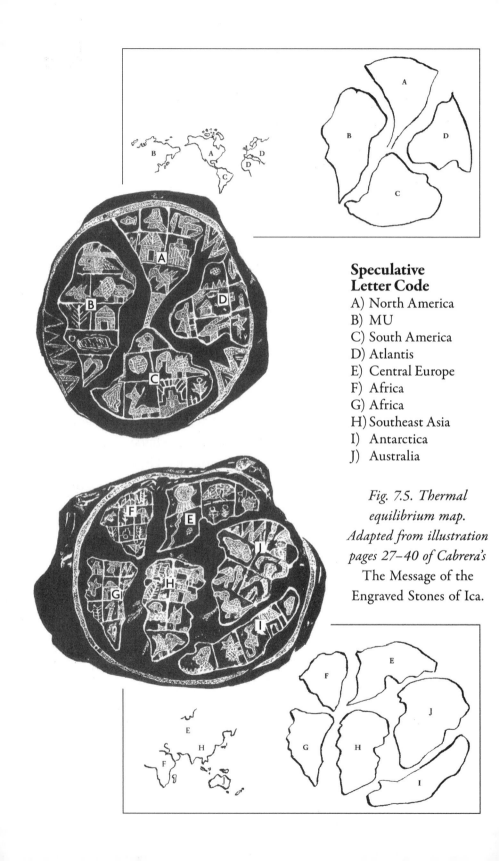

**Speculative
Letter Code**

A) North America
B) MU
C) South America
D) Atlantis
E) Central Europe
F) Africa
G) Africa
H) Southeast Asia
I) Antarctica
J) Australia

*Fig. 7.5. Thermal
equilibrium map.
Adapted from illustration
pages 27–40 of Cabrera's*
The Message of the
Engraved Stones of Ica.

with a corresponding letter-coded drawing. The Ica Stone continents are rather accurate for current North and South America, yet they are very different for the Eastern Hemisphere. This suggests greater subduction in the Eastern Hemisphere—uplifting and splitting apart—which, in fact, occurred there during the past 60 million years.

Figure 7.6 is a speculative map of Pangaea, the proposed supercontinent of 220 million years ago (Paleozoic) by Cambridge geologist Tjeerd H. Van Andel based on conventional geological theory. I ask readers to take a moment to compare Allan and Delair's tentative map of the prediluvial world in figure 2.4 (p. 51) with Van Andel's map of Pangaea, and then compare them with the lower Ica Stone map. You really have to wonder about what these people knew! According to Cabrera, the symbols on the continents can be read by glyptolithics (even if it is a map of a planet in the Pleiades). Cabrera said that these are maps of a *planet in a state of thermic equilibrium* inhabited by humans who are technological and adept at managing its resources. Plants and animals, *including dinosaurs* and domesticated animals, are prevalent, large cities are shown, *and there are pyramids that capture, accumulate, and distribute energy.*[73] The glyphs indicate that this is a "planet that is ideal for human life."[74]

Since the first edition of this book came out in 2001, an Egyptian researcher, Edward F. Malkowski, has developed a comprehensive Egyptian

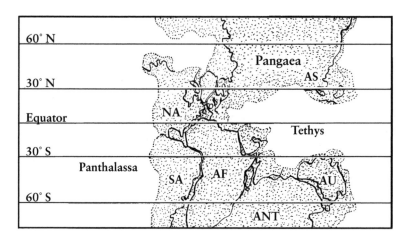

Fig. 7.6. Pangaea. Adapted from figure 7.1 of van Andel's
New Views on an Old Planet.

pyramid hypothesis that may shed some light on both the prehistoric vase in figure 7.3 (p. 190), and the depictions of pyramids on these stone maps. Readers may want to compare these pyramids to the artistic rendition of the pyramids on the 6,000-year-old Egyptian vase depicted in figure 7.3. Malkowski argues that the ancient Egyptians used granite technology for pyramid construction in order to direct Earth's gravitational and magnetic fields. The pyramids, he writes, "were designed to focus electrical currents that were naturally occurring in the ground from the pyramids' base to its peak."[75] By methods too complex to cover here, Malkowski says the pyramids generated a "blanket of ionization" over the Nile Valley that was "perhaps twenty miles wide and forty miles long."[76] Other researchers, such as John Burke and Kaj Halberg and the entomologist Philip Callahan have explored how ionization was generated in megalithic monuments in order to enhance seed germination and plant growth in general.[77] Malkowski comments that the Great Pyramid and all the other pyramids were "part of an ELF-based [extremely low frequencies] fertilizer system."[78] Back to the stone that is a planet that is ideal for human life, we can see visually that *glyptolithic humans may have used the same technology* as the ancient Egyptians and Holocene megalithic humans!

Like the astronomical stone, Cabrera said the stone in figure 7.5 shows men projecting energy into the cosmos. They are depicted uniting with serpents and assuming various animal forms, which means *they are shamans working with serpentine energy.* As we all know, the pharaoh and the priests were famous for their work with serpentine energy, such as the meaning behind the Uraeus on the pharaoh's third eye. We don't really know whether the pyramid ionization technology was used during the dynastic era or much earlier, or both, and it is impossible to date this map. Certainly it is pre-cataclysmic, and it is loaded with climatic, paleontological, and geological information. Regarding the lower map, I'd have to guess that it is a depiction of the Eastern Hemisphere before 200,000 years ago, the time of Pangaea.

On the second map (figure 7.7), Earth is in a very different state. The Eastern Hemisphere is radically different, yet the Western Hemisphere, with Mu and Atlantis, is somewhat recognizable; the Western Hemisphere is above and the Eastern Hemisphere below. There are letter-coded

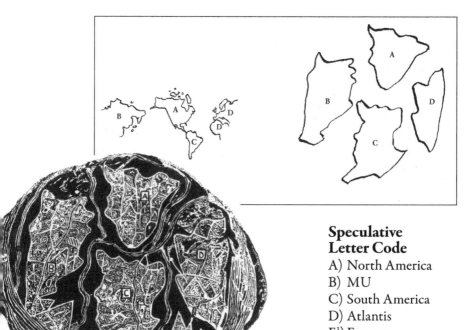

Speculative Letter Code

A) North America
B) MU
C) South America
D) Atlantis
E¹) Europe
E²) Australia
F) Africa
G) Southeast Asia

Fig. 7.7. Closed thermic system. Adapted from illustration pages 30–35 of Cabrera's The Message of the Engraved Stones of Ica.

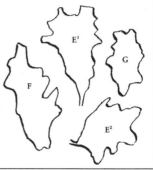

drawings of the landmasses on the stones above and below. By glyptolithic analysis, Cabrera posited that this is Earth in a *closed thermic system* at a "critical point at which the water vapor precipitated in the form of unending rain that released a correspondingly large amount of mechanical energy that resulted in the beginning of the shift of the enormous continental masses; that is, a cataclysm of monstrous proportions."[79] The closed thermic system is depicted by the thick waves of water around the maps—in the atmosphere—that form a vapor cap or black body formed by the clouds; and the thermic energy of the sun is captured but cannot radiate back out."[80] The maps depict even more continental landmass in relation to seas, and they may depict Earth before a great cataclysm in the remote past, or more recently. Possibly it is 10,500 BC during the Younger Dryas. By glyptolithic analysis, it records a difficult time for glyptolithic humans, and certainly it is concerned with too much technology. There are no ice caps, and this closed thermic system could make one think of global warming. Cabrera pointed out that the pyramids used for power are on the continents in the first map, but in this map, the bottoms of the pyramids aim to the sky, "indicating that part of the energy of the atmosphere is being captured in a complex technological system."[81] The vertices of the pyramids point toward the continents, indicating that humans use the power, and the strange canals seem to be part of this system.

Dr. Cabrera was certain that the makers of the Ica Stones were from the same cultures as the first people of the Andes who built Tiahuanaco and other Peruvian-Bolivian cyclopean structures. This suggests links between the global seafaring culture and the pyramids in general in these maps. Graham Hancock notes that the "clean-sided step-pyramid of earth faced with large andesite blocks" at Tiahuanaco "might have functioned as some kind of arcane device or machine" that archaeologists think has something to do with fast-flowing water, because it has a "complex network of zigzagging stone channels, lined with fine ashlars."[82] Interpreting the glyphs, Cabrera sees robotic controllers who are dealing with failing, overly managed, controlled agriculture and animal domestication; houses where there are groups of humanoids, called the *Notharctus* (a small tree-dwelling primate that lived 50 million years ago),[83] who are having their intelligence raised to the minimal level. These controllers could fly. This seems to be a time when humans lived on Earth during an environmental crisis.

Other stones not depicted show advanced surgical methods, such as brain and heart transplants, advanced knowledge of human and animal reproductive cycles, and even dinosaur farms! Glyptolithic humans did not quiver in fear of the great reptiles—they understood the dinosaurs' physiology, and they used advanced technology to farm them for food.[84]

I began this chapter by stating that humans have the potential to create reality with thought, yet it would appear that these people were *controlling* the planet with technology, just as today. The mysterious Stones of Ica must be prediluvial. *I think they depict the core basis of the forbidden knowledge of the Fallen Angels.* As discussed in chapter 3, Chris Dunn in *The Giza Power Plant* has built a powerful case for the usage of power tools in ancient Egypt, and he speculates that the Great Pyramid was one of their power plants. The depiction of pyramids as power plants on the Ica Stones supports Dunn's hypothesis.

Astute readers will notice that there are many suggestions of ancient humans coexisting with dinosaurs depicted on the stones of Ica. When I try to put the two species together, intuitively I am inclined to side with Dr. Cabrera's conclusion that the humanoid beings depicted on the stones are from the Pleiades, because they may have visited Earth over millions of years. If this is so, then they were on the planet to assist Earth during a time of near-extinction, and they left records of their advanced science for us to find today. As it turns out, Charles Hapgood gave some consideration to the possibility that humans once coexisted with dinosaurs.

Hapgood investigated a ceramic collection found at Acambaro, Mexico, called the Julsrud Collection.[85] The items depict humans interacting with dinosaurs, like the Ica Stones; however, carbon dating indicates they are approximately 7,000 years old.[86] In 1972, just before the first edition of *Mystery in Acambaro* was released, Hapgood was visited by a few archaeologists who showed him slides of the Ica Stones and a few stones that Dr. Cabrera had loaned to them. Hapgood could see many parallels between the two collections. About the Acambaro collection, Hapgood says, "One obtains from the collection itself a sense of the dark forces within the human psyche, an emphasis on the negative power of fear, and a suggestion of witchcraft in an elementary state of development. *There may also have been a true, positive rapport with nature that our society does not understand"* [italics mine].[87] We must seriously evaluate these kinds of wild findings now that consistencies between them are becoming apparent. Otherwise, there is a shadow hidden deeply in the human mind that can erupt any moment in evil actions. The fact is, many ancient artifacts suggest levels of advancement that we do not understand, and that are contrary to the conventional historical paradigm. Others have seriously investigated Chris Dunn's hypothesis of the Great Pyramid of Giza as a power plant.

The Great Pyramid Is a Power Plant!

Following the path of the great Egyptologist Sir William Flinders Petrie, Chris Dunn studied granite structures and artifacts at Giza Plateau, as well as stone vessels made of diorite, basalt, quartz crystal, and metamorphic schist, some of which are more than 5,000 years old. Both Petrie and Dunn conclude that the makers had used motorized machining.[88] In his day, more than 100 years ago, Petrie could not imagine how they did it, so he wrote detailed descriptions of stone-cut artifacts that absolutely could not have been made with hand tools or any tool technology of his day. The modern engineer Chris Dunn examined Petrie's evidence himself, and he concluded that ultrasonic machining was the only method they could have used to cut and drill the stone.[89] He points out that these machine-made artifacts suggest that the Great Pyramid was built by an advanced civilization.[90] With this in mind, he examined the Florida laboratories of Edward Leedskalnin, who built Coral Castle by lifting and maneuvering blocks of coral weighing as much as *30 tons* because Leedskalnin claimed that he knew the secrets of the ancient Egyptians.[91] Dunn believes that Leedskalnin figured out how to work with Earth's gravitational pull by aligning the magnetic elements within the coral blocks; that is, he built an *antigravity device!*[92] Dunn published more articles and gave interviews about Leedskalnin's discoveries. Then he asked the big question: What provided the power that ran the ultrasonic tools 5,000 years ago in Egypt?

The Great Pyramid is located on the center of Earth's landmass, and its builders used *the exact dimensions of Earth in its design, so in that location the pyramid is a harmonic integer of the planet.* That is, it responds to Earth's vibrations by resonance and harmonics.[93] Resonance means that it is in sympathetic vibration with the planet, which makes it a *coupled oscillator* that can draw on Earth's energy once it is primed—*the Great Pyramid vibrates with Earth.*[94] As Dunn summarizes, "The Great Pyramid was a geomechanical power plant that responded sympathetically with the Earth's vibrations and converted that energy into electricity. They used the electricity to power their civilization, which included machine tools with which they shaped hard, igneous rock."[95] The logical next step would be for other scientifically inclined researchers to follow up on Chris Dunn's research to determine how the ancient Egyptians cut the stone and moved multiton blocks, which is exactly what Edward F. Malkowski did.

Malkowski points out that the high-quality granite workmanship that Petrie and Dunn studied points to a "grand unified ancient civilization" that he calls Civilization X.[96] He makes the point mostly by analyzing high-quality photographs of granite remnants all over Egypt, the same ones

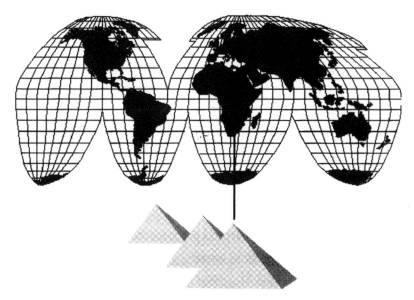

Fig. 7.8. The Great Pyramid in the center of Earth's landmass. Figure 32 of Dunn's The Giza Power Plant.

my teacher Abdel Hakim loved to show us. Malkowski's most intriguing evidence is his analysis of a beautiful concave black granite stone that lies by the side of the unfinished pyramid at Abu Rawash. Malkowski calls this stone the New Rosetta Stone, since he demonstrates that only a high-powered circular saw could have fabricated it.[97] For example, the machinist feed lines are visible, which cannot be denied in Malkowski's photos of the stone.[98] Both Dunn and Malkowski think that the deep-cut trench into the bedrock near the stone is a trench that was originally used to mount a huge saw.[99] Archaeologists say these pits are boat pits, and some of them are. But this pit is way too narrow, and the ratio between its width and depth is exactly right for a circular saw. When I went to Abu Rawash with Hakim in 1993, I didn't see this curved stone, but we spent some time looking at the deep-cut trench. I've observed granite cutting with this technique at a quarry in Massachusetts, and I'm sure Dunn and Malkowski are right.

This chapter began with some ideas about creating realities with thought. Then we followed the activities of the Fallen Angels and explored the Ica Stones, and we've ended with considering ancient Egyptian stone technology. The Elite archaeologists laugh at and ridicule these incredible discoveries by scientifically informed researchers. The question is, *Why?* It would appear that some kind of high-stakes game is being played on the Giza Plateau. Next, we will look at how the Elite chess game is played. Of course, they are the kings, queens, knights, and bishops, and we are the pawns. Mysteriously, all of us living on the planet now are on the chessboard—the geodetic center of Earth's landmasses—because we are global and connected again by technology. As you can see by the Stones of Ica, when human civilization attained this level before, pyramids were a vital aspect of its technology. Could that be why the Great Pyramid is on the America dollar? Now that we have considered the Great Pyramid's technological aspects, *how* did the Egyptians obtain the technology? This question will be taken up in chapter 9, since we can't even approach it until we examine how the Global Elite game is played. Enter the Global Elite plan for the Age of Aquarius.

THE STARGATE
CONSPIRACY AND
THE KOSMOKRATER

*With the changes that will be wrought, true Americanism,
the universal thought that is expressed and manifested in
the brotherhood of man, as in the Masonic order, will be
the eventual rule in the settlement of affairs in the world.*

EDGAR CAYCE[1]

Support the Heretics!

The comprehensive cover-up of the real story of the Fallen Angels, the Stones of Ica, and the power-driven Egyptian granite technology are all excellent examples of Elite information-control programs. Archaeological remnants of an advanced prediluvial global culture have been found and analyzed, yet this exciting story is suppressed and hidden. The public is totally bored by the stupid, spoon-fed story of the past, so they increasingly turn to shallow stimulation of their minds. Controversial researchers like Hapgood, Allan and Delair, Cabrera, Dunn, and Malkowski are either greeted with total silence or debunked. However, in spite of the consistent efforts being put into this cover-up, more and more people are realizing they are being lied to, and they sense an elaborate plot. There are hundreds of books about the Elite's financial, social, and political programs, such as lately those by

David Icke and William Cooper, which I've included in my bibliography. The details of what the Elite have been doing—when and where—are really tedious, so I will single out some of the more entertaining aspects. No matter how much they are observed, they just change into new forms, because they are *shape-shifters,* a skill from the Fallen Angels. It makes perfect sense that the Elite would cover up their current activities, since they have most of the money. But, *why do they go to so much trouble to cover up the past?* This is the central question asked in this chapter. Later, we will look at how any one of us can transmute this serpentine energy, since it takes form only amid ignorance and confusion. Here, I explore how the Global Elite program got started in the first place, and how it has taken over realities in the world.

The Elite stays one step ahead of people by carrying on an elaborate disinformation campaign. As we've seen, the Elite ignore, harass, or debunk anyone who gets too close to scientific or spiritual information that could free the people. When anybody gets close to divulging the secrets of harmonic resonance, such as Chris Dunn, one of the Elite creative agents—writers, filmmakers, or media stars—simply picks the most flawed part of the person's research (all research has some weak points) and blows it all out of proportion to make the person look like a fool. Another favorite tactic is to convince the public that an extraordinary find or happening was faked, such as the Stones of Ica or the crop circles in England. The Elite goal is to consistently *dishearten and disempower* the public, so that people will lose hope and even forget there is any hope. For example, the book *Giza: The Truth* attempts to take down Chris Dunn, yet he was able to refute it successfully, and Dunn and Malkowski are not going away.[2] *There is a continual mental wounding going on that tests the fortitude of inventors and avid seekers.* The public gets excited about a new theory and gets turned on by the possibility that they might finally get some information that could improve the planet or answer some deep questions, and then the theory gets shot down and its inventor is crucified. Why? I ask you to consider that the Elite *disheartens* the public because the most direct route to cosmic resonance is to awaken your heart, which has a more profound intelligence than your mind. The Elite live in their minds, and we can beat them at their own game by giving our full attention to the ideas and individuals that they debunk and or attack. This disempowers them, because they are heartless. (NO CONSCIENCE?)

The Elite show you the way! Simply turn your attention to the *heretics!* Whenever an exciting discovery is greeted with stone-cold silence by the media and academia, assume that it is of extreme importance. Certain finds, such as the Stones of Ica, are considered in detail here to teach you to study the Elite program in reverse: While they play their games to stupefy the public, why don't you get smart? Another tactic in the Elite chess game is to push a dunce into the limelight, such as Thomas Edison, while they secretly cull the mind of the real genius, Nicola Tesla. Tesla's resonant energy technologies were stolen, and his discoveries were developed in secret, such as the so-called Philadelphia Experiment, in which a ship and its crew were vibrated into another dimension during the Second World War. Albert Einstein and his bomb were the focus of the twentieth century, while Wilhelm Reich's research on the primary life force was debunked and stolen for future reference. Reich was a psychoanalyst who discovered the organizing force that enables the soul to take bodily form—the orgone—and Reich was close to scientifically defining what real health is. Those who have gone against the official paradigm have lived lives of great pain, yet *this outcome would shift if smart people turned their attention to the real inventors.* Charles Hapgood's colleagues shunned him until his death once he published *Maps of the Ancient Sea Kings,* which is the most significant cartography book in modern times. Wilhelm Reich died in prison after his laboratory and books were destroyed, and Nicola Tesla died penniless in a ratty hotel. Ironically, Albert Einstein wrote the foreword for the first edition of *Path of the Pole* by Charles Hapgood, and it was stripped out for the second printing![3]

The Stargate Conspiracy

The Stargate Conspiracy by Lynn Picknett and Clive Prince was published in England in 2000, a deeply disturbing and insightful work that lays bare the Elite plans for the new religion of the Age of Aquarius. The authors show how "the CIA, Britain's MI5, occult groups, and even some of the world's top scientists" are working together in a vast conspiracy that exploits human "craving for contact with the numinous and the ineffable."[4]

Whenever the Great Ages shift, the new core beliefs arising among the people seem to be absolutely unique, such as extraterrestrials visiting Earth. The recent fad has been watching out for spacemen in the backyard, yet *extraterrestrials are probably just new forms of the Fallen Angels and the Watchers.* The way to follow the moves in this elaborate chess match is never to forget for one second that the strategy is a huge political and religious conspiracy that "checkmates" anybody who moves independently. Humans seek spiritual contact above all other things, so *usually the conspiracy comes out of religious movements,* and politics is merely the front. We arrived previously at this point when the Roman Catholic Church superseded Judaism in the West at the beginning of the Age of Pisces. The obvious question for us is, what's the plan for the main religion this time? Like a reverse Exodus, the hot spot is the geodetic center of the planet—the Giza Plateau. When I wrote the first edition of this book in 2000, a fanatical search for the Hall of Records of Atlantis was happening on the Giza Plateau. American New Agers were hooked into the drama because they are linked to Giza by the almighty dollar with its pyramid capped by the all-seeing eye. Meanwhile, *the recently verified granite technology of Egypt is the Hall of Records!* Many people miss this astounding breakthrough because the discoveries are not what they expected to get; they were lead astray by the Elite and Edgar Cayce. Cleverly, the search for the Hall of Records was presented as a modern form of the Arthurian quest for the Holy Grail, "the ancient, elusive object of the heart's desire," according to Picknett and Prince, and when it is found, "somehow magically the whole of our civilization will be transformed."[5] This diversion effectively used the desire to find the Holy Grail, so it "has now effectively become a new orthodoxy with an equally unyielding doctrine of its own."[6] Ironically, the granite evidence just bakes in the sun all over Egypt, and credible scientists are laboriously deciphering it.

Picknett and Prince discuss popular writers like Graham Hancock and Robert Bauval, who seem to be knights seeking the Holy Grail. It's nearly impossible to know whether they realize they've been swept into the mythical quest, or whether they are cynically orchestrating it. I stopped teaching in Egypt in 1996 when I realized something very murky was going on around my ceremonial work. *The Stargate Conspiracy* helps me understand some of my own experiences in Egypt from 1985 through 1996: We are all part of the mystical quest as the Aquarian energy permeates the planetary field, and Giza is the focus for this infusion. If we can figure out what's really going on, then we can grasp our heart's desire, which is to know our story. We don't have to be reduced to being pawns in a very nasty and transparent global game, so let's look at the main players.

The Sirius Mystery by Robert Temple (1976) is an erudite book about Egyptian, African, Greek, Babylonian, and Sumerian legends. Temple's main thesis is that the Dogon culture of central Africa was given its symbols and rituals by actual visitors from the Sirius star system.[7] Temple's book gave me some new ideas about what I call the *Sirian mentality*. However, I paid little attention to his ideas about spacemen, since any shaman can go to Sirius anytime he or she wants to, which was obviously a favorite sport for the Dogon stargazers. Oddly, Temple radically revised the book for a new edition in 1998, adding claims that the British secret service, the MI5, monitored him after its initial publication. He says the CIA harassed him for fifteen years, and a major Mason asked him to join the fraternity so they could discuss his book as equals and keep the discussions private.[8] This is probably because *The Sirius Mystery* greatly influenced the New Age movement by causing countless people who read it to honestly believe the Dogon and Egyptians are extraterrestrial cultures. I thought this was mere silliness on the part of a very intelligent man, since I've been in contact with Sirians, and they've never landed a spaceship in my backyard! The realms they exist in are nonphysical and nonlocational, which means they are always there and accessible if their resonance can be felt, which happens to be the sixth dimension in my *Alchemy of Nine Dimensions*.[9] I've seen "spaceships" near military bases or research labs like Los Alamos, and I believe most sightings are scientific conjurings.

The scariest thing I've ever seen in my life happened when our family was driving on New Mexico's Highway 25 by the White Sands testing ground in 1984. Suddenly, a mile or two to the left side of the car, at a thousand feet high or more, a giant black shining vulture manifested out of thin, clear daylight and flew along by the side of our car! We didn't know what we'd seen until the B-2 Spirit stealth bomber was rolled out of a huge hangar and wheeled over a gigantic red pentagram on television a few years later. Mass culture is conditioned by Hollywood to believe extraterrestrials are real and that they intend to harm us. I think most sightings are part of an Elite disinformation program. So, what is somebody trying to distract us from?

There is a widespread belief within the counterculture that Mars hosted an ancient civilization that was connected to the ancient Egyptians. This leads to the conclusion that "the ancient gods were extraterrestrials *and they're back*"[10] [italics mine]. *The Sirius Mystery* convinced a lot of intelligent people that extraterrestrials influenced African culture.[11] But this implies that the ancient Egyptians could not have built the pyramids. The ancient astronaut hypothesis feeds a very dangerous conspiracy that has sucked in countless unwitting people. The agenda is to convince the public that extraterrestrials colonized Earth and Mars, and they are coming back as soon as the Hall of Records is found at Giza. People talk about how spacemen will rescue the Chosen People of God before the prophesied cataclysm and take them away in spaceships, warmed over Judeo-Christian fanaticism. Such airhead nonsense encourages people to wait for gods in the sky who will come and unleash an apocalypse. *This is advanced catastrophobia all dressed up for the New Age.* How could such silliness ever have gained any credibility? Enter the Sleeping Prophet.

Edgar Cayce and the Search for the Hall of Records

The famed "Sleeping Prophet," Edgar Cayce, is the driving force behind the search for the Hall of Records, and then he linked this discovery with the *coming* Earth changes, which injected great fear and urgency into the quest.[12] I ask readers to reread the opening quotation for this chapter, which shows that *Cayce's agenda was Masonic.* Widely presented to the public as a simple Christian who was deeply disturbed by the weird occult information that came through his trances, Cayce had been exposed to this information beforehand: He worked in esoteric bookstores where he constantly read the books, he was exposed to many occultists who sought him out, and he was gifted with a prodigious memory. Cayce and his father were high enough up in the Masons to found new lodges, and they were salesmen for Masonic insurance.[13] As a great example of how the Elite knits elements together, Cayce advised Woodrow Wilson on the formation of the League of Nations. Colonel Edmund Starling, head of the Secret Service and a friend and possible fellow Mason along with Cayce's father, introduced Cayce to Wilson.[14]

The content in Cayce's readings is stuffed with the esoteric ideas of Alice Bailey, Madame Blavatsky, H. C. Randall Stevens, and many other current stars.[15] Channels often bring through material they've already studied, since esoteric data is the perennial wisdom, and this process is a form of teaching and rediscovery for the channels and their groups. The problem with Cayce is that he was presented as an innocent and sleepy Christian, so *ordinary good-hearted people took his occult ideas and prophecies as gospel truth.* Mysteriously, the search for Cayce's fabled Hall of Records (Atlantis) is central to the Elite agenda, which means this quest is the ideal tool for cloaking conspiracies. Most people simply can't believe that intelligence agencies are involved, since such psychic quests are "woo-woo" psychobabble, which is consistently debunked by the Elite.

Cayce's son, Hugh Lynn Cayce, started the well-funded Association for Research and Enlightenment (ARE) to house, analyze, and promulgate Cayce's readings. ARE is located at Virginia Beach in front of Cayce's little hospital, where he worked as a dedicated healer. Cayce was a fantastic medical intuitive, and it would be a shame if that part of his work were discredited. Meanwhile, ARE has been deeply involved in the explorations in Egypt for the Hall of Records, because Cayce said it would be found there by around 1998. Zahi Hawass, director of the Giza Plateau since 1987, was educated in the United States by ARE, and he regularly lectures at its headquarters in Virginia Beach, which makes it easy for ARE big shots to explore the plateau.[16] Other projects at Giza have been carried out by the Stanford Research Institute (SRI), which is closely linked with the Department of Defense and the intelligence community.[17] Dr. James J. Hurtak, the author of a bizarre fundamentalist tome, *The Keys of Enoch,* is the new messiah to millions, and he has been deeply involved in the Giza explorations.[18]

Hurtak already explored the correlation between the pyramids and Orion in 1973, more than twenty years before the publication of *The Orion Mystery*.[19] In 1977 and 1978, strangely, Hurtak was allowed to use lasers to measure the airshaft angles in the Great Pyramid to see if they align with Orion and Draco; but the results have been kept secret.[20] There are persistent and well-founded rumors that the Egyptians are carrying out clandestine digging all over the plateau and that many things have already been found but kept secret.[21] In the middle of this bizarre drama is Zahi Hawass, who shows selected "discoveries" on American television that are smoke screens to divert attention from clandestine explorations, and to draw attention away from researchers like Dunn and Malkowski. Hawass is a classic front man for an elaborate game. These people are shape-shifters, and it is impossible to know what the various players are really doing. Meanwhile, *affiliations with the military and intelligence communities are always signs of the vast conspiracy that distracts the public by means of rumors and planted lies.*[22]

In 2000, the Internet brought the heated Giza Plateau rumor mill to a boil in cyberspace while the temples in Egypt were being raided. Sucked unawares into the quest for the Holy Grail, people end up being bitterly disappointed by not finding their heart's desire while they are being subtly conditioned to buy into the Aquarian Age religion. This culling is more broad based than it may seem: The pyramid on the American dollar, the obelisk in Washington, and other such Masonic symbols have been imprinted in the brains of Americans for more than 200 years.[23] *This symbolic imprinting makes the whole American culture messianic,* as millions of unwitting people are led by these planted thoughts because they are so curious about the ancient lost civilization. Next, enter the Martians.

The Lost Civilization on Mars

In 1972, the *Mariner 9* probe took some photographs of an area on Mars called Cydonia, which reveal a huge sculptured human face, some pyramids, and a circular henge and mound that resemble Avebury Henge and Silbury Hill in England. By fractal analysis, natural forces did not make these Cydonia structures.[24] The possibility that there are ruins of a civilization on Mars that contain a big humanlike face staring at Earth really got the ancient astronaut hypothesis going! J. J. Hurtak linked Cydonia with Giza in people's minds by describing the face as "Sphinx-like," even though it has no body, much less a lion's body.[25] Various players made new careers as researchers of the Face on Mars, particularly Richard Hoagland—a NASA consultant, who was once an NBC, ABC, and CNN consultant—who has become the public champion for the Face on Mars.[26] Hoagland is largely responsible for convincing the public that there was an ancient civilization on Mars that was once connected with Giza.[27] Strangely, he said, "The 'Message of Cydonia' could significantly assist the world in a dramatic transition to a real 'new world order'. . . if not a literal New World."[28]

Regarding the very real possibility that evidence for an ancient civilization *does* exist on Mars, the Elite are barely more than a step ahead of the pack in space exploration. There are many things the Elite desperately want to figure out before anybody else does, so much of space exploration may be reconnaissance missions to retrieve ancient artifacts and technologies. Of course, in the context of this book, this evidence suggests that the global maritime civilization even made it into space! Maybe the Elite are looking for the remains of extraterrestrials that were all over the solar system. In 2007, Richard Hoagland and Boeing engineer Mike Bara published an astonishing book on the secret history of NASA—*Dark Mission*. In this absolutely mind-boggling analysis of the Mars and moon explorations, Hoagland and Bara outrageously expose NASA as a publicly funded science that is run by the secret brotherhood, the Masons. For example, the flag that was brought to the moon in July 1969 by astronaut Buzz Aldrin is a Freemasonic flag, and Aldrin, who is a thirty-second-degree Mason himself, brought it back and presented it to the Scottish Rite Headquarters in Washington, D.C.[29] In *Dark Mission*, the authors argue that "in the warped vision of these 'ritual elitists'—who have, if we are right, *literally stolen the entire space program* for themselves from the rest of all Mankind—'Space' is destined to remain the *sole possession* of only those with these 'proper bloodlines and perspectives.'"[30] This statement shows the real depth and range of the conspiracy to control the Age of Aquarius. As you will see in a moment, it also aims to strangle our right to know the real story of our past.

The discovery of the remains of an ancient destroyed civilization on Mars with ruins that are similar to the Giza Plateau and Avebury Circle *is the ultimate proof of Allan and Delair's cataclysmic theory.* Figure 2.1 (p. 45) indicates that Phaeton ripped close by Mars and changed its orbit. The current slow rotation of Mars—twenty-four hours when it should be eight hours—suggests that this flyby caused its crust to fracture and its magnetic field to drop. Astronomers say "something quite profound has happened to Mars in the not so distant past."[31] The Martian surface is damaged more profoundly than Earth's surface, yet similar effects suggest that both planets must have been traumatized by an external agency like Phaeton. The Martian surface was so destroyed that probably no life survived. Enough Earth species survived, and we on Earth have arrived at the moment when we can realize that *this recent disaster altered the whole solar system.* Clearly the Elite doesn't want this realization, and strangely Graham Hancock comments, "The notion that the terminal Mars cataclysm might have occurred recently—perhaps less than 20,000 years ago—is an astronomical heresy that raises peculiar resonance for us."[32]

What could Hancock mean by an "astronomical heresy"? This is where I bring Hoagland and Bara back in, because I think they push the date for the destruction of the constructions on Mars and the moon way too far back; they date it to 3 million years ago. Hoagland and Bara describe truly incredible ruins on the moon, such as a rough crystalline spire that is over a mile and a half tall, "making it a truly inexplicable wonder of the Moon, if not the universe."[33] And Hoagland has effectively proven that the face and the henge on Mars are not works of nature. Why doesn't everybody know about this? Why aren't we celebrating these great discoveries? Hoagland and Bara have made the case for the huge NASA cover-up, but also the reason this story is not getting out is *because it has not yet been put in the right time frame.* The main source of the faulty timeline is the astronomer

Tom Van Flandern. He has presented good evidence that a planet that was once between Mars and Jupiter exploded, and what's left is comets and asteroids—the exploding planet hypothesis (EPH).[34]

Van Flandern dates this event back 3 million years because comets that are coming back to the sun for the first time are traveling in orbits with periods of 3 million years.[35] Van Flandern argues that this event is the cause of the damage in the solar system that Allan and Delair attribute to Phaeton 11,500 years ago. However, while there probably was a cataclysmic event 3 million years ago, the ruins on Mars and the moon *cannot* be that old. In fact, the design of Cydonia on Mars has too many elements that we see in early megalithic sacred sites on Earth, such as Avebury and the Giza Plateau. Ralph Ellis argues that Avebury Henge is a model of Earth floating in space and *tilted on its axis,* as if somebody out there wanted to show what recently happened to Earth![36]

Following Tom Van Flandern, Hoagland and Bara date the Mars/ moon destruction back to 3 million years ago, and this is where they lose the thread. They also lose the public interest, because any smart person can see it is untenable. The remains that have been found and photographed cannot be 3 million years old considering the storms, meteorites, solar flares, and other damaging events; and secondly, by their very nature, they are *culturally* related to Earth. This is incredibly important for this book because Mars, the moon, and other bodies in our solar system are the background for our story on Earth. We not only have the astrophysical hypothesis in Allan and Delair's description of Phaeton, we also have archaeological evidence for cultural connections in the solar system. By putting this event too far back in time, Hoagland and Bara lose this critical link, the very line that can take us back through our story in our solar system. It turns out there is more to the sweeping nature of this cover-up—Graham Hancock's astronomical heresy. Previously in this book I commented that I understand why the Elite want to cover up their current activities, such as these NASA explorations, but I struggle with why they want to cover up the past. Hoagland and Bara conclude that "ritual elitists" are stealing the whole space program for themselves. Maybe they think there is oil and gold on the moon and Mars? Or maybe they are doing this is to make sure we never get the real facts about the cataclysms 14,000 to 11,000 years ago?

The Mars Announcement

Regarding the Elite attempts to cover up what they know about Mars, on August 7, 1996, NASA mysteriously staged a news announcement by a group of scientists that evidence for life on Mars has been found in a meteorite that landed on Antarctica about 13,000 years ago. This event had full media attention, including excited comments by Bill Clinton and Al Gore, which are typical signs of a big Elite plot.[37] This announcement was probably part of the program to get the public to buy into extraterrestrial influence, or possibly it was a smoke screen to distract public interest away from Cydonia. This announcement is a perfect example of high-level Elite tactics, which many people recognized instantly: Anyone following this scene knew that the discovery of possible life on Mars had *already occurred and been announced to science* by scientists Vincent Di Pietro, John Brandenburg, and Bartholomew Nagy.

Nagy published a paper about the chemical compounds in meteors (although he did not yet know they were Martian) in 1975, and he added the Martian aspect in a paper with scientist Colin Pillinger in *Nature* in July 1989.[38] Nagy died in December 1995, a few months before the Mars announcement validated his research. All scientists in the field know what *Nature* publishes, yet Nagy got the silent treatment. With his Pinocchio nose growing longer on television, Bill Clinton said about the big new discovery, "Its implications are as far-reaching and awe-inspiring as can be imagined."[39] Why was he so surprised? A Washington prostitute, Sherry Rowlands, immediately did press interviews, and contributed some pillow talk: She said that Clinton's close adviser, Dick Morris, had told her all about this discovery when it was still a military secret.[40]

What is going on? Notice that the mysterious Martian meteor landed on Antarctica *about 13,000 years ago.* Sound familiar? The fact is, Di Pietro, Brandenburg, and Nagy may have gotten too close to the truth: This big distraction was created to make sure nobody figures out that *this is a meteor from the surface of Mars that was flying along with Phaeton 11,500 years ago!* Consider figure 2.1 (p. 45): When Phaeton tangled with Earth, some Martian meteors fell on Antarctica. The official story is that this meteor formed 4.5 billion years ago when the Martian crust first formed; then supposedly 16 million years ago, a comet or asteroid struck Mars and ejected the piece of rock off the surface; and then 13,000 years ago, it fell on Antarctica.[41] This is classic Elite disinformation—a silly story that the public will believe because they've been trained to believe that the solar system formed 4.5 billion years ago. The suggestion that a meteor from a Mars impact took 16 million years to land on Antarctica 13,000 years ago is then used to foster the theory that the cataclysmic features of the Martian crust are not recent. The fact is, *the Mars meteor fell on Antarctica 11,500 years ago, a solar-system proof of Allan and Delair's cataclysmic theory.*

What's at stake here? As the magnitude of what happened so recently comes out, many scientists and writers are inventing all sorts of cyclical disaster theories. One of the reasons Van Flandern's EPH has been bought lock, stock, and barrel is that finally somebody came up with some good ideas about the asteroid belt. Obviously there was a planet that was destroyed, and by the way, I don't think planets just explode. It is only human to conclude that if something so horrible happened before, it will happen again, which is true, but when? I think galactic astrophysics is what we need more of, and we are getting it with more sophisticated satellites. As the solar system goes around the galaxy, it moves above, through, and below the galactic plane approximately every 30 million years like a dolphin swimming through stars, molecular clouds, and other bodies. When the solar system moves through the galactic plane, cataclysmic encounters are much more common than usual. There *were* mass extinctions of species when we traveled through the galactic plane 94.5 million, 65 million, 29 million, and 11,500 years ago. Allan and Delair have shown that the most recent major cataclysmic phase of the 30-million-year galactic plane cycle *already happened 11,500 years ago.* We probably are in the very beginning of 25 to 30 million years of relatively undisturbed evolution while the solar system reestablishes equilibrium. Regarding the orbital and axial derangements in the solar system, uniformitarian scientists, according to Allan and Delair, would have us believe that "these anomalies have accumulated over aeons of time," which enables them to convince the public that the solar system is "recurrently catastrophic."[42] Yet, if the anomalies are the result of a recent great disaster, the solar system's history "can be best defined as normally quiet and orderly but punctuated recently by a single tremendous cataclysm."[43]

The August 1996 Mars announcement involved all levels, even the subtle ones. This great controversy is a sign that our planetary mind is awakening. Meanwhile, incredibly invigorating cosmic waves are reaching Earth now, which the Elite is measuring.[44] Whether individuals can receive the waves, and whether their subtle glands can be activated by these powers, depends on whether they are focused or distracted—that is, whether they are grounded in their bodies. The condition that people will be in during any period of time can only be known by examining astrological patterns that influence the collective mind; that is how the solar system influences humans. Since 2002, I have been giving an analysis of these patterns in the context of time acceleration on my website, *handclow2012.com,* a new form of emotional astroforecasting. This continual reporting has given me many unexpected insights into Elite tactics. Due to various planetary factors, patterns hold for a few days, weeks, or over a few months, and they are of varying potency that can greatly increase or decrease potential freedom for individuals. My students consistently report that by being informed about these patterns, they take greater advantage of these moments. Astrology is one of the most transformative tools available to individuals, and the Elite knows all about how people are strongly affected by astrological patterns.

Of course, after a few years of emotional astroforecasting, I began to notice that the Elite was staging managed events during the influential periods that I was calling out. I noticed that during times of great creative opportunity, often horrible things happened, such as the murders of JonBenet Ramsay, Nicole Simpson, and Princess Diana; the Waco and Columbine massacres; the Oklahoma City bombing; Y2K; and 9/11. So I concluded that these were *mass events orchestrated to distract the public from the powerful transformative energy* coming in during the culmination of the Mayan Calendar. Y2K is especially interesting, because people were all tied up in worrying about whether their computers would fail them during 1999. Yet 1999 was the first year of the Eighth Underworld time acceleration—the Galactic Underworld. Regarding the 1996 Mars announcement, it was a brilliantly constructed diversion. I gave a series of lectures from May through early August 1996 about the amazing astrological potential of August 1996, a time when there was a great cross in fixed signs in the sky formed by the lunar nodes (where the moon crosses the ecliptic), and Jupiter, Saturn, Chiron, and Mars conjoined Venus. This was a period when there was great potential for men to face their own participation in female suppression. The potential to heal this Promethean pain with the women in their lives was so great that it was possible to catalyze healthy male-female polarity and sink into intentional love. I think the Mars announcement was timed to distract men by overwhelming them with martial energy, the vibration that holds them the most captive. I noticed that some men I knew and many of my students *did* begin removing the armoring around their hearts in August 1996. This book began with the premise that the Galactic Winter Solstice—1987–2012— is activating Earth, so next I wondered, are the Elite using these potent opportunities for their own purposes? Enter the Council of Nine.

The Council of Nine

The search for the story of time is driven by the human desire for enlightenment. The *Stargate* authors argue that noncorporeal intelligences—the Council of Nine, or simply the Nine—hold great power over "top industrialists, cutting-edge scientists, popular entertainers, radical parapsychologists, and key figures in military and intelligence circles."[45] J. J. Hurtak has been heavily influenced by the Nine: The Nine is Hurtak's source for *The Keys of Enoch,* which then caused millions to be open to the Nine. Recall the Fallen Angels in the Book of Enoch described in the previous chapter, and notice that J. J. Hurtak's book is titled *The Keys of Enoch.*[46] So, what are the Nine, and where did they come from? A primary source is Andrija Puharich, a parapsychologist who began the Round Table Foundation in Glen Cove, Maine, which is devoted to channeling and other esoteric pursuits. At the Round Table, Puharich set up channeling sessions for an Indian mystic, Dr. D. G. Vinod. The Nine Principles or Forces identified themselves and explained that they are a group of nine entities that make up a whole that is godlike.[47]

The Nine through Dr. Vinod never said they were extraterrestrials, but Puharich declared this was so after a young psychic convinced him. *Notice how this leap blocks our free access to the numinous and ineffable,* because it concretizes divine beings not meant to be material. Because of the awesome size and power of these beings, the contactee becomes confused and may go insane. Puharich was initiated as a full-fledged Hawaiian Kahuna; he studied many methods for altering consciousness, including the use of psychedelic drugs; and he may have been a real seeker. Regardless of his merits, he was deeply involved with the Elite.[48] He used hypnosis to cull the minds of many brilliant psychics, such as Uri Geller, and he was involved in Stanford Research Institute (SRI) experiments on Geller during the same period when the CIA was involved in remote-viewing experiments with SRI.[49] Speaking of strange bedfellows, Lab Nine was founded at Puharich's estate in Ossining, New York, with J. J. Hurtak as his second in command. This spawned a series of people who were primarily channeling extraterrestrials with wealthy backers, celebrities, and SRI physicists hanging around.[50] Books were written; the Nine gave seminars through a channel at Esalen; the group continued even after Puharich died in 1995; and channelers around the world, including me, brought in the Nine with no knowledge of each other. In my case, I brought in a nine-dimensional scientific system, and I was not at Puharich's estate or at Esalen.

The gods of the Egyptian Heliopolitan Mysteries were called the Nine, and they are still potent cosmic forces that have really inspired my work.[51] The level of interpretation of these forces is in direct proportion to the spiritual level of the channel. Since at this time individuals, groups, and cultures are in a very low state of moral and spiritual consciousness, often what comes through channels is distorted. Through the Round Table channels, the Nine claimed that they were going to return to save humankind, and this salvation was all mixed up with apocalyptic fear, racism, the Chosen People, and the battle between good and evil. Supposedly, humans are flawed because extraterrestrials messed up their genetic programming. The Nine have come to fix all this, because humans are so helpless. How will the Nine fix everything? First, the apocalypse will cleanse the planet, and then, according to Hurtak, America will be the location of the new "Spiritual Administration," the rise of the new "JerUSalem."* Here we go again! The big problem with Puharich's presence in Lab Nine is that, as Picknett and Prince note, he "was also carrying out secret research for the defense and intelligence establishments in two main areas: techniques for psychological manipulation using hallucinogenic drugs; and the military and intelligence potential of psychic skills."[52] He was deeply involved in the mind-control experimentation projects of the military and CIA for many years, and his use of hypnosis was unethical and dangerous.[53] This is a classic example of how the Elite co-opts greatly needed healing methods: for example, hypnosis is an incredible tool for removing phobias, clearing emotional blocks, and sharpening intelligence.

The Nine are the center of an orchestrated plot to implant a series of ideas into individuals, cults, and the culture to create a new religion. This has spawned organizations, such as the Institute of Noetic Sciences at Palo Alto, which are used as intelligence organs to influence powerful individuals and the world. Why? The *Stargate* authors note that Puharich "was obsessed with the space gods," he was fascinated with the Heliopolitan Mysteries, and he believed that "it was possible to open the stargate," which would force extraterrestrials to enter this reality so he could meet with them.[54] This is *conjuring*, or calling in energies that are normally nonphysical into the linear space and time. These forces operate by their own dimensional laws, and properly trained shamans are very wary and respectful of them. Puharich and Uri Geller carried on so many weird experiments at the Lawrence Livermore Laboratory in California that the physicists there began to see apparitions of huge, ravenlike birds and flying saucers.[55] They

---

*Picknett and Prince, *The Stargate Conspiracy,* 197. Word formation—"JerUSalem"—is by J. J. Hurtak.

caused a temporary break in the barriers between dimensions, and were probably conjuring the Fallen Angels, perhaps intentionally.

Such experiments are a hideous spiritual distortion. The Heliopolitan Mysteries are eternal and available, and contemplation of their structure and laws can gift anyone with exquisite mystical communion. Because of the personalized interpretations of Puharich, Cayce, Hurtak, and others, I think some very real spiritual forces were diverted and perverted just when they are coming back into this dimension. The Elite plan seems to be that once the extraterrestrials have been conjured, then they will be the new messiahs. Some people are even waiting for the Sumerian god Anu to return and rule Earth! Many channels obsess on the "coming" Earth changes, and people think what they say must be true because everybody says the same things. The herd mentality in cyberspace blinds people. Meanwhile, a deeper and more profound contact with spirit is building and building. For example, Spiritualism was a huge movement in the nineteenth century that was devoted to reaching people who had died to comfort their loved ones; mediums helped people experience loved ones in the nonphysical state. This is comforting, and it helps living people experience the numinous quality of life in other dimensions. There is a great difference between Spiritualism and occult conjuring, yet distortions like the Nine rob the public of respect for legitimate contact with other dimensions.

Symbols as Transmitters of the Divine Mind

The working hypothesis of this book is that Phaeton tilted Earth's axis 11,500 years ago, which disarranged the solar system and began an entirely new form of human evolution. Approximately 11,000 years ago, abstract symbols began to appear, and by studying the mythology and artifacts from this time, we can detect signs of the Great Ages. Before this time we see animals, depictions of plants, and human hands, but not abstraction. What are symbols? Symbols *translate ideas from other dimensions into ours.* The sages saw that symbols have great power, and people enjoyed using them for art and decoration. Before the cataclysm, people seemed to have been in direct contact with nature, and then our access was shattered. The myths that have come down from that time right after the disaster—which are contained within more recent myths like cosmic seeds—are stories of great dramas in the night sky. The constellations and various star systems contain a very rich mythology, which may derive from the global maritime civilization, and then was nurtured by early Holocene cultures, such as Çatal Hüyük.

During the Age of Cancer, the astral realm opened as a great theater of mystery plays that loomed over the world. The sages observed this development with amazement. Next, during the Age of Gemini, kosmokraters or *lords of time* appeared, and then the sages could see that the symbols changed when the ages shifted. Based on the Çatal Hüyük discussion in chapter 6, we can speculate that the symbolism for the Age of Gemini was available in toto exactly when the age opened. *The sages could see that symbols were influencing people to create realities with thought.* For example, the great reformer of human civilization, Zarathustra, used symbols very effectively to encourage people to improve their lives by adopting agriculture. Anthropologist Felicitas Goodman notes, "What all agriculturalists have in common is the illusion of power, of being able to exert control over the habitat."[56] People were experiencing power over nature during the Age of Gemini; they used its inherent creative potential by means of complex and exquisite symbolism.

We can feel the numinous quality in symbols because they lure our minds into connections with other worlds. Responding to symbols was an unconscious process for people during the Age of Cancer, perhaps because they were still numbed by surviving, or perhaps because symbols were opening new areas of their brains. Now it is time for *many* people to understand these gateways to other worlds, since they have been used for thousands of years to control people who are unconscious of them. It is important to see how symbols affect people in general. After all, the Internet could create global waves of positive symbolic connections, or it could create a collective insanity—the most likely "cataclysm" at this time. Since symbols bridge realities, they are *divinized;* they can manifest out of nowhere because they are formed by pure thought, such as *Apple* taking us back to the Garden of Eden, or *Amazon,* leading us into a forest of reading. Great beings like the Nine have had no problem returning at any time, but there are few vehicles that can receive them clearly and/or avoid the temptation to profit from them. Where are our Michelangelos, Beethovens, and Bachs? It is easy to answer that question: the culture that used to support the arts now supports pornography, fear, and violence. Each Great Age births a body of potent symbols that can be doorways to numinous worlds, and we can identify each Great Age by its symbols. Just as there are layers of time in myths, symbols all over the planet manifest in geographic zones by time; they are *geomorphic*. Amazingly, symbolic systems really do show up in toto right when an age opens. Symbols have been used to inspire beautiful potentials, and they've been used to limit and pervert human potential, which is what Hitler did with the swastika. I think evil manifests through symbol-control programs: Evil comes into the world when symbols are used to manipulate and mind-control humans by the select few who happen to know how this process works; kosmokraters, the timelords, are the crafters of this game. They enjoy playing it, so they keep it secret because they'd rather be the king than a pawn. In other words, *evil begins with thought manipulation.* Those who wish to avoid evil influences must observe every single thought that comes into their own heads. We have seen how symbols, such as the all-seeing eye in the capstone of the pyramid on the dollar, can be used for good or evil. Great forces use symbols for thought manipulation for their own purposes. We live in an age in which it is obvious that huge forces are controlling people for power, money, and sex. Most people even know exactly who is doing it, but they can't figure out how to stop it. The information we need now is, how did this happen to our world, and when? The master program that enslaved the world during the Piscean Age is from the Roman Empire.

Perseus Slays the Medusa

Mysteriously, about 200 years before the beginning of the Roman era, when the Age of Aries was ending, a potent brew of forces in the ancient classical world—Stoic philosophers, Greek astronomers, and Cilician pirates—created a new religion called *Mithraism*. Mithraic scholar David Ulansey

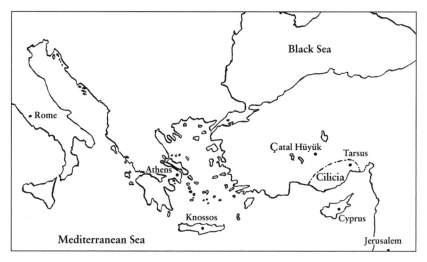

Fig. 8.1. The Black Sea region and the eastern Mediterranean

comments that Mithraism and Christianity arose at the same time and spread through the Roman Empire in the same places, because they were "two responses to the same set of cultural forces."[57] Mithraism was the "road not taken" by Western civilization.[58] Gnosticism is also a road not taken, but I think Mithraism is *the secret road running deep in the bowels of Roman Catholicism,* a road the Elite would just as soon keep private because it was the genesis of militarism during the Age of Pisces. The Cilician pirates were 20,000 sailors who controlled the Mediterranean Sea during the Roman Empire, and their new religion spread like fire through their ranks and the Roman legions. This religion of soldiers was inherited from the Age of Aries when war was the favorite sport for 2,000 years. The Cilician pirates were wealthy men of illustrious lineage who used the stars for navigation. They believed they possessed superior intelligence as blue-bloods; they had inherited the right to live adventurous lives and pursue knowledge.[59] These strapping pirates burned with occult curiosity, just like the Cayce knights today.

Tarsus was the capital of Cilicia, and during Hellenistic and Roman times, it rivaled Athens and Alexandria. There an exciting intellectual community developed around the Stoic philosophers, because the natives were fond of learning. Tarsus hosted many famous Stoic philosophers. Among them were both Posidonius and Athenodorus, and the famous Zeno of Tarsus, who was influenced by the famous astronomer Aratos of Soli (315–240 BC).[60] According to the Stoics, stellar patterns greatly influence human affairs. They believed in the Great Year determined by the constellations on the ecliptic, and they preached that the "entire cosmos was periodically destroyed by a great conflagration *(ekpyrosis)* and subsequently re-created *(palingenesis)*."[61] They allegorized gods and mythical figures to represent cosmic and natural forces; they mastered symbolism and mystery plays. For example, for them Phaeton was an allegorical being who drives the chariot of the sun at the end of an age, the agent of ekpyrosis.[62] It is fair to say that the scientists of today who preach that a cyclical cataclysm will be coming soon are Stoics.

Stoicism was the primary philosophy of Tarsus, the city of the Cilician pirates. Therefore, when Hipparchus supposedly discovered precession in 128 BC, it had a huge impact on both the Stoics and the pirates because of their interest in the stars.[63] In fact, I have pointed out throughout this book that precession was understood in some form at least 10,000 years ago, but it was the way that Hipparchus *described* this influence that matters. Of course, Hipparchus was the dunce shoved into the public eye. Because he believed that Earth was fixed in space and everything in the cosmos moved around it, then precession was the movement of the "structure of the entire cosmos" around a cosmic axis.[64] Because the current belief was that stars were fixed and unchanging, and because the real precessional knowledge was hidden within secret cabals, this announcement by Hipparchus would have been shocking to the public. However, just like the Mars announcement, this was merely what the public was being told. I am suggesting that this form of lying and public manipulation has been endemic for more than 2,000 years. Meanwhile, the real power brokers—Cilician pirates, Roman soldiers, and Stoics—took these new ideas and formulated a potent astral religion; the Stoics allegorized divine beings to carry natural forces. Which great god would be selected as the mover of the cosmos, the kosmokrater! When the Age of Pisces began more than 2,100 years ago, everything was in flux, and there were many strange bedfellows. If we keep the *Stargate Conspiracy* in mind, it is possible to conjure up a *tauroctony conspiracy*. Tauroctony means "bull slaying," and we will see what this means in a moment.

As the Age of Aries waned, the Stoics scanned their inner minds for a suitable archetype to embody the kosmokrater, the awesome force that moves the heavens. Ulansey argues that *they used Mithra in public and*

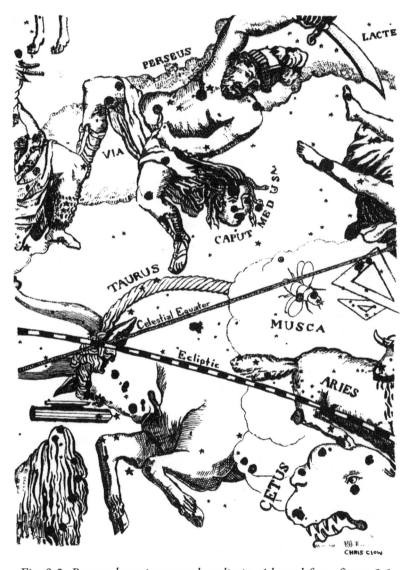

Fig. 8.2. Perseus hovering over the ecliptic. Adapted from figure 3.1 of Ulansey's The Origins of the Mithraic Mysteries.

Perseus covertly.[65] Within the exquisite Mediterranean deep-blue sky, the great god Perseus—who looms over Taurus, Aries, and Pisces on the ecliptic and holds the severed head of the Medusa in one hand and the sword of Damocles in the other—was infused with the light of many dimensions. Impelled by the great cosmic whirlwind as the Age of Pisces approached, Perseus was cast as the force that encapsulated both Taurus and Aries, and then his sword even points to Pisces. Contemplate figure 8.2 and imagine the potency of this warrior god wearing a Phrygian hat (meaning that he is a Magus) as he looms over two or three Great Ages and slays the Medusa. The Perseus constellation within the Milky Way may be the axis the whole cosmos turns on, so this is where the last remnant of the ancient goddess culture, the Medusa, is decapitated. Medusa also represents ancient snake shamans, who were often females just like vulture shamans. Medusa turned people to stone just by looking at them, so some scholars suggest that the Medusa is an archaic form of Tiamat, the destroyed planet.[66] Perseus slayed her, so he is a cataclysm figure. Consequently, after thousands of years of war and oppression that eventually suppressed the goddess, Medusa loses her shamanic powers during the Age of Pisces.

Perseus turns the wheel of time, bringing in woman-slaying for the Age of Pisces. A divinity of such power could control Earth, the agenda of the Roman Empire. Exactly how the Cilician pirates and the Stoics got together and developed the Mithraic rituals is not clear. Yet we know more about the actual rites than we do about most secret religions, because they built Mithraeums in Roman towns and cities from northern Scotland to Libya. These are underground temples that feel like ancient caves, with huge altars called tauroctonies, which depict Mithra slaying the bull surrounded by numerous astral and mythological symbols. So why was Mithra the public hero and Perseus the covert one? Perseus was an ancient Persian god, and the legends about his birth and life are very similar to the story of Zal in chapter 7. Danae, the mother of Perseus, was seduced by her uncle, her father's twin, who was her father's rival. Danae's father locked her away in a tower where Zeus seduced her, and then Perseus was born, who was sent away just like Zal. This story is an early Greek version that was derived from the earliest phases of Iranian and Indian religion back at least 10,000 years, the survival phase after the cataclysm during the Age of Cancer. Perseus and the tauroctony were chosen in secrecy because they are potent archaic archetypes that would numb and dumb down the people during the Age of Pisces. As you will see in a moment, Mithra is named after an emperor, a political god, so the people were to pray on their knees in church and obey. Perseus as kosmokrater would be the secret ruler of time, so that the core initiates could control reality by conjuring in secret caves. The sacrificial rituals in caves and underground temples were the places for the great mysteries—sacrifice and slaying.

The predynastic Narmer Palette from Hieraconpolis (Nekhen) dated circa 3500 BC is a very early rendition of the pharaoh slaying his enemies—in this case, Semites—who periodically came to the Nile because they were starving. The Palette is made with exquisite skill, and the concepts expressed are clear and complete: It depicts pharaonic kingship that developed after

*Fig. 8.3. The Narmer
Palette*

the opening of Taurus in 4480 BC; the passing of Gemini is denoted by twins in the lower level of the Palette. I have included it here for comparison with figure 8.2; I propose that the Mithraists adopted Perseus because the dynastic Egyptians had already used this potent archetype to depict the *pharaoh as Perseus slaying his enemy.* Rome planned to conquer Egypt, so the Mithraists probably selected this archetype to extend their power back to the Age of Taurus. The Narmer Palette shows that the Egyptians used the precessional ages to organize their empire, and the Romans knew how successful they had been for a few thousand years. The enemy being slain in the Palette is an invader of Egypt, but the Mithraists slay the Medusa. Perseus is a very archaic Iranian god, so the Narmer Palette may be a record of the Elder Culture's sojourn in the Middle East before it returned to the Nile. From this, we can infer that the Elder Culture was deeply involved in the shifts of the Great Ages. Back to Mithraism, this religion was intended to be the secret society that controlled symbology 2,000 years ago, while the empire and the Catholic Church would be visible to the world. Recall that conspiracies operate through religion, and politics is the game that is seen by the public. Let's flesh out this story more.

Mithridates IV Eupater was the king who controlled Asia Minor from 88 to 66 BC, and when the Age of Pisces arrived, his name was used for the god. Mysteriously, Perseus was a direct ancestor of the Iranian line of kings begun by Zal, the line from which Mithridates was also descended, and Mithra was also an ancient Iranian bull-slaying god.[67] Mithridates was also a great rival of Rome during the Mithridatic Wars, and he used the Cilician pirates as allies against Rome. Perseus was the secret divinity, and naming the god in public after the great king empowered the cult. Since Mithra was a god way back during the horrible time of the struggle with the Watchers, the cult was *chthonic*—imbued with powers from the inner Earth. Once the Stoics had formulated this potent allegorized deity with Mithradates IV, the Cilician pirates adopted Mithra as their god, and the bull-slaying rituals and the slaying of the Medusa activated chthonic forces: Amid the blood, new ideas were formulated and imprinted with potent astral symbols. Forces were conjured from the deep past that still possess the dark side of Roman Christianity. For example, the Mass is a symbolic sacrificial eating ritual in public. Meanwhile, there is a hidden tauroctony exactly below the Bernini Altar in the Vatican, just as there are hidden caves under the altars of many old churches that may have Mithraeums. The actual existence of a ritual cave with a tauroctony below the Vatican was revealed to me by a Jesuit who said Mass there, and he shared this with me on the condition that his identity would not be revealed. He said there are four altars to the four directions in this ancient cave, and a priest says Mass every hour at one of these altars. In other words, this potent chthonic energy was still being activated hourly under the Vatican in the 1970s.

The tauroctony in figure 8.4 is typical of tauroctonies in general. The bull is dying an agonizing death, while the sword of Mithra sprouts wheat in the wound. The followers of Mithra participated in bull-slaying rituals in front of tauroctonies such as this one. Because this was done in caves, it revived distant Paleolithic and Early Holocene memories when humanity was forced to live underground, and the sprouting wheat in the wound reminds people that adopting agriculture was traumatic. *Mithraism was incredibly atavistic,* as the Nazis were; Mithraism was very strong in

Fig. 8.4. Tauroctony. Adapted from figure 5.5 of Ulansey's
The Origins of the Mithraic Mysteries.

Germany, which made it an ideal place for the rise of Hitler. As we've seen, because of the horrible struggle to survive during the Age of Cancer, the early stories about the activities of the Fallen Angels suggest that people endured terrible suffering that led them into cannibalism and sacrifice, and sex with their children, siblings, and parents. Some of the hideous crimes we observe in modern times come out of sick minds that are filled with chthonic urges that possess minds that have been denied the story of the past. Earlier sacrificial and orgiastic cults—such as the Orphics and Dionysiacs—were religions that may have helped people process chthonic powers. But Mithraic rituals and iconography use many of the practices of the old orgiastic religions to cull atavistic powers to be used for power and control instead of ecstatic release. We have to wonder why soldiers developed such a potent cult that carried out blood rituals that obviously conjured up very great chthonic forces. We may never know exactly why, but we can be sure of one thing: These soldiers and their esoteric masters created an intense wave of misogyny, which still grips the Roman Catholic Church and military systems today. As long as women are the Medusa, men will be warriors, and eventually the world will run out of mothers.

Zoroaster and the Age of Asa

Going back further into the Age of Gemini, the Earth changes were settling down, people moved beyond the survival level, and reforms came naturally; people prefer more refined approaches to life than basic survival. Meanwhile, shamans—the mediators between Earth and sky—worked with these forces for collective balance, so that ordinary people could go about their business. *People do not seek, want, or allow these chthonic powers in their lives except when they are afflicted with catastrophobia.* The Age of Cancer was ending, and various spiritual teachers and sages came forth to create new religions that could diminish chthonic practices and help people animate their lives with finer vibrations. Zarathustra of India (Zoroaster of Iran) was this kind of great reformer. He goes all the way back through to the Age of Gemini, since there was a lineage of Zoroasters who assumed this enlightened role. Zoroaster and Zarathustra mean "watching the stars," so this is a lineage of astronomers, who knew about precession, as we've seen with Çatal Hüyük. Following Zoroaster through the stages of time by symbols and mythology is a great way to see how the patterns of the Great Ages change, since these star-based reforms reflect the evolution of humanity. Magism may be the earliest form, because in later times, Magi priests were wild rainmaking shamans, which comes from the Age of Cancer. The next form was Zervanism, and the double ax and the wheeled cross of Çatal Hüyük in figure 6.10 (p. 165) may actually depict the opening of the Age of Gemini. Settegast believes Çatal Hüyük was one of many sites where Zervanism was actually taught, possibly by the line of prophets.[68]

Zoroaster was a very successful reformer during the Age of Gemini. Agriculture was sorely needed because of the condition of the land and the burgeoning population, and he and his emissaries taught people how to care for the land and to work hard and value a simple life. He encouraged people to cease invoking chthonic forces in orgiastic rituals, and he taught them how to live in a state of order by being a good person enjoying a good life. He called the principle of order and peace *Asa,* and his concept of it was the same as the Tao and Maat. According to Settegast, "The cultivation of the earth was looked upon by Zarathustra's followers as a kind of worship."[69] Settegast argues that the Samarran and Halafian farming communities from Greece through Turkey to Iraq and Iran began exactly when the Age of Gemini began, and they were inspired by the religion of Zarathustra.[70]

As you can see in the illustrations from the Halafian culture (figure 8.5), their pottery designs are very geometrical with great contrast between dark and light. They are beautiful and inspiring and show the need to

Fig. 8.5. Halafian geometrical pottery designs. Adapted from figure 138 of Settegast's Plato Prehistorian.

balance the dark and light; religious awe must have inspired them. Because Zarathustra taught about bringing in the light and encouraged people not to invoke dark forces, pottery was used as art in the household to teach people how to blend these forces in their lives. Asa and Maat are similar concepts, and both these cultures used exquisite art to draw down high spiritual forces into the people's everyday lives.

In the previous chapter, I commented that Zoroaster stifled further discussions about Angels being involved with humans, yet they remained in the sacred literature and folk tales. *This suppression of the dark forces may be the first cover-up of the Fallen Angels.* This phase in Zoroaster's teachings probably comes from the beginning of the Age of Taurus, when theocracies created cities and temples where priests and kings worked together. Modern Zoroastrians keep priestly control and rituals to a minimum, and Andrew Collins notes that over the centuries the Muslims of Iran and India have systematically attempted to eradicate their faith.[71] As we know, there are difficult tensions today in the Middle East, which may be the result of the suppression of these dark forces. Collins visited a Yezidi sacred cave on the Turkish border with Syria. The Yezidis are *zaddik* priests, ecstatic nomadic rainmakers claiming descent from Noah, and their records go back at least 10,000 years.[72] On the floor, Collins saw a rendering of an early zodiac, and he saw shrines with ancient figures wearing conical caps like the ones the Tibetans wear. This conical cap is the earliest version of the Phrygian cap that Perseus wears. We will return to Perseus/Mithra now that we can see how ancient and potent these archetypes really are. They are the forces that were hidden totally during the Piscean Age after being progressively suppressed through the previous Great Ages.

Blood Rituals and the Ahriman

Considering the tauroctony in figure 8.4 again, notice that there is a scorpion pinching the genitals of the bull, a long snake is under the bull's right leg, and wheat is coming out of the bull's body where Mithra slays him. Hundreds of tauroctonies have been found, and they all contain the same grouping of symbols. In this tauroctony, the scorpion on the genitals of the bull suggests that his sexuality is part of the energy of the ritual, and the long snake under his leg is astronomical. The bull's leg or thigh commonly depicted the Great Bear constellation, and the snake is Draco writhing around the North Pole by precession. Notice the twins, who represent the ecliptic and the Age of Gemini. On many tauroctonies, one twin carries a scepter at a 90-degree upright angle, and the other tilts his about 23.5 degrees.[73] Based on Iranian mythology, the dagger in the shoulder means that the slain bull is creational—he bleeds out the plants and herbs as he dies. If we look at the Perseus constellation astronomically in figure 8.2, Ulansey says that the Pleiades are located right where the dagger goes into the bull's shoulder. The knowledge that Phaeton came in through the Pleiades is even depicted in Mithraic secret teachings.[74] Because they carried out the bull sacrifices hidden away in caves, they were free to record what they knew by symbols that they figured nobody else could identify.

When we conceive of the darkly shamanic Age of Cancer as a survival and struggle period, then the process of reform during the Age of Gemini shows that it was a heroic age for humanity, a time when many of the great religions began. It was an age when people strived for peaceful community and artistic and mental freedom after a very dark and mystical experience with Earth's powers during the Age of Cancer. When thinking of Zoroaster as an agricultural and religious reformer who influenced religions in the Middle East including Judaism, we have to ask: Isn't it odd that Mithraism, which is based on the older chthonic forces from the Age of Cancer and Leo, would be reinvoked at the beginning of the Age of Pisces? This sacrificial ritual religion of soldiers, which centers on the slaying of the female, would have horrified Zoroaster: *It represents everything he and his followers reformed thousands of years before.*

I am not the first or the last person to wonder if the dark forces—the Ahriman of Zarathustra—rule the Roman Catholic Church. I would not even mention this without offering some solutions in the final chapter. The most important thing to recognize here is that *evil forces are real, yet they cannot come into this world unless somebody conjures them.* Powerful chthonic forces were invoked in the Mithraeums right when the Piscean

Age began. There is always a zodiac in the Mithraeums, which is not illustrated here, and usually Mithra slays the bull under a zodiac. So this ritual sucked up the archetypal forces of the previous five Great Ages and loaded them directly into the Piscean Age. *These are the occulted Elite forces that humanity is becoming objective about now.* And a really exciting book about this strange shift from Aries to Pisces is *Not in His Image* by the philosopher John Lamb Lash.

Lash portrays the Gnostics as the last wisdom school of the ancient mysteries that existed all over the world for thousands of years. He traces their suppression and final obliteration by Roman Christianity. Lash details exactly what the Gnostics believed, which is shocking but can be absorbed in light of the rest of the material in this book. The various Gnostic strains believed that the Hebrew god Yahweh or Jehovah was the "Demiurge"—a false creator god who is a demented and violent imposter. On this basis, when Jesus arrived and founded Christianity, the Gnostics wanted a new religion that was separate from Judaism, which worshipped Yahweh in the Hebrew scripture. Lash says that central to Gnostic theology are the Archons, an alien intrapsychic species, the source of subliminal intrusion that deviates humankind from its proper course of evolution. "Archontic interception of humanity," he writes, "was initiated in the meeting of Abraham and Melchizedek, the premier moment in Jewish salvation history."[75]

The Gnostics said Yahweh is the head Archon, the principle of evil in the world, and I think the Archons as described by Lash came into our world as a result of the cataclysm and the disarrangement of the solar system. Lash's book is excellent and also extreme, but the Gnostics were very extreme. They were deeply worried about what would happen if Christianity just absorbed Judaism two thousand years ago and became Judeo-Christianity, the religion of the Piscean Age. The Gnostics wanted a truly new religion for the Piscean Age, a religion of peace. Now that we are bringing in Aquarian symbols and archetypes, this it's time to examine all the things that have been piled onto religion for thousands of years.

Christianity may have been the light force and Mithraism the dark force during the Piscean Age; however, as we consider these forces in our times, they are both fundamentally misogynist. The long-lasting Elder Cultures of the Athenians and the Egyptians and the prediluvial goddess culture of the Magdalenians were adamant about one thing: the importance of the veneration of the goddess. The Gnostics revered Sophia, the goddess of wisdom, and what they disliked the most about Judaism and Christianity was the adoption of a father god that everybody must obey. As the Aquarian vibrations penetrate our planet today, we have some grand opportunities. First, the Age of Aquarius forms a trine to the Age of Gemini, which means it will naturally foster enlightenment and leadership by sages. Second, the Aquarian energy is so androgynous that it will tend to balance male and female powers. Third, and most importantly, the great data convergence described in this book suggests that *humanity is on the verge of being able to transmute the control forces that have been building for thousands of years.* Sometimes I wonder if the end of the control program is what the end of the Mayan Calendar is all about. I don't think very many people will be swept along in *The Stargate Conspiracy* because it is so transparent and sophomoric. The knights might chase the grail all the way to the end, since Faustian pacts are lucrative, but informed people will not follow along. The great challenge is to invoke the Great Goddess in balance with the new harmony of Earth that is forming as the planet establishes equilibrium. The greatest challenge will be to bring the goddess back into our world without conjuring chthonic forces. She is best found in the love between people, in our communications with animals, in the eyes of children, and in the natural world around us.

9

GODDESS ALCHEMY AND THE HELIOPOLITAN MYSTERIES

Feelings are the only way you can move yourselves outside of linear space and time while you are in body, since they are the access point for beings in other realities to communicate with you.

BARBARA HAND CLOW[1]

The Pleiadian Agenda Model and Interactive Time

The central consciousness model of *The Pleiadian Agenda* and *Alchemy of Nine Dimensions* shows how our bodies receive frequencies from nine dimensions simultaneously when we are grounded in linear space and time (3D).[2] It is a *model of the awakened human.* The first dimension (1D) is the iron-core crystal in the center of Earth, which pulses 40–60 times per second, or 40–60 Hertz. This pulse moves out in magnetic waves into the rocks, magma, and microbial essences that live in the area beneath the surface of Earth—the *telluric elemental world* (2D). On Earth's surface, the magnetic waves emerge to be charged by the electricity in the atmosphere, and they become electromagnetic fields that support all living beings, such as the person shown lying on a massage table in figure 9.1. This person in 3D emotes thoughts and feelings that all weave together into the collective consciousness. The collective consciousness (4D) emanates an etheric energy dome over the individual, or groups and communities. We all participate in this group mind, which is not solid or physical, and it is palpable. This group mind is *real* but less dense than our bodies, and it is textured and colored by each person's sense of time and history; it is fluid and changes as cultures and people evolve. The 4D emotional body is greatly shaped by events in 3D, such as events staged to manipulate people, for example, the search for the Hall of Records. If one is unaware of the big game that is being played, events and quests incite people to take actions, or they influence them to shut down. Meanwhile, any person can read this game and choose to work with 4D in a wide spectrum, which means accessing many realities through feelings.

Egyptian sacred science is invaluable because it teaches us how to detect the 4D archetypal realm in 3D by learning to recognize the influence of the gods (neters) in ordinary reality. When Earth's field is balanced and people live in cultures that hold the field of the Tao, Asa, or Maat, the individual is profoundly grounded, intensely stimulated by feelings, and can read events brilliantly. When cultures achieve these levels, people spend most of their time telling stories, making art, and carrying out ceremonies that bring the gods into everyday life on Earth. At present, humanity is grossly unbalanced and out of touch with the spiritual realms, the upper five dimensions (5D–9D). This is why I chose to explore how we can reestablish Paradise on Earth—Maat/Tao/Asa—in this book. Simply by tuning ourselves to the frequencies we all are capable of holding, we invite divine intelligences into the human world, which is what I think is happening during the end of the Mayan Calendar. We have forgotten about these subtle beings, and they are lonely when they cannot play in our solid world. My nine-dimensional model is a simple and accessible new method that is inspired by the Heliopolitan Mystery School. This is why the distortions by the Council of Nine described in the previous chapter are a concern to me.

All existence is a matter of perspective, and my nine-dimensional model examines realities as dimensions in which our consciousness locates itself, whether we are aware of it or not. These days most people experience reality in their 4D feeling and mental states, and *they are not well located in their 3D physical bodies.* This causes them to be totally confused and lost in the archetypal realms, where the Elite easily manipulate them. You really have to be careful about getting caught on this 4D game board, which is carefully maintained by the Elite on the black-and-white-checked floors of Masonic Tracing Boards.[3] When you *are* grounded in your body, you are fed by tremendous flowing energy from Earth, and the 4D dome becomes diaphanous—easily permeated by cosmic consciousness in the higher realms. Clear and open feelings are the bridge between the tangible and intangible—between body and spirit. Then our 4D feeling bodies access cosmic frequencies of the fifth through ninth dimensions, and we can actually comprehend the spirit world by becoming adept at reading divine manifestations in our world. We are designed to live in a delicious cocoon of subtle impulses that soften 4D while our cells regenerate by potent lower forces, such as crustal movements, magnetism, and microbial forms of life. Think of how much energy we miss when we block the lower dimensions because we fear cataclysms. In the Pleiadian Agenda model, 5D through 9D are shown as lines coming right into our 4D dome because these higher frequencies activate the 4D dome, which opens our emotions. *We receive cosmic information first by feeling it in our bodies.* Simply put, we are designed to play with the gods all day long by reading our feelings and expressing these forces through art and ceremony. According to the ancient Egyptians, these gods love to eat, have sex, work, and organize realities! We are *designed to have total access to divine essences and create with them in our world.*

I show a person lying on a triangle that is also healing table, because so many of us have first detected these feelings during a healing session; however, this person could be standing, sitting, or swimming. The dimensions that humans can interact with are progressive, such as moving from 1D to 9D, yet here we are interested in how we detect these dimensions with our bodies. The lower dimensions are dense and charged with the most intense energy. The higher dimensions vibrate with progressively faster frequencies and are less dense, and they translate down into our bodies through the

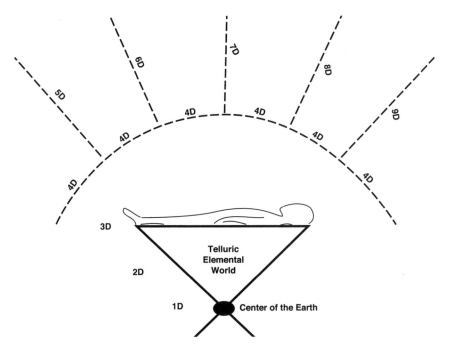

Fig. 9.1. The model of the awakened human. Adapted from
Clow's The Pleiadian Agenda.

4D dome. That is, this dome has gateways for the higher dimensions that open or shut according to our feelings. *Radical density differentials are the cause of the split between body and spirit; yet, ironically, there is no split in someone who is emotionally clear.* As the iron-core crystal pulses Earth, we in 3D vibrate with waves coming through the telluric realm (2D), and by these waves we take physical form by our soul's intention. Meanwhile the pulses in the sky penetrate Earth by waves, such as gamma rays, which vibrate at much higher frequencies than 1D through 4D and contain amazing intelligence coming in from cosmic worlds, such as the Pleiadian, Sirian, or Orion star systems. Our 4D bodies feel these higher-dimensional vibrations, which have been identified by the perennial wisdom, and sages insist we need this knowledge now.

Our *feelings* pick up these signals, so if we do not understand our personal emotional response patterns, the 4D collective mind translates what we feel in weird ways, which blocks the reception of higher frequencies.

That is, we perceive reality *through* 4D instead of *in* 3D, but 3D is where we experience life. Considering John Lamb Lash's exposition of the Gnostic teachings, I would suggest that the Archons are not real in 3D, yet they take form in 4D and can totally possess people. I think this is the same thing as David Icke's famous Reptilians.[4] When we pick up contacts in 4D, our personal fears *cloak* them. For instance, feeling an awesome numinous presence, a fundamentalist Christian might think the Archangel Michael has arrived; an Orthodox Jew might think Melchizadek has landed; and a blissed-out New Ager might think an extraterrestrial from Zeta Reticulae is at the end of the bed. These appearances often exhibit snakelike characteristics, like the Reptilians. Meanwhile, a spirit in another dimension that wants to communicate is contacting this person, which is a marvelous opportunity for playing and learning. Since most people are out of their physical bodies and stuck in a 4D media swill, divine forces are reduced to dark/light, good/evil, and positive/negative. The Elite know this, so television is a favorite tool for conjuring forces in other dimensions.

People are thrown into *dualistic confusion* by these appearances because we live in a culture that debunks the perennial wisdom. Meanwhile, we can befriend these forces when they are good for us and screen them out when they are of no use. Fully embodied humans are naturally able to see, hear, touch, and smell these appearances; yet most of these exquisite higher consciousness avenues are dormant because of the education system. Usually, a person occasionally has at least one doorway open and can receive one or more of the higher dimensions. For example, you may be able to hear the divine seventh-dimensional sounds in a late quartet by Beethoven. Yet for the time being, the 5D emotional domain of your heart may be too complex for you because your heart is shut down by grief or trauma. Many of us may be easily transported by the 6D divine geometry that is the source of all creation in this world, yet we might have a heart attack if we *really* fell in love! The nine-dimensional model shows that we are capable of receiving any one or all of the five higher dimensions, and once we learn to receive any form of divinity, we are open to more. This is the goal of life.

Bringing the Divine into Everyday Life

You might be able to discover the numinous in the idealized 6D forms or hear God in the 7D sound codes, yet you might be almost incapable of finding the divine in passionate 5D love. However, once you experience how the divine *feels,* eventually more aspects of this exquisite elixir come to you. For example, the seventh dimension structures itself by vertical octaves, and its coherency is detectable in the musical scale. So if your consciousness resonates with the divine in music, as you respond to it you scale up the octaves and feel exquisite high frequencies. Since 7D sound creates the geometry in 6D, you may descend into geometrical visions, or you may ascend to pure 8D light. Regarding sound's ability to create forms in 6D, this has been demonstrated by cymatics—the study of sound, which shows how patterns are formed by sound waves, such as in sand. As sounds are transmitted, the sand moves around and makes patterns on the disk of the cymatics machine. This proves that *each one of us can hear and see divine sages.* When a person is in a conversational relationship with the sages, the political and religious agendas of the Elite are easy to decode because they all function in 4D: They are split into black and white, and they are much less complex than the immanent divine light. The eighth dimension actually creates the material world by clear intentionality—the divine Word, just as the Bible says. When we hear these words, we know the purpose of the divine plan and our role in it, and we would never confuse it with dualistic 4D vibrations.

In the ninth dimension (9D) we experience cosmic time, which links our world with the Milky Way galaxy; knowing this realm helps us know when it is *time* to take action. The most incredible thing about this moment in time is that Carl Johan Calleman has enabled us to understand the meaning of the Mayan Calendar, the ninth dimension. *We can comprehend the nature of the 9D perennial wisdom,* and we know how to cocreate with the divine when we are conversant in this high dimension. This is why indigenous people have always revered their calendars, and they follow them in 3D time because real calendars are doorways to divine purpose. Then you are not stuck as a pawn on the 4D checkered field, you are enveloped in light and love. The universe loves you! This all makes more sense when we go from the top down in the vertical axis: The galaxy pulses from its center where the 9D divine intelligences live, and they speak to humans through 8D councils, which offer excellent advice. Often these councils are circles of nonphysical sages, animals, stones, or even microbes, and there are wisdom councils in all nine dimensions. If we absorb this knowledge, it generates 7D waves of intelligence, the actual sound of creation. These tones pulse into 6D geometrical forms, which are pulled down into pulsing 5D biological fields of love. These feelings intensify when they are stretched by the 4D span of collective energy, our species karma. When we feel things, it is contagious, and once we truly know our own feelings, we are seized by a creative vortex that invites the divine into the material world. At any moment in the flow, you may be pierced by 5D love, expand this into resonant harmony in 6D geometry, be transported by the 7D music of the spheres, find communion with 8D divine beings or guides, and meet the 9D sages in the center of the Milky Way galaxy.

We humans are the keepers of Earth, a place where all these intelligences may visit and play. As nature awakens, the polarity is intense, because the higher dimensions activate the 4D archetypal realm with cosmic frequencies while the telluric activates our bodies, and we are sandwiched between them. During the cataclysm, our 4D emotional bodies went into shock, which locked out higher frequencies because we were so afraid of the chaotic forces. Now the *light is moving into these shadows, releasing catastrophobia in our cells.* Our emotions are flowing again, we feel overenergized; millions drug themselves just to calm down. Yet drugs move awareness out of our bodies and plug it into the 4D archetypal dome, which blocks our bodies from regeneration by 2D telluric powers and the connection with 1D Earth records. *Drugs steal the will, our mind's ability to guide us, and we become pawns of the collective mind.* Sometimes drugs are needed to keep emotions under control during a crisis, but everything should be done to get off these substances as soon as possible.

As the Pleiadian Agenda model shows, we can be conscious receivers of many dimensions, which is how we differ from animals. As higher dimensional forces arrive, we polarize them by our feelings in order to process their meaning. Our minds play with the issues, such as considering that the Angels once walked among us. Then suddenly, in the midst of the mundane world, exquisite dramas and mystery plays emerge like huge emotional mushrooms. We become children in a dark room peering at a puppet show as the forms on the strings begin to dance. Our minds awaken by the primordial archetypes, such as the Minotaur or Medusa, when we find these characters and stories right in our ordinary lives. I think we need mythological and archetypal breakthroughs because without this penetration of the sacred, we get bored. Our mundane world is too limited without its expansion by the higher dimensions. However, because we are so fearful, we try to stifle the awesomeness of our own personal dramas and monsters—the contents of the right brain. We remain small and fearful beings who hide in our little personal worlds and look out through periscopes into the great 4D emotional realm. Yet now after a long narrowing, we are ready to have more courage. We must stretch our emotional bodies now by staying grounded in our physical bodies so we can contain these great forces and free ourselves of manipulation. Otherwise, our 3D lives are simply hysterical theaters for events that actually exist only in other dimensions.

We are always on one side or the other of any drama, and this misplaced duality splits 3D into all good or all bad. In this darkened theater of life, lower-dimensional (2D) forms seeking freedom are sucked in to occupy the side of ourselves that is judged or denied. These materialized 2D forces are distorted in 3D, and cancer is a very good example of this problem. *Cancer is an emotional disease.* The telluric invasion of the material realm causes disease and violence in the material world, which *will not cease until each one of us recognizes that the realm of dark and light simply expresses both the positive and negative aspects of ourselves.* If we work with these aspects of ourselves emotionally without allowing these aspects to manifest in the physical world, then our world is a joyful home to play in. In the Celtic and Balinese worlds, the gods are everywhere in the house helping solve problems, and home is a magical place. Divine forces become demonic when they are denied creative participation. The second and fourth dimensions need to work together to energize 3D;

people with mature emotions integrate 2D and 4D in their daily lives.

We are indeed alive in an amazing moment. As you can imagine, I have studied emotional healing methods my whole life, and to my utter amazement, author Karla McLaren has described the full range of human emotions and how to attain mastery of our feelings in her book, *The Language of Emotions.* Far beyond all the excellent self-help and emotional-processing books that we've enjoyed since the 1970s, McLaren has distilled all this knowledge into this one book. She fully knows the depths of the dark side because she was hideously abused as a little girl, and she has thoroughly healed her own pain. As she says, "I was brought into full-body contact with human evil."[5] Her approach is holistic and accurate because she bases emotional healing on the five elements—earth, air, fire, water, and ether—the fundamental basis of the perennial wisdom. But what I love about her approach is that the esoterics are stripped out. We may need esoteric information in a book like this one, but we have little use for it when people just need compassion, clarity, and a sense of direction.

As she says, "When you move away from imbalance and diminishment (where you saw yourself as primarily intellectual or spiritual or emotional or physical), an entirely new world opens up. When the village of elements is in balance inside you, a fifth element or a meta-intelligence—your intelligence *about* your intelligence—arises at the center of your psyche. This new element is called *nature, wood,* or *ether* in various wisdom traditions. . . . You no longer swing wildly between being too mental or not smart enough, too physical or too ungrounded, too emotional or too frozen, or too spiritual or too coarse. When you're standing upright in the center of your four elements, you're something and someone new."[6] This is a model for how we can be grounded in our world.

The archetypes that filter divine forces into this world reveal themselves by art and symbolism, the library of collective human evolution that links us to the divine realms. Higher dimensions are simultaneous realities that penetrate our world with waves that we may or may not detect. To receive these waves, we each need to learn to feel their specific frequencies, and then our feelings can decode them, just as a radio or a screen translates waves. *The nine-dimensional model shows how humans can be receptive devices for multidimensional frequencies when our deep memory awakens.* This is why Egyptian sacred science says that the first step is Maat, or balancing the polarities, and the Mayan Calendar announces the time is now. This is why a stupendous struggle is occurring in our 3D world.

As one Great Age ends and another begins, the great sages return to this world bringing the perennial wisdom, such as Karla McLaren. Then, it is up to us to bring in an age of enlightenment, such as the Age of Gemini, which can only happen if everyone participates and cocreates with divine forces. Without knowing the feelings of archaic people, we cannot imagine how they were in contact with greater realms of being. But, we can be sure they were in touch by their art and symbolism. This is why we are so moved by Paleolithic art that came at the end of tens of thousands of years of cosmic contact; then the link was shattered.

The Collective Awakening

When we have a clear and responsive emotional body and receive higher frequencies, we discover rich resources within. If we are emotionally split, eventually archetypal collective forces can possess us, and we become exhausted and deenergized. According to the wisdom of the sages, we are completing 11,500 years of a collective degeneration, and we are rapidly moving into an exciting regenerative phase. This news is what the Maya managed to save for us. The key to the whole process is the awakening of each individual, because each one of us must hold resonance within the morphogenetic fields of creation as we ascend collectively to higher levels. The great creative gods are returning and looking for meetings with us in our reality. Will there be anybody home when they arrive? This book discusses secret, arcane, and superhuman abilities because humans have already experienced these potentialities. Clearly, *we are preparing for the return of ancient wisdom.* However, something is still missing, and I think it is time to realize that we live many lifetimes.

We may also be living many lifetimes simultaneously. Whatever is going on, the lost parts of our psyches are filled with knowledge and rich emotionality. Christianity eliminated reincarnation so that people would think the knowledge they've attained during life dies with them, but it does not. As we've seen, anybody can go into a trance and access esoteric knowledge, and you can find the perennial within yourself just by accessing your "past" knowledge. The church wants to be the only source of wisdom, and so it cuts off personal access to inner wisdom. Our planet is attaining global consciousness again, and each one of us has gifts for the gods. Egyptian sacred science actually describes how the gifts of the gods are seeds that are contained in mundane human activities. Each individual—farmer, priestess, architect, or pharaoh—was an artist. These days, people resist the movement of creative energy through themselves because they are conditioned by religion to fear dark forces. These forces are real, yet they are not a problem for people who have balanced emotions. Let's look at what goes on when clear individuals respond to the collective mind.

People who clear inner psychological blocks form a *group alchemy*, which supports all those who continue to struggle. I am very optimistic about our future, but we are right in the middle of the most difficult passage: As humanity faces the true depths of its inner pain, disassociated archaic memory from old wounds comes up, and some of it is bizarre, such as the antics of the Fallen Angels described in chapter 7. For example, many people have become obsessed with the return of the gods in 2012. Egyptian sacred science understood the antics of the gods in the human realm, so they instructed the people all about the gods. Stories about the sexual behavior, personal dramas, or sickness and suffering of the gods contain brilliant instructional information for handling problems, which offer humans more developed and complex solutions.[7] The gods are not perfect, but they aspire to a more ideal order because their dimensions are without space and time, which offers perspective on human dilemmas. This information was freely available to everyone through storytelling, and it often enabled people to heal themselves. For example, symptoms were a sign from the gods, and the ancients interpreted their messages by reading their own bodies as much as possible. It was a matter of concern if anybody was suffering or unbalanced because this could destabilize Maat, so the strong people looked out for the weaker ones. They knew the gods were acutely sensitive and that their subtle qualities existed only in happy and kind homes. Altars were kept in the home to invite the divine into ordinary reality, and they came to visit.

The Elite stole the perennial wisdom from the people over the past 2,500 years. Yet lately, people who aren't even aware of occult ideas find themselves flooded with rich and arcane memories. Those of us who understand what is happening must have great compassion for those who go into shock. When we first awaken inner memory, our nervous systems reconnect with the planetary mind, and our bodies have to learn how to handle greater flows of energy. Each receiver grounds these forces for the alchemy of the whole. Through a spinning module of biological intelligence, plant and animal species know when it is time to regenerate within an ecological zone, and so do we. Our ecological zone is the collective mind, which is calling us to regenerate. Many gravitate to the experiences needed for growth: When we find a way to be in harmonic resonance with Earth, our bodies, emotions, minds, and souls quicken as our energy fields adjust to the qualities in the planetary mind. As more of us come to terms

Fig. 9.2. Megalithic spirals

with emotional blocks and physical traumas from the past that inhibit growth in the present, free intelligence floods through us into the collective. Reincarnational knowledge connects us to the flow of time, and we participate in the collective mind through great spans of time; this frees the current personality from guilt and judgment.

By traveling back into the past by means of past-life regression, I found that archaic Egyptian, Minoan, and Paleolithic initiates were always guided through their previous lifetimes when they were ready to awaken. Also, their knowledge from the past was used to advance their cultures. This was how they protected the oral traditions, especially after the cataclysm. This was how cultures avoided making the same mistakes over and over again. As a result, certain cultures experience *spiralic evolution,* which is why spirals are so common in megalithic art. As we regain memory, the coils on the spiral thicken, and we become serpentine. We have forgotten this excellent venue of cultural transmission until recently. Cultural continuity will be lost unless we remember who we have already been. We need to lie down on our beds and reweave the time dream.

Past-Life Regression Under Hypnosis

Past-life regression (PLR) is a therapeutic method for recalling our "past lives," and whether these stories are thought of as "real" does not really matter. PLR helps us access the themes of our lives. In a typical regression session, clients are hypnotized, or induced into a light trance, and they are encouraged to go back in time to seek information that might assist them in their current life. Often, by simply remembering key themes in the past, we can experience psychological breakthroughs that stimulate new growth in our current life. Crippling phobias can be eliminated—such as fear of water or heights—by having the client reexperience a drowning or fall in a past life. Sometimes overweight people achieve their normal weight after experiencing a past life when they starved to death. Some clients access lifetimes in which they experience terrifying cataclysms. *PLR significantly reduces catastrophobia* when people get in touch with cataclysmic lifetimes.

PLR emerged during the 1960s out of standard hypnotic therapy and psychological counseling, and now it is widely used by therapists to help clients access deep emotional themes. Beyond receiving symptomatic relief, some clients seek spiritual growth and transformation from PLR sessions. When spiritual growth is the goal, PLR is greatly facilitated by using the concepts of karma and reincarnation, which teach us that we live many lives to work out emotional blocks. We return again and again, guided by our soul's desire to learn, express love, and find spiritual meaning. I've lectured to thousands about reincarnation and karma, and so far the biggest objection to the concept is that people say they hate the idea because *they never want to be born again!* This is why Western culture is ecocidal. Why bother to care for the forests and streams, the animals and insects, and the fertility of the soil if you believe you will not return again to this world? This one-lifetime mentality causes people to destroy the world.

Gregory Paxson of Chicago was my first PLR therapist. Although PLR is a recent practice in our culture, it is actually an ancient and sacred tradition that was used to train adepts for thousands of years. Most people who do PLR sessions report past experiences in the linear space and time context, which surprises people. This is what makes me think there must be a central, time-coded library that contains all our past experiences that anybody can visit at any time. We seem to be souls who create experiences amid collective events, as if being alive is like being in a movie. Since 1999, when the Eighth Underworld opened, computer technology has made it easy to imagine ideas like this. Computer files are organized by linear time based on crystalline clocks that are the essence of this Underworld's resonance. By traveling through various times and experiencing different phases of time acceleration, I encoded the mental-emotional qualities of the fifth, sixth, and seventh underworlds going back 102,000 years. Anyone can reawaken these dormant capacities. PLR is tremendously helpful for clearing your emotional body and going beyond duality, because the therapist is trained to help you see all the aspects around a particular dilemma and seek resolution.

Greg Paxson thinks of memory as a "power of refreshment, of new life in harmonic resonance with the ancient earth of the heart."[8] When we explore this harmonic resonance, we experience ourselves as pure energy, which is what happens when we have a clear, diaphanous emotional body. Realizing that your feelings are the energy field that holds you in physical form is very liberating and expansive. I hardly need mention that millions of meditators attain these levels of awareness day after day. Paxson once said to me that our bodies of consciousness—physical, emotional, mental, and soul—are "holograms of different densities, co-occupying the same physical space, vibrating independently and in harmonic interaction around the reference-frequency of Self." For him, an initiation is when higher energies are received into the person, permanently changing the energy frequency and functioning of that personality—that is, accessing nine dimensions simultaneously. For me, memories are like imagistic musical chords, and when we experience them again, we enrich our current resonant frequency. Accessing our inner memories is like listening to Beethoven's late quartets or Bach's fugues. By feeling past vibratory fields existing deep within our brains, our current nine-dimensional structure tunes up. Like an old violin in the attic that is oiled, restrung, and played again, we become cosmic instruments. To accomplish this, PLR leads the client to experience the body, feelings, thoughts, and spirit aspects of forgotten lifetimes that lurk deep within us, waiting to tell their stories. Paxson discovered that the easiest way to advance a client's consciousness was to have him or her experience past initiations, because those were the previous times that we had advanced our consciousness.

As I relived past initiations, I could feel my current body responding to these activations. Everyone has experienced initiations in the past, since ancient cultures were initiatory; this is how they encouraged personal growth. These initiations are encoded in our bodies, and anyone can relive them. When I went out to interact with my readers, I was amazed to hear them tell me that while reading *The Mind Chronicles,* they experienced their own initiations, which were often the same initiations as mine! Many readers said the shifting vibratory fields fascinated them, and they sometimes went into trance while reading these descriptions. They felt they were being initiated with me, and I am sure they were. I noticed that some people described initiations I had just gone through in PLR sessions with Greg, but I had not yet shared this information with anyone in any form. This is a great example of group alchemy; that is, we must have all been tapping in to the awakening collective mind. This process follows certain laws of progressive levels of attainment that alter the group mind. Eventually I got to the point where all my lifetimes became interactive! My current reality kept changing whenever I removed a block in the past, and finally I fell into a resonant field that is quite remarkable—I can feel myself in simultaneous times: If I make an emotional breakthrough in my current life, it seems to free up blocks in a past life, and when I make a change in a dormant personality, I am freer. No one can free that entity except you; freeing your soul now offers your current state of mind a wider view.

The recovery of PLR in the mid-twentieth century began clearing the collective mind, I'm sure of it! Theologians removed reincarnation from Christian practice 1,600 years ago, and since then the one-lifetime mentality has created a huge glut of unprocessed emotions. Individuals erupt ever more ferociously and irrationally with desperate and violent cries for help because they feel they must get married, have children, succeed at work, and be famous all during one life. They drug themselves, the frustration builds, and like a dam, the weight of the water means it will be breached. These intense inner complexes must be expressed eventually, which is why the initiation process has always been used in healthy cultures. As Paxson puts it:

An existential schizophrenia has evolved in our own society, which is manifested in the inner lives of many of its inhabitants. Judeo-Christian culture is founded on the accounts of men to whom God spoke directly, or through a burning bush, or prophesied through their dreams, and reaches its height of fervence in the Teacher who raised the dead, restored sight to the blind, and, as a climax in a long series of miracles, resurrected himself after death. The binding thread that runs throughout is that there is a higher source and value to our existence than we can perceive by physically objective means. The chasm between these fundamental roots in "the Seen and Unseen" and the realm of scientific, rational knowledge of the tangible world "where we actually live" is broad and deep. This polarity in our minds and bodies has been expanding and intensifying for the last two centuries.[9]

Dancing on Turtle's Back

Many respected scholars, such as Julian Jaynes, have feared that awakening the powers of the dark and light drives people to racism and collective insanity.[10] However, mass movements have polarized cultures by getting people obsessed with great archetypes, such as National Socialism and Aryan Supremacy in Nazi Germany. Many thoughtful people fear that similar forces will possess people if they expand their awareness. Yet I believe we must all awaken and understand how these powers influence our reality. Otherwise someone will always use them again to control humanity and influence people to engage in a collective insanity. The nine-dimensional model is a surprisingly easy way to avoid possession by dark forces, because it can't happen when your consciousness is operative in the solid world. As we've seen, the Global Elite insidiously divide and conquer people and countries by conjuring the dark forces. Once divided, people think of themselves as victims or victimizers—neighbor will kill neighbor, brother will kill brother. *The Elite cannot trigger people into fighting each other if people understand these forces within themselves.* The vast majority of people on the planet participated in the twentieth-century world wars physically and/or emotionally. This has generated a huge collective insanity, which has enabled the Elite to use the world as their military game board. If there had been less emotional involvement in the collective during these insane wars, peace might have been found by now; the general public would recognize the moves by the game masters and put them where they belong—in jail or on the battlefield themselves. We have arrived at a turning point now because many people know that the only winners in wars are the financiers and manufacturers of weapons.

Sages have helped people discover the sweetness of peaceful vibrations within themselves once they clear their own emotional conflicts. Now in the early twenty-first century, the Elite are still trying to whip up the deadly whirlwind of dark and light forces. Yet each person and country that opts out of the game reduces anger, judgment, and hatred. *The world is becoming intelligent about the sources of the conflict.* Many are thinking that the genesis of the Arab/Israeli conflict may be in the unresolved battles between the Fallen Angels that were hidden by Judeo-Christian-Islamic religion. What if the Elite selected Palestine for this atavistic conflict because many participants in this region are still caught in the survival mentality of the Age of Cancer? Possessed by the survival times while praying for the end of time, people fight over the caves and portals to the Underworld like vultures stripping a carcass.

People living outside this field can emote compassion while observing their own participation in their minds with this hot vortex. This region holds the ultimate wounds of humanity; pain soaks the soil. Who would dare visit the sacred sites in Jerusalem without first purifying their emotions? Assuming that the people who are fighting it out there are fed by energy in the collective mind, imagine what could happen if the unresolved emotions coming there from the outside were to vanish. Wouldn't that reduce the charge? After thousands of years of migrations, this whirlwind exists to be processed by the people who live there until peace comes. Harmony arises when each one of us cares for the land where we live. Courageous souls live there who work with this dilemma, and many people are leaving the Middle East because it is not their battleground.

We've seen that Earth once hosted a global maritime civilization that mastered geomancy, resonant forces, astronomy, geography, and community. This world collapsed 11,500 years ago, and the survivors settled around the planet to renew their cultures. They realized that the position of the stars in the sky had changed, and the amount of heat coming from the sun now varied when seasonality began. Very soon hunter-gatherer and horticultural cultures adopted agriculture for survival, and they became less free. In spite of many great changes, these people saved the Elder knowledge, and temples were built everywhere to save these records and to continue the ritual practices. The knowledge that the ancients developed, such as using geometry, sound, and light to contact advanced beings in other dimensions, was critical for balanced life on Earth, and it still is. Many are participating in the massive collective awakening of Earth's intelligence.

Turtle Medicine, the indigenous records of Earth changes discussed in chapter 1, suggests we withdraw our consciousness from the global field temporarily to feel the building intensity of the second dimension in our own geomorphic zones. This process began February 11, 2011, when the people's revolution drove Hosni Mubarek out of Egypt. This revolution awakens our own bodies when we are grounded and triggers astonishing waves of feelings. As our bodies vibrate with the intensified field coming in, our hearts open, and we are flooded with geometrical forms, sound, and light; then we perceive time agendas from higher dimensions that will guide us through our evolutionary leap. We must be home in our own bodies first before we push our consciousness into other places, especially into places as juicy and coded as Palestine or Afghanistan. The memories of the survival times and the Great Angels pull the people there right out of their bodies. The Middle East is the most difficult energy zone on the planet because the Elite have whipped it into a vortex for the massive collective insanity—the end times. In truth, we are like Osiris experiencing a great global dismemberment. The goddess Isis found the parts of Osiris's body and made temples where she found them by the Nile. So, we can put ourselves back together again and be whole. Instead of being torn apart by vultures in the land of duality that will trigger the dark and light until the Holy Land is pacified, we can heal our own pain and move our consciousness into the vertical axis of enlightenment. The divine will live in our peaceful hearts.

The activated fields in Egypt instruct us to plug into Earth where we live. Osiris was the most popular god in Egypt because he modeled dismemberment in life and eternal renewal of the soul. Osiris in his battle with his brother, Seth, is a teacher for facing the dark within and making peace with neglected elements. Seth carries the powers of the second dimension, and now these powers are intensifying, so we must pacify our shadows. These dark vibrations pulse deeply in our bodies and connect us to Earth. When we realize that making peace with them enables us to ascend to spiritual realms, we learn to love the dark. The fetish of Abydos (figure 5.6 on p. 144) was carried through the crowds of people to the temple, because it taught them how the vertical axis forms by the activation of the lower dimensions. They were allowed to see how Earth energies are born out of the lower and deeper dimensions, and how living in the third dimension and praying to the four directions propels our consciousness into contact with the divine. During the festival of Osiris, the common people were allowed to contemplate this most potent path to enlightenment. The ancient Egyptians all knew that their land—Khemet—was sacred, yet this teaching was not just about Egypt. They are located in the geographic center of Earth, and so they are the ideal guides for everyone on Earth to be at home in their own geomorphic zones. It is exciting that they grasped enlightenment in 2011. As was true in ancient Egypt, *Maat can be created today only by the people who make peace in their home.* Osiris was a popular god because he was a male who was made whole by his goddess, his wife. (Isis)

The rest of this book is devoted to a few of my own techniques for establishing Maat; we begin with astrology.

Chiron as the Wounded Healer

Western rationalism has split the tangible and intangible. Our bodies have become so bound in material things that many of us can't feel the subtle vibratory fields. This began to change in November 1977: Mysteriously, a cosmic vehicle for healing this split was sighted by astronomer Charles Kowal at the Pasadena Observatory. He sighted a new planet that orbits the sun between Uranus and Saturn, and he named it Chiron. Whenever a new planet is sighted, a new archetypal field awakens in human consciousness. Astrologers use the planet's name for mythological analysis, so immediately a group of astrologers investigated Chiron's mythology.

Chiron was a centaur (half horse and half human), and in Greek prehistory before 1600 BC he was an astrologer who initiated healers, astrologers, and warriors. The founder of natural medicine and energetic healing, Chiron was a guide for adepts who went out on the alchemical quest.[11] *Chir*—or the Greek form, *Cheir*—means "hand," and it is the root word for many healing modalities, such as chiropractic, chiromancy (divination), the chiral wave (the energy that moves between the hands of healers), and choroid plexus (the deep cranial wave), which should really be *chiroid*. Surgery is *chirurgie* in French as it was in English until the twentieth century, but it is too difficult to pronounce. In historic Greek times, Asclepius claimed Chiron's healing mantle and founded allopathic medicine in 600 BC, which was based on the idea that the doctor heals the patient. Chiron was the founder of natural healing and medicine, which is based on the belief that patients heal themselves. Thus, Chiron's discovery in 1977 heralds the return of subtle-healing modalities in the West, such as the emerging forms of vibrational medicine. The Greeks had forgotten their own past, just as Plato said; so when they came out of their dark age around 600 BC, Asclepius replaced Chiron. This was the beginning of the split between our bodies and minds, which is finally ending.

In the ancient world, Chiron initiated warriors during the survival period, which goes back to the earliest times. More significantly, *Chiron went into its current lopsided orbit when Phaeton smashed through the solar system 11,500 years ago!* That is, *Chiron is the carrier of the cataclysmic archetype.* In the Enuma Elish, which describes the great cataclysm, Phaeton is the same as Marduk, and Marduk pulled Gaga, a moon of Saturn, free from its orbit. Then Gaga assumed its current orbit as Chiron. Allan and Delair agree that Gaga is Chiron, which I'd already concluded myself in 1986 by consulting the key Akkadian Seal—VA/243—and studying the Enuma Elish. VA/243 shows the whole solar system *after* the cataclysm, and the Earth and its moon are clearly represented. Allan and Delair note that the key section of the Ninevah Tablets, the Third Tablet, describes Gaga/Chiron being pulled out of its orbit as a moon of Saturn and then gaining its own orbit.[12] That is, Chiron became a planet during the cataclysm—the Wounded Healer. Chiron was sighted exactly when the body/mind healing movement really got going. Therefore, *Chiron is the planetary archetype for healing catastrophobia!* According to astrology, the planetary archetype that is being born comes during the first orbit of that planet since its sighting. Chiron will complete its first orbit around the sun since its discovery in August 2027. Chiron was the astrologer's astrologer, so many modern astrologers use its guidance for healing purposes.

The body/mind dichotomy in the West began to heal in 1977 when the power of Chiron came in. Psychologists remembered that what goes on in people's *bodies* is relevant to what is going on in their *heads*. Simultaneously, body workers realized that what was going on with people's feelings and thoughts affects their bodies. Suddenly, in the late 1970s, like Humpty Dumpty putting himself back together again, we began rebuilding our fractured wholeness. For the last few hundred years, the body/mind split has been so disturbing that nothing will stop this holistic fusion. Chiron is the Wounded Healer because Hercules shot him with a poisoned arrow. Since Chiron was immortal, he had to reside in his eternally pained body. Chiron wanted to die, so in exchange for his descent into Hades, Zeus freed Prometheus, the fire god who was hanging off a cliff while vultures ate his liver. This legend reaches way back to vulture shamanism during the survival times. By this exchange, Zeus liberated the Promethean creative fires, and the centaur healer died after a long time of great pain. Aren't these still big issues for us now? Millions are trapped in bodies tortured by allopathic medicine. The medical system makes a person feel guilty unless they battle against their inevitable end with chemical and radioactive weapons, and they must even replace worn-out parts in their bodies; people get liver transplants instead of just letting go. *We must regain power over our own bodies to be free.* We must demand the right to choose our time and way of death; we were not born to be fodder for medical systems. Chiron was a classic shaman, who refused to live in pain and misery.

Next we consider the remarkable work of Felicitas Goodman of the Cuyamungue Institute in New Mexico who has brought archaic shamanism back to our world.

The Alternate Reality and Ecstatic Body Postures

Dr. Felicitas Goodman discovered a technique for modern people to access the alternate reality by using sacred body postures. Her discovery is playing a major role in healing the world. Universally, shamans and medicine people understand that they contact an alternate reality that is "the twin of the ordinary secular one, a sacred reality where the spirits dwell."[13] Assuming ritual postures while in trance is a great way for modern people to connect with archaic consciousness because *these same postures were used by shamanic cultures for thousands of years.* Assuming a ritual posture and going into trance is a way archaic shamans met with the spirits and sought information for solving problems. Once she discovered this by accident in 1977 (Chiron's discovery year), Goodman realized that many figurines and representations of figures in rock art around the world "are not simply expressions of creativity, but in fact are ritual instructions."[14] If the posture of one of these artifacts is combined with rhythmic stimulation, "the body temporarily undergoes dramatic neurophysiological changes, and visionary experiences arise that are specific to the particular posture in question."[15] Neurophysiological changes include stress-related hormones in the blood that initially rise and then drop dramatically during the rest of the trance, and blood pressure that drops while the pulse increases. This is what usually happens when you die, which may be why many shamans say that they die in trance. She found that the trance should be maintained for fifteen minutes, and the induction and cessation instructions teach people how to go in and then out of the other world safely.

Goodman has developed the easiest, fastest, safest, and most direct way to enter and leave the alternate reality. While doing PLR work, our psyche selects the past life that can give us the solution for a current dilemma. By selecting the sacred posture we need, our body experiences journeys, cultures, or meetings with animals and spirits that can help us. The postures are a great way to bring in the sages and learn from them because they tap into archaic sacred cultures that worked with the spirits. They are also an ideal way to maintain your constant self-awareness while in ordinary reality. The first dimension is the iron-core crystal, which vibrates at 40–60 cycles per second, and remarkably, while in trance, the brain waves have been measured at *exactly the same frequency! The person in trance is synchronizing with the center of Earth*. Remember, Greg Paxson said that memory is new life in harmonic resonance with the ancient Earth of the heart, as if he too was intuiting the pulse of Earth's center. As far as I can see, the alternate reality just opens up when humans pulse with the planet.

Statues or drawings of the Bear Spirit posture, which is used for healing, have been found at hundreds of sites around the planet; the oldest ones are 8,000 years old. Thirty-four examples were found on the

*Fig. 9.3. The Bear Spirit
posture, from Gore's*
Ecstatic Body Postures

Cyclades alone.[16] Appendix E explores the Paleolithic Bear Clan, which goes back 100,000 years, so the wide spread of the Bear Spirit posture in Holocene times connects it to the Paleolithic. Some postures are more than 30,000 years old, such as that of the Venus of Galgenberg. Paleolithic artifacts indicate that this ritual art form began way before the cataclysm. Using the Venus of Galgenberg posture gives direct access to the precataclysmic mentality. Shamanic cultures retained the postures during the survival period, and they were still being used until the conquerors ended ritual practices. Now Goodman has brought them all back to us. The Cuyamungue Institute is still finding new postures and testing them in groups, and as of 2011, students and teachers can use well over 100 significant postures. The postures access nine different realities: healing, divination, metamorphosis, spirit journeys to the upper or lower worlds, death and rebirth initiations, living myths, and celebration. For example, if you or someone you love is ill, you can assume the Bear Spirit posture or six or seven other healing postures, each of which have special spirits attached to them that are known by the institute's research. If you need to let go of old realities and just allow change to come, you can undertake a metamorphosis posture, such as the Olmec Prince. All the postures are shown and the technique described in *Ecstatic Body Postures,* written by Belinda Gore, who is a psychologist and director of the Cuyamungue Institute.

What is the alternate reality, and why would we want to enter it?

Fig. 9.4. The Empowerment posture, from Gore's Ecstatic Body Postures

Chapters 7 and 8 consider a titanic struggle over human access to ancient wisdom. Because we've forgotten our story, people are obsessed with the end of the world, and they are afflicted with what Goodman calls "ecstasy deprivation."[17] We are cut off from the ancient lineage of spiritual contact that goes back at least 40,000 years when we were gathering hunters, who were in balance and harmony with their environment, the Fifth Underworld time of Eden. We were in balance because we sought the advice of the spirits, which is the same as being able to consult with the sages. As Belinda Gore notes, "It is a powerful lesson to realize that today, when we are at the brink of ecological disaster, it is within our human power to enact rituals that can help bring the natural world back into harmony."[18] The alternate reality where the spirits live is eternally there and available just by assuming a posture and using your body as a magic carpet to enter this nonordinary reality.

Felicitas Goodman noticed that the postures came from only two kinds of societies—either hunting societies or horticulturist. Although pastoralists and agriculuralists have certain poses during religious ceremonies, "they are symbolic, and do not mediate entrance into alternate reality."[19] Changes came in the Early Neolithic period, and as populations increased, people began to control the cycle of plants and regulate their societies more; they lost their sense of unity with the natural world that had characterized their hunter-gathering ancestors. Gore believes people in Neolithic societies refined the postures to restore their connection to the more free life of the past, and Goodman sees this as a system they passed along to us so we can enter the alternate reality. Eventually, large-scale agriculture took over in many places, and control over the natural world dominated. Geologist Andrew Sherratt argues that plate tectonics is why this happened. He shows that agriculture began with three tectonic global bottlenecks—Central America, the Middle East, and the Far East, that is, it merged out of trauma. This would have changed the ritual postures because people had different needs.[20] As Gore puts it, "Duality became the focus in spiritual and secular visioning of the world. . . . The world of ordinary reality and the spirit world were split between good and evil, heaven and hell, above and below, spirit and body, God and Devil."[21] This primal duality splits our emotional bodies and cuts off access to the spirits.

People are starved for the numinous and the ineffable, for shamanic access to other worlds. Modern tribal shamans access these worlds by drug-induced ecstasy, and we know the shamanic Egyptian priests contacted other worlds, since the Pyramid Texts describe ascension to other worlds. During ayahuasca journeys in the Amazon, when the processed plant is ingested that creates psychotropic effects, the women sit with the ayahuasquero shamans and go into the other realms with them. But they do not take the drug, because they "have no need of chemical aid for their spiritual flights."[22] When we take flight while assuming sacred postures, whether we are male or female, we also do not need to use drugs. Amazonian shamans receive specific answers to specific questions in their trances; likewise, the postures are so specific that one can select a certain posture for a specific purpose.

At the Cuyamungue Institute and at other locations where sacred postures are taught, students participate in masked trance dances. A group of fifteen or twenty of us go into sensory deprivation—simple diet, withdrawal from the outside world, praying with the sunrise and sunset, and exhaustion by doing trances and making art all day and into the night—to prepare for a dance of the spirits. To create a dance of the spirits, we must live with them in their world for many days by gradually withdrawing our attention from ordinary reality. We go into trance day after day in specific postures, often divination or metamorphosis, to learn about the story of the dance from the spirits. That is, *the spirits teach us the elements of a dance that we will bring into our world.* We discover which animal, plant, or being each one of us will become in the dance, and for days we learn to become the animal by making a clay mask and using various materials to become our animal from head to toe. When the time for the dance arrives, we no longer conceive of ourselves as humans. A new story for Earth emerges that will be danced, a teaching from the alternate reality for our world. When we've donned our costumes and we understand the form we're creating with the spirits, then it is time to dance in the sacred field. The drummers signal a reality shift by beating the great council drums, and the dance begins. I've danced three times, and each time the story of the dance was happening simultaneously in the ordinary world while we were dancing in the alternate reality. For example, in August 1994, the spirits brought us the dance of the birth of the White Buffalo Calf from Lakota tradition. When we went home after the dance, we read in the newspapers that the sacred White Buffalo Calf was born near Janesville, Wisconsin, exactly while we were dancing! The Lakota say the birth of White Buffalo is a sign of new hope coming to Earth, and it certainly felt like it in New Mexico at the Cuyamungue Institute.

The spirits enter our world if we invite them. The dances of the Cuyamungue Institute, the Egyptian mysteries, art and music, shamanism and meditation are all ways to bring the spirits into our world. Most of the archaic sources illustrated and discussed in this book emerged after the cataclysm, such as Çatal Hüyük, megalithic cultures, and the dynastic Egyptians. We have glimpses into the world before the cataclysm with the Magdalenian cave painters and the Ica Stones. I will always wonder what Earth was like before it was nearly destroyed 11,500 years ago and the axis tilted. If the disaster began the split between the ordinary reality and the alternate reality, then perhaps the spirits enjoy our new complex, emotional experiences. From my experiences in masked trance dances, I've discovered that they find our world is better than ever. If we invite them in and learn their wisdom, our experience with Earth can be peaceful, harmonic, blissful, and much more fun!

According to Carl Johan Calleman, we complete the Mayan Calendar on October 28, 2011, which is when this book appears. For the last few years, many people have been asking me what I think the world will be like when the time accelerations caused by the World Tree are complete, which suggests a completion of evolution itself. I have a few ideas, and I do have a good sense of how I will live in the coming world. Shamanic traveling accesses the World Tree; indigenous cultures have been doing this for at least 50,000 years; we still are. When we visit the World Tree, we go into the roots to enter the Underworld; or we align our bodies with the solid realm by means of the trunk; we visit the higher realms by going into the branches and leaves. In the new world, we will continue to dance with the Tree.

Since the cataclysm, the four seasons are a great gift. The great teaching that came with the tilting axis is that we can use its spiral structure to create reality. Indigenous teachers have instructed people in this art for more than 10,000 years, as I do today. It is simple: The new season begins with the spring equinox north of the equator, and this is all reversed for people living south of the equator, where spring begins in September. With spring's arrival, we carefully select three things we want to create, and we imprint them in our consciousness, and then we get right to work. During summer, we intentionally deepen these creations, and during fall we balance our creations with everything else in our lives. During winter, we go into deep contemplation about the meaning of our work in the whole world. Then it all begins again in the spring. If you adopt this practice, you will be cocreating with the divine, the new way to work in the new world. Meanwhile, in the middle of seasonal manifestation, we can use the new moon each month to plant a new seed that grows through the full moon and then wanes before the next new moon. If you adopt this process, man or woman, you will be a birthing human creating life on Earth. Welcome to the new world beyond time.

EGYPTIAN TIMELINE

- 39,000 to about 9500 BC—The **First Time,** or Zep Tepi, when great mythical sages called the Shemsu Hor ruled Egypt.[1]
- 9500 to about 4000 BC—The **Egyptian Elder Culture exile** in the eastern and western deserts and in the Middle East.[2]
- 5500 to about 3200 BC—The **predynastic archaic period** when the Egyptians reemerged by the Nile, first as the Gerzean culture, who by predynastic times had claimed descent from the Shemsu Hor, the mythic gods and goddesses of the First Time. The tomb of Uadji was built during this period.[3]
- 3150 BC—The **unification** of Upper and Lower Egypt under Menes (who may be Narmer) when the First Time was reestablished by the Nile and continued for 3,000 years.*
- 3150 to 2700 BC—The **Archaic Period,** which encompasses the First and Second dynasties with named pharaohs such as Narmer, Menes, and Djer.
- 2700 to 2200 BC—The **Old Kingdom,** which encompasses the Third through Sixth Dynasties. This is known as the Pyramid Age, when the power of Egypt greatly intensified, whether the pyramids were built during that time or not. Djoser was a famous Third Dynasty pharaoh, who built the pyramid of Saqqara, which was said to have been designed by the great sage Imhotep. Khufu was a famous Fourth Dynasty pharaoh who supposedly built the Great Pyramid. Unas was a famous Fifth Dynasty pharaoh who built a pyramid temple at Saqqara, which is incised with the earliest version

---

*The Dynastic Chronology is the basic standard used by Egyptologists that is derived from Manetho and the King Lists, and the interpretation of events is my own.

of the Pyramid Texts. The Old Kingdom was characterized by the religious practices of the Heliopolitan, Hermopolitan, and Memphite mystery schools, mostly directed from Lower Egypt.

- 2200 to 2000 BC—The **First Intermediate Period,** which encompasses the Seventh through Tenth Dynasties, when royal power declined and there was much anarchy and chaos, when Upper and Lower Egypt divided.

- 2000 to 1750 BC—The **Middle Kingdom,** which encompasses the Eleventh and Twelfth Dynasties, when Egypt was reunified. Thebes became a new capital where the priesthood of the god Amun became a political and theological power that rivaled the Old Kingdom mystery schools.

- 1750 to 1550 BC—The **Second Intermediate Period,** which encompasses the Fourteenth through Seventeenth Dynasties, when unity broke down again when the Hyksos occupied much of Egypt from their kingdom at Avaris in the Delta. This movement of people was probably caused by massive Earth changes in the Middle East.

- 1550 to 1070 BC—The **New Kingdom,** which encompasses the Eighteenth through Twentieth Dynasties, when Egypt carried on organized warfare for the first time in its history. Some call this period the Golden Age of Egypt. Egypt unified again, and because of the previous occupation by the Hyksos, it conquered territories beyond its borders by campaigns in the Middle East. Famous pharaohs were the Tutmosids I–IV, Amenhoteps I–III, Hatshepsut, Akhenaton (who was Amenhotep IV but changed his name), Tutankhamen, and Seti I and his son Ramses the Great. This period was characterized by constant power struggles between the pharaohs and the priesthood of Amun.

- 1070 to 525 BC—The **Third Intermediate Period,** which encompasses the Twenty-first through Twenty-sixth Dynasties, when pharaonic power declined and the Amun priests ruled Egypt from Thebes.

- 525 to 332 BC—The **Late Period,** which encompasses the Twenty-seventh through Thirty-first Dynasties until Alexander the Great conquered Egypt in 322 BC.

EARTH CHANGES DURING THE HOLOCENE EPOCH

"A HOLOCENE SNAPSHOT" BY J. B. DELAIR[1]

Even a cursory glance at the Holocene record shows that, coming after the allegedly glacial 2-million-year-long Pleistocene epoch, its duration has been exceptionally short: only about 11,500 years. This dating and the epoch's brevity are confirmed by field evidence straddling several disciplines. Within this brief period, however, a whole series of profound environmental and climatic changes has occurred in quick succession. Naturalists have coined names to distinguish the different episodes, while prehistorians, studying them from anthropological and social perspectives, have given them other names. Appendix C tabulates these chronologically.

Outstanding among these changes have been globally rising sea levels, oscillating water-tables, fluctuating glaciers and snow-lines, recurrent volcanic and seismic episodes and cycles of desertification. All these have either engendered or resulted from often quite acute climate changes—including monsoonal shifts—with widespread effects on plant and animal life and also human activity. Superficially of great permanence, many existing environmental systems initiated by these changes have been accorded great antiquity, but modern researches tend to demonstrate the opposite: *with few exceptions these systems have been proved to be remarkably youthful and anything but permanent* [italics mine].

Particularly prominent examples are the North Sea, the Saharan and Arabian deserts, the bed of the Persian Gulf, the Indonesian archipelago,

North America's Great Lakes and the Amazon jungle. Indeed, in their present guises, none of these "permanent" geographical features actually predates the Holocene.

The North Sea, resulting from progressive subsidence of its site (40), only achieved its present configuration about 6500 B.C. (41) Before that date, men could walk across continuous dry land from Flamborough Head to western Germany's Elbe estuary. In those days the Isle of Man was still joined to mainland Britain (42), the present Bristol Channel remained land-filled as far West as Westward Ho, and Cardigan Bay's western coast followed a nearly straight North-South line from western Anglesey to the furthest extremity of the Pembroke peninsula. (43)

A network of river channels on the sea floor between Sumatra, Java, and Borneo (44) and other Indonesian islands (45), many of them submerged extensions of the rivers still active on those islands, testify with drowned offshore peats and undisturbed tree stumps (46) to the extreme geological recency of a crustal subsidence and marine invasion of huge tracts of Southeast Asia (47) around 8000 B.C.

Generally coeval analogous effects also separated northern Australia from the island of New Guinea (48, 49, 50), while the slightly earlier drowning of the territory now submerged between eastern New Guinea and Melanesia (Bismarck Archipelago and the Solomon Islands) and extending northwards to neighboring Micronesia (now mostly represented by the Caroline Islands) is part of the same story. (51) Not surprisingly, marked sea level changes accompanied these developments in French Polynesia (52) and as far eastwards as the Society and Tuamotu Islands. (53) The disappearance of so much continuous terrain (collectively almost as extensive as Australia) represents a land loss of continental dimensions.

Similar changes involved the separation of Sri Lanka (Ceylon) from mainland India approximately 9,000 years ago (54) and, perhaps a little before then, the drowning of much land now occupied by the Persian Gulf (55, 56), as well as of the Atlantic Coast of Canada's Maritime provinces. (57)

In geological parlance the terms "Holocene" and "postglacial" are essentially interchangeable. It is significant that, more or less coevally with the aforenoted crustal subsidences, "post-glacial" uplifts of the lithosphere occurred in North America (58, 59), Scandinavia (60, 61)—including the Gulf of Bothnia (62)—and northern Estonia (63, 64), to list just four examples.

Of these, the Scandinavian uplift in particular was uneven and apparently quite abrupt, insofar as huge portions of Earth's crust supporting large lakes were, especially in Norway and Sweden, heaved up *en bloc.* Otherwise undisturbed, the lakes were brought to rest with differently-tilted shorelines. (65, 66) The exact positions of the pre-tilt shorelines are clearly visible on the adjacent hillsides. Several millennia later, many of the great Alpine lakes were also tilted, but, in their case, on two separate occasions. (67) Lake-village communities grouped around these lakes were severely disrupted by these events.

Still further South, far away in upland Peru and Bolivia, tilted strand lines noted for extraordinary "freshness" (68) were left on the flanks of the Andes by a formerly much greater and deeper Lake Titicaca. Interestingly, Titicaca's water level has fluctuated quite markedly several times during the past 7,500 years (69) and even today it submerges the impressive ruins of cyclopean stone structures made by some ancient, now forgotten, civilisation.

With tectonic (crustal) movements of this magnitude, it is hardly surprising that the sole egress of the waters of North America's Lake Michigan was, until some 10,000 years ago, the Mississippi River (figure B.1). Following a temporary coalescence of the waters of the Great Lakes some 8,000 years ago, when they formed super-lake Algonquin, the seawards flow of Michigan's waters was along a now defunct channel known as the Ottawa Outlet. A further 4,000 years elapsed before the Great Lakes began to assume their modern outlines and Michigan's waters reached the sea by their present route—Lakes Huron, Erie, and Ottawa, Niagara Falls, and the St. Lawrence River. (70) Niagara Falls, incidentally, are actually little more than 5,000 years old (71, 72), no older than Sargon-of-Agade's unification of the early Mesopotamian kingdoms of Sumer and Akkad! (73, 74)

These crustal and lake changes inevitably affected local hydrographies. Among other effects, the Alpine tilts diverted the original courses of Tyrolean rivers (75), damned others to produce new waterfalls as at Jajce in Bosnia (76), or altered Holocene water-tables at innumerable localities, causing rechannelling or draining of countless rivers and minor streams. Of these we may note the hydrographic changes in Zambia's Kafue valley (77), the extinct waterways of the English fens (78, 79, 80), a now dry former channel of the River Lea near Wheathampstead, Hertfordshire (81), and the successive changes in the course of China's mighty Yellow River, some of which relocated large sections almost 100 miles from their previous route. (82, 83)

These hydrological changes had widespread repercussions. In many instances—including inland Australia (84, 85), Africa's Namibian (86) and Kalahari (87) areas, Syria (88), Arabia (89, 90, 91, 92, 93) and

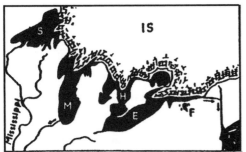

The ancestors of Lakes Superior, Michigan, Erie, and Huron forming at the southern edge of the Laurentian ice sheet about 10,000 years ago. Lakes Michigan and Superior drained into the Mississippi River and Lakes Huron and Erie into the Hudson River.

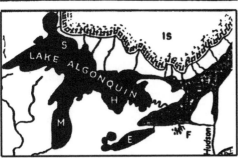

Lake Algonquin in its heyday about 8,000 years ago, formed by the meltwater of the retreating Larentian ice sheet and emptying into the swollen St. Lawrence seaway. Lake Erie had become separated from Lake Algonquin though it also drained into the St. Lawrence valley.

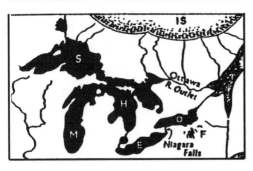

The Great Lakes began to assume their present outlines about 4,000 years ago, as the ice sheet retreated still farther and Lake Algonquin diminished in size. The upper lakes still drained into the St. Lawrence seaway, though via the Ottawa River valley. Lake Ontario and Niagara Falls had formed by this stage.

Fig. B.1. Lake Algonquin and the Great Lakes
(E=L. Erie, F=Finger Lakes of New York, H=L. Huron, IS=Ice Sheet, M=Lake Michigan, S=L. Superior, O=L. Ontario)

virtually the whole of the Sahara—entire, often extensive, lake and river systems disappeared.

The immense size of some of these networks was highlighted in 1981 when ground-penetrating radar sweeps of the Sahara by the Columbia Space Shuttle "discovered" several of them buried just below the desiccated surfaces of southern Libya and western Egypt. (94) Similar defunct systems had been found earlier in the western Sahara (95) and were traced in the desert's central region as far back as the 1920s. (96)

Elsewhere, as with the bygone sources of various still extant rivers such as the Nile, tributaries shrank, reversed their direction of flow, or altogether ceased supplying the original parent rivers. (97, 98)

Lakes as large as the huge freshwater one occupying Egypt's celebrated Fayum vanished only around the close of Neolithic times. (99) Unfossilised remnants of modern animals and plants congregated in the beds of these extinct lakes and rivers reveal the equally recent demise of the organic life sustained by these lost hydrological systems. They show that, just a short geological time ago within our own (Holocene) epoch, large areas of these now desert regions hosted thriving fauna and flora. Even as late as 4000 B.C., woods still flourished in now dehydrated areas of the Sudan (100), the Nubian sector of which has had no continuous rainfall since about 3500 B.C. (101)

Before then, in Neolithic (middle Holocene) times, the (currently bare) Red Sea Hills were well wooded and irrigated by rivers—now nearly all dry—well stocked with fish. Several distinct predynastic Egyptian cultures successfully availed themselves of those conditions. (102) As now known to us, much of the Saharan desert regime dates from only around the astonishingly recent datum of 5,000 years ago. (103) The desertification process developed unevenly, since a few oaks and cedars, which formerly dominated many Saharan districts, contrived to survive in small isolated pockets, e.g., south of El Daba, in Egypt's Qattara Depression as late as 500 B.C. (104)

To the East, a similar story unfolds in Arabia where, in middle Holocene times, vanished civilised peoples utilised the once active river and lake networks in the peninsula's currently parched "Empty Quarter" and environs. (105, 106)

These developments were unquestionably connected with a northwards pan-Asian shift of the early Holocene's monsoon belt (107) about 5000 B.C., before it slowly returned to its present latitude in late-Atlantic times or by 3500 B.C. Of particular interest is the sensitivity of the monsoon system to orbital changes. (108) As already noted, the Earth's rotational speed varies and its orbit is eccentric. All these factors are inextricably linked.

While extensive early Holocene desertification was seriously affecting contemporary vegetation in the Old World, quite different developments occurred in the New.

Earth's largest rain forest fills South America's Amazon basin. Modern studies of fossil pollen there reveal that, until very recently, large areas of the forest were occupied by typical savannah flora and that the similarities of the plants in the still extant but widely sundered patches of savannah actually demand a former continuous contact between them. (109, 110) This conclusion parallels that of ornithologists investigating Amazonian bird speciation (111), herpetologists investigating lizard evolution (112), and archaeo-ethnological studies across the region. (113)

This environmental change appears to have proceeded in stages. Radiocarbon dates of masses of fallen subfossil timber underlying today's rain forest, examined at several widely separated localities, show that, generally speaking, three main episodes of sudden change have occurred, involving destructive violent flooding quite unlike the region's present seasonal flooding. (114, 115) These arose around 8000 B.C., 5200 B.C. and 3600 B.C. (116) Before those dates, the Brazilian rain forest, as we know it, with its extensions into lowland Venezuela, Colombia, Peru, and Bolivia, simply did not exist. This "snapshot" of the Holocene does no more than highlight the remarkable geological modernity of many of the world's most celebrated natural features and indicates dates for when at least some began life.

[J. B. Delair's notes for this article are included in the notes section for those who wish to consult them.]

APPENDIX C. HOLOCENE CHRONOLOGICAL HIGHLIGHTS[1]

Dates BC	BIOGEOGRAPHICAL Episodes	BIOGEOGRAPHICAL Significant Events	Egypt/Nubia	Levant	Mesopotamia/Iran	India
c. 687		• Acute meteorological upsets			Sennacherib's army destroyed	
c. 1000	**SubAtlantic**					
c. 1630		• Thera (Santorini) erupts				Indus Valley civilization ends
c. 1700	**Transitional**		**NEW KINGDOM** Dynasties VII–onward			
c. 2300						
c. 2500			**OLD KINGDOM** Dynasties III–VI		Ur-Larsa Akkadian	Apogee of Indus Valley civilization
c. 3000		• Niagara Falls begin life	**EARLY DYNASTIC** Dynasties I–II		Early Dynastic I–III Jemdet Nasr	
c. 3500		• Asian monsoon belt shifts back to the South	Nagadian Gerzean / Pre-dynastic	Chalcolithic	Late Uruk	
c. 3600	**SubBoreal**	• Catastrophic land floods in lowland South America		Chassulian	Early Urrk	
c. 4000		• Scandinavian lake beds tilted/Woods still flourish in Nubia	Amratian			
c. 5000		• Saharan/Arabian deserts assume modern images	Badarian / Late Fayum	Jericho (*level viii*)	Late Ubaid	
c. 5250		• Asian monsoon belt shifts northward	Early Faylum		Ubaid	Indus Valley civilization begins

IRON AGE BRONZE AGE NEOLITHIC

Date	Climate	Global events		Mesopotamia / Near East
c. 5400–	Atlantic	• Brazilian rain forests assume present form		Ubaid (*Eridu*)
c. 6000–		• Saharan/Arabian/Australian lakes/rivers begin to dry up		
c. 6500–		• Britian severed from mainland Europe		Khuzistan
c. 7000–		• Sri Lanka severed from South India	QUARUNIAN	Jamo
c. 7500–	Boreal	• General retreat of glaciers/snowfields	TASIAN	
c. 8000–		• Indonesian archipelago forms		
c. 8200–		• Catastrophic floods in lowland South America		
c. 8300–	PreBoreal	• Australia/New Guinea/Melanesia become islands		Jericho (*level i*)
c. 8600–		• Apogee of "Little Ice Age"		Zawi-Chemi & Karim Shahir
c. 8700–				Natufian
c. 9000–		• Slow sea level rise begins globally		Ali Kosh
c. 9400–	Younger Dryas	• Glaciers/snowfields form on most elevated areas		Mallaha
c. 9500–		• Sea level much lower than now		Shanidar cave dwellers
c. 9550–	Pleistocene		—Global Disruption—	

NEOLITHIC MESOLITHIC PALEOLITHIC

APPENDIX D

REFLECTIONS ON EARTH'S TILTING AXIS

J. B. Delair's thoughts about why Earth's axis must have tilted 11,500 years ago from his recent "Planet in Crisis" article are next.[1] I also describe Alexander Marshack's research on Paleolithic and Neolithic bone markings as well as some very avant-garde Neolithic astronomical research by a few other scholars. This material could have been a whole chapter, but I chose to put it in an appendix because of its highly technical nature and because axial tilt theory is a working hypothesis that I have by no means proven. We begin with J. B. Delair.

"The most immediately striking image of the Earth is that it rotates on an axis inclined at 23½ degrees from the vertical. Its orbit is not a perfect circle and it is not strictly concentric with the Sun. The axial tilt accounts for the variation in daylight hours per day between different parts of the world through the year. Combined with the Earth's eccentric year-long revolution around the Sun, the tilt accounts for the seasons and the difference between the average summer temperature North and South of the equator. Earth's axis of rotation does not coincide with its magnetic axis. This is also apparently connected with Earth's variable rotation, which fluctuates over a 10-year period. (28, 29)

"While following its orbit, Earth also oscillates cyclically: the 'Chandler Wobble,' with a cycle of 14 months. (30, 31, 32) This wobble is also associated with viscosity at the Earth's Core (33), so it is an intimate part of Earth's present internal mechanism.

"Because the Earth ought, theoretically, to rotate on a vertical axis and may actually have done so in the geologically recent past (34, 35), *these details suggest a planet which, in not very remote times, has been seriously disturbed.* [italics mine] If true, these 'ill-fitting terrestrial cogs' [i.e., Earth's inner core rotates significantly faster than the rest of the planet], which appear to function only through the presence and action of inner-Earth viscosity, may be regarded as abnormalities.

"Yet a number of these features, including axial inclinations and eccentric orbital paths, are shared by several of Earth's planetary neighbors, so are the terrestrial equivalents really 'normal' ones? The evidence suggests otherwise. A selection of this evidence and its pan-solar ramifications, has been discussed by Allan and Delair (36) [and further considered in the main text of this book, especially chapter 2].

"*There ought to be no reason why any Earth-like planet undisturbed for untold ages should not have a vertically positioned axis.* [italics mine] This would unify the locations of the geographical and magnetic poles, ensure equal daylight hours in all latitudes and virtually eliminate the seasons. There would be no necessity for various subcrustal layers to function differentially and the present rheological mechanism would not be required. However, an equatorial bulge would remain as an essential stabilising feature and the retention of a non-circular and non-concentric orbit would probably still cause small 'seasonal' climatic differences when Earth was nearer or further from the Sun."

What follows next in "Planet in Crisis" is a few comments about the implications of these abnormalities, and then Delair describes the Holocene Earth changes in detail, which is in appendix B. He notes that these relatively recent global Earth changes must be the result of other forces operating deep within Earth, and he speculates on the "cause or causes of the Holocene cluster of catastrophes" in this section, which is titled "Rupture."

"Earth's essential instability, as mirrored by its structural and behavioral 'abnormalities' must reflect some persistent internal imbalance not yet fully accounted for. However we have already seen that the boundary of the solid Mantle with the liquid outer Core is irregular, perhaps to the point of being topographic (119), and that the outer surface of the solid inner Core is also not smooth. (120) Indeed, it is uncertain whether the inner Core is actually spherical: as it moves within the viscous medium of the outer Core it need not necessarily be. A non-spherical or irregularly surfaced inner Core would, however, generate further instabilities.

"Given these details and the inner Core's higher rotational speed [400 or 500 years for one complete turn by the inner core!], its surface irregularities must be in continuously varying opposition to those of the slower moving Mantle's inner boundary. The plastic material of the intervening outer Core must therefore undergo displacement as the distances between the opposing irregularities alter. Continuous compression and release of this material must occur as the outcome of such differential rotation. Inner Earth movements of this kind are now being investigated deductively. (121)

"It is not unreasonable to infer that peaks of acute outer Core compression and troughs of compensatory relaxation should alternately develop to differing subsurface intensities at different times in different hemispheres. Likely results, which could sometimes arise quite suddenly, would include events that have often been termed mid-Holocene catastrophes. Lithospheric adjustments such as the Scandinavian, Alpine and South American lake tilts, extensive regional subsidences such as the Indonesian/Australasia/Melanesian area [see appendix B], large-scale water table changes as in the Arabian and Saharan regions and earthquakes and severe vulcanism, such as the Santorini eruption and its widespread aftermath effects (122), are typical examples. There is also no doubt that large earthquakes such as at one time racked the Roman Empire are closely associated with the Chandler Wobble (123, 124), itself intimately connected with viscosity activity at the Earth's core. (125)

"Why does the inner Core rotate faster than the rest of the planet and why doesn't the inclination of its axis coincide with that of Earth as a whole (cf. the different locations of the geographic and magnetic poles)? *It strains credulity to suppose that any Earth-like planet, undisturbed by external influences for millions of years, could have naturally acquired, unaided, a tilted axis, an offset magnetic field, variable rotation, or a Chandler Wobble.* [italics mine]

"Most geoscientists who have studied this broadly agree that any event or series of events resulting in characteristics as profound as these would almost certainly have to involve some influential outside agency. In other words Earth would need to be subjected to some powerful extraterrestrial force—a force severe enough to rupture its previous internal mechanism without actually destroying it.

"Down the centuries precisely such a source has been repeatedly advocated to account for traditionally catastrophic events like Noah's Deluge, the loss of a primaeval Golden Age, the advent and also the demise of the Ice Age, the sudden refrigeration of the Siberian/Alaskan mammoth fauna and even the foundering of legendary realms such as Atlantis, Lyonesse, etc. (126–135)"

Next the article discusses the main catastrophic scenario, which is already synthesized in my main text, and advances these events as the cause of Earth's abnormalities, such as the axial tilt.

"After apparently adversely affecting many of the Sun's outer planets, the postulated cosmic visitor was seemingly able to temporarily retard the rotation of Earth's Mantle and lithosphere but could not halt the rotation of the inner Core, due to the viscosity of the outer Core. As a consequence of this disruption, Earth's thermal and electromagnetic levels increased enormously, with all kinds of unwelcome effects. Among these appear to have been an *axial slewing of the Mantle and crust to an inclination differing from that of the solid inner Core.* [italics mine] Indeed, the latter may itself have been wrenched, gravitationally, within the liquid outer Core to an off-centre position, causing the Earth to yaw or tremble (or both), as some traditions recalling the events actually state. Such movements were *only* possible because of the viscosity of the outer Core. It is also probable that the cosmic assailant pulled the entire Earth over to its present inclination, since any former *normal* planetary regime *must* have developed over a more vertical axis.

"The resumed rotation of the Mantle/Lithosphere around a still rotating but slight off-centre inner Core (the liquid outer Core is immaterial at this point) at different speeds round different axes (the geographical and magnetic poles) imposed huge strains and stresses on the Earth. Prominent were fluctuating rotation and the Chandler Wobble. An off-centre Core would ensure only a very slow and stuttering return to planetary normality, punctuated sporadically by catastrophic terrestrial adjustments. Holocene history is littered with these. While often alarming, they are really the coughs and wheezes of a world still in crisis."

Catastrophobia is my name for a psychological syndrome resulting from great Earth changes over 14,000 years. This book explores the possibility that we can heal this syndrome by remembering the original events as well as the brave struggles of Holocene people. The memories of these catastrophes were saved because the people knew their descendants—us—would need this information to be able to achieve the next stage of our evolution. Recently, some amazing new theories about ancient astronomy have been advanced that highlight how Holocene humanity came to terms with the new Earth. I cover some of these new ideas briefly, since they may be fertile ground for others who want to consider whether Earth's axis may have tilted recently and made life on Earth into a whole new ball game.

Leaders in the space program asked science writer Alexander Marshack in 1962 to cowrite a book to explain how humanity had reached the point of planning the first moon landing. When Marshack interviewed many of the key movers and shakers in the space program, he realized none of them knew *why* we were going into space; all that mattered was they had the skills to do it. He was supposed to write a few pages on the dawn of civilization and how the development of mathematics, astronomy, and science leads up to entering space. He studied the orthodox interpretation of our historical emergence and ran right into all the "suddenlies" that begin 5,000 years ago, such as the instant-flowering model of Egyptian civilization.[2] He went back into Paleolithic cultures, and then he had the big awakening that changed his whole life, as well as our current understanding of Paleolithic and Neolithic science: Marshack discovered he could read and decode the markings by early humans on ancient bones. Ironically, he was working on a project that was to explain how we could get to the moon, yet he discovered that Paleolithic carved bones are lunar calendars! Eventually he became intrigued by the fact that from the earliest times until 9000 BC, the bones are lunar calendars; then about 11,000 years ago, the solar factor is added to the lunar notations. The soli-lunar phases are divided into six-month phases, which are either equinoxes or solstices.[3] *Marshack's research and the research of many other paleoscientists indicates that early humans show no signs of being aware of the existence of the four seasons until 11,000 years ago.* I think it is unrealistic to surmise they just didn't notice the sun traveling back and forth on the horizon and the changing seasons, especially since they suddenly became obsessed with this factor approximately 11,000 years ago.

Marshack's laborious decodings of the bone markings as lunar calendars from before 11,000 years ago have been widely accepted over the past forty years by most prehistorians.[4] Eventually, he focused on the fact that the bone notations were lunar calendars until the end of the Paleolithic, and then the seasonal factor appears 11,000 years ago. He spent twenty years trying to decipher the marking of a plaque found in 1969 at the Grotte du Tai that is 10,000 to 11,000 years old because it has the typical lunar cycles with some new elements. Marshack decoded it by his knowledge of Upper Paleolithic notations and art combined with the art and notations of Neolithic preliterate cultures. This plaque is one of the earliest and most complex scientific Early Neolithic objects, and it probably is one of the first objects that records attempts by humans to show that there are about six lunar cycles between the solstices and equinoxes.[5] Anthropologist Richard Rudgley notes that the Tai notation fills the vacuum "before the apparently sudden development of astronomical observations in the Neolithic period in north-western Europe, epitomized by alignment of megalithic monuments, such as Stonehenge."[6] Regarding Early Neolithic astronomical notations, what strikes me the most is Çatal Hüyük wall art, complex geometrical Natufian designs, and the incised spirals and chevrons of New Grange, which show the year divided into the light and dark halves with the phases of the moon deliniated.[7]

We have only barely begun to realize how advanced Neolithic astronomy was because we only now are deciphering their monuments, notations, and artifacts. It is very hard for us to take their obsession with the sky seriously because we can barely see the night sky in our modern cities. A great change is evident in Neolithic renditions of the sky, which I believe was caused by the tilting axis that introduced the equinoxes and the solstices. Maybe now we can see what was right under our noses because our own perspective is expanding. For example, Robert Temple, in *The Crystal Sun,* definitively proves people have been using telescopes and lenses for improving eyesight for thousands of years. Many of these lenses have been on view in museums all over the world for hundreds of years, but nobody could see what they were for.[8] In *Thoth,* Ralph Ellis argues convincingly that Avebury Circle is a representation of Earth floating in space that *exhibits Earth's axial tilt!*[9] These diagrams and text by Ellis need to be studied by interested readers. In the 1980s, I noticed that the north/south avenues coming into Avebury tilt about 23 degrees to the east/west avenues, and I wondered why. Why would they go to so much trouble to model Earth in space tilted in its solar orbit? Temples were teaching centers in those days, so probably people were being instructed about axial tilt. Megalithic astronomy exhibits a virtual obsession with the solstices and equinoxes. For example, New Grange captures the first light of the winter solstice when the sun sends daggers of light deep into its chambers that illuminate the centers of complex spirals. Many other megalithic chambers capture the light at the exact moment of the spring or fall equinox. Even the center of the Vatican is constructed to capture the spring equinox light, which I noticed when I visited the Vatican in 1979.

In *Uriel's Machine,* Christopher Knight and Robert Lomas argue that early cultures went to almost unbelievable lengths to comprehend, record, and anticipate light from the sun and also Venus. They show that the shapes of various lozenges depicted on Neolithic Grooved Ware pottery and incised stone balls actually convey astronomical information. The shape of the lozenges created by sunrise and sunset through the year changes with latitude, which suggests these lozenges depict the latitude of the makers![10] Suddenly latitude became important because the solar angles by season change so dramatically in the northern latitudes. The ideas in *Uriel's Machine* need much testing, and their conclusions about the megalithic stone chamber Bryn Celli Ddu on the Isle of Anglesey (3500 BC) have attracted serious attention. Using archaeoastronomy, Bryn Celli Ddu is a sophisticated chamber that was used to correct the time drift in solar and lunar calendars by calibrating the time of year by the eight-year Venus synodic return cycle with the winter solstice. Venus shines a bright dagger of light every eighth year into the chamber at Bryn Celli Ddu when it is the brightest. According to the Roman historian Tacitus, this was when the goddess appeared, and since Venus is the most accurate indicator of the time of the year, what does time have to do with the goddess?[11]

In *The Dawn of Astronomy* Sir J. Norman Lockyer reported in his exhaustive study of the star temples of ancient Egypt that various temples are aligned to certain key stars as far back as 6400 BC (see chapter 3). He also demonstrated that the "apertures in the pylons and separating walls of Egyptian temples exactly represent the diaphragms in the modern telescope," and comments that they "knew nothing about telescopes."[12] Robert Temple has subsequently demonstrated that the ancient Egyptians *did* have telescopes, so perhaps their temples were used like the large telescopes in modern observatories.[13] Regarding this book's cover showing an ancient astronomer clearly using a telescope, it would seem telescopes were in use many thousands of years ago.

I bring together these related details here because I believe that *the tilting axis inspired a preliterate scientific revolution* that we are now decoding. Axial tilt would have changed the way we receive light on Earth. When Alexander Marshack looked for the reason modern humanity could get to the moon, he discovered that archaic people were already profoundly in touch with the moon. A way beyond catastrophobia is to awaken archaic intelligence, which is encoded in the Light itself; the Light is infused with cosmic information. Modern science has discovered that photons carry cosmic information. Megalithic astronomy suggests that the Light is more potent and transmutative for humans during the equinoxes, solstices, and the new and full moons. Perhaps they awakened cosmic intelligence by intentionally attuning their consciousness during certain cycles. A new evolutionary form began when the tilting axis cracked Earth open, as if Earth is a cosmic egg ready to hatch in the universe. And now our species is waking up to cosmic intelligence.

THE PALEOLITHIC REVOLUTION AND THE FIFTH UNDERWORLD

The purpose of this appendix is to investigate the 102,000-year-long Fifth Underworld of the Mayan Calendar, as defined by Carl Johan Calleman.[1] I have lightly added Calleman's Mayan Calendar hypothesis to the text of this revision, and this appendix offers a deeper reflection on his idea. I discovered Calleman's research in 2004 after the initial edition of this book came out, when I found that his work adds significant new insight to this book's exploration of our planet mostly over 20,000 years. For example, a central thesis of *Awakening the Planetary Mind* is that a great dichotomy in human evolution was caused by the cataclysms 14,000 to 11,500 years ago. Before these events, we lived in Eden, a Golden World that we still long for today. Then Earth's axis tilted 11,500 years ago, and we've become very confused about what happened to us. Calleman's 102,000-year-long Fifth Underworld *is* this Golden World, and viewing its developmental stages is a great way to lift the thick curtain on the Paleolithic of the last 100,000 years. Also, Calleman's Days and Nights of the Fifth Underworld bring us some ideas about *why* the great cataclysms occurred. Previous to this approach, one might argue that destruction has to occur as well as new creation. Yes, that is true, but we seek better answers. Many religions preach that the Flood occurred because a vengeful god punished humankind for its sins—Original Sin—an idea that we can now see leads directly to waiting for an apocalypse. This appendix uses Calleman's idea of the Seven Days and Six Nights in his Calendar analysis to find the themes of our growth over 100,000 years, the first period when our species is recognizably like us. When we investigate the Regional Night Six—15,800 to 7,900 years ago—we have a better reason for why our planet and our species have suffered. The Regional is the Fifth Underworld.

Calleman's Calendar analysis adds significant new insights to my previous understanding of the last 100,000 years. When you adopt the Days and the Nights as a directive and thematic tool, you'll see that the archaeological and anthropological finds of the last 100,000 years fit into a very distinctive pattern. This enables us to better imagine what our close forebears were really like, and it yields remarkable insight about what we've apparently lost—a scientifically advanced global culture that was in harmony with nature. This essay is not meant to be comprehensive in covering the rare Paleolithic finds because it would be too long. I encourage you to dig into some of my sources for this appendix, because they are a gold mine.

Before getting into dates and details, it is helpful to start with Calleman's belief that our planet is completing nine time accelerations or Nine Underworlds that began *16.4 billion years ago.* Each new Underworld is characterized by a radical speed-up in evolution, and each one is twenty times shorter than the previous one. So, by the time we get to the Fifth, the span is 102,000 years, which occurs during the final one-twentieth of the 2-million-year-long Fourth Underworld of hominid evolution. Hominids moved along slowly and steadily while chipping their tools for a few million years. Then as of 160,000 years ago, biological evolution was complete, and our next advance was *emotional.* This next step came 102,000 years ago with the Fifth Underworld when we suddenly see that Neanderthal has feelings and a sense of the soul, expressed in their burial rites. Later, Cro-Magnon comes along, which will be discussed, but we need to begin with the awareness that there was a significant *cultural* shift mostly accomplished by Neanderthals that moved everything at a much faster pace after the long, slow phase of tool-making humans.

Who was Neanderthal? Neanderthal has been treated very badly until very recently, while Cro-Magnon man has been thought of as the reason we are so developed today. First of all, judging by how we care for the planet, how developed are we really at this time? If we conceive of our lost ancestor so negatively, we lose the fact that we are derived from *both* Neanderthal and Cro-Magnon. Going back through 102,000 years, 70 percent of the development is Neanderthal and 30 percent is Cro-Magnon: Cro-Magnon appeared around 40,000 years ago and then bred with Neanderthal until 25,000 years ago. A Cro-Magnon-Neanderthal hybrid skull that is 35,000 to 40,000 years old was found in Pestera cu Oase Cave in Romania.[2] The most recent hybrid finding is a four-year-old boy dated to 24,000 years ago unearthed in 1999 in Portugal.[3] Until very recently, anybody who suggested that modern humans carry Neanderthal genes was kicked out of the university, but now the Swedish biologist Svante Pääbo has proven that modern humans carry Neanderthal genes.[4] If you have wild red hair, are from the Levant, are significantly left-handed, psychic, or have a heavy ridge above your eyes, you probably have some Neanderthal genes. Neanderthal's cranium was 1,600 cc, and modern human's is 1,360 cc, so Neanderthal's brain was larger. He had a huge *cerebellum,* the protrusion at the back of the skull that is the source of being psychic. I could go on and on about him, but now it is time to examine his culture by using the laws of the Fifth Underworld. Using this method enables us to spot the significant shift 100,000 years ago and then trace its development. Remember, all the advances until about 40,000 years ago are Neanderthal.

Figure E.1 is a pyramid that indicates the dates for the Seven Days and Six Nights of the Fifth Underworld, the Regional Underworld. Looking at the figure, the First Day (*sowing*) is dated as 100,700 BC. Each one of the Days and Nights is about 7,900 years, and the pyramid progresses up to the midpoint in the Fourth Day—49,350 BC. The qualities of each Day are described as cycles of growth—*sowing, germination, sprouting, proliferation, budding, flowering,* and *fruition*—and the Nights are periods when major advances are being assimilated and processed. All Nine Underworlds have these stages, each one is shorter and spans less time than the previous, and all nine of them culminate simultaneously on October 28, 2011. This may seem to be an exceedingly wild idea; however, the Maya actually said this about the nine

Underworlds in AD 700 on an inscription—the *Tortuguero Monument 6*.[5]

The 2011 edition of this book will be in your hands when this culmination is occurring, and of course we shall see what it is like. This simultaneous completion is expected to be a global revelation of our long climb from cosmic creation and single-celled animals.[6] As things culminate, knowing what we've been and come from will help us dive into all the work ahead of us on Earth. The Fifth Underworld climb is the most significant one for us now because this was when we became spiritual and emotional beings, the faculties that were reduced during the cataclysms. We will use this pyramid to slot in significant archaeological finds that show the progression of cultural time acceleration during the last 100,000 years. Remember that in light of the ferocity of the cataclysms, *any* discoveries from long ago are very significant.

Going back 102,000 years to the opening of Day One (*sowing*), suddenly large-scale red ochre mines and quarries were established in southern Africa. Red ochre is a red pigment that was used by Neanderthals to bury the dead. Bodies, sacred objects, and grave pits were painted with it because it symbolizes the blood of the mother, the life of Earth, which

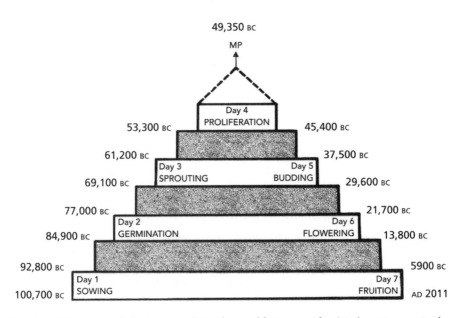

Fig. E.1. The Days of the Regional Underworld. From Clow's The Mayan Code.

is the *first usage of symbolism*. The use of red ochre appeared 100,000 years ago globally—the foundation of early mining and trade. You may be thinking I am talking about little pits in the earth. No, a million kilos of ore were removed from one of the largest sites, and at another site a half-million stone-digging tools were found. In all cases the mines were painstakingly refilled, and the Neanderthal researcher Stan Gooch points out that the Swazi do the same thing today to placate the spirits.[7] In other words, Neanderthal cared for the Earth. So, the Day One innovation was a global system of obtaining red ochre for the sacred burial of loved ones.

A young Neanderthal man was buried in central Asia 100,000 years ago and his remains were encircled by goat horns.[8] This suggests they had a sense of the soul, because they felt connected to and honored their loved ones when they passed. Of course, the next question would be, how did they quantify or measure this ore? Colin Wilson believes that the *"disque en calcaire"* found at the LaQuina Neanderthal site in southwestern France indicates that its maker 100,000 years ago was measuring by the same system as Alexander Thom's megalithic yard! Colin Wilson comments that A. E. Berriman has successfully argued in *Historical Metrology* that ancient measurements are evidence for a Neanderthal *ur*-civilization.[9]

Following Day One, Night One would have been a phase of integration of this great shift in consciousness. Day Two (*germination*) opened in 84,900 BC. The Bear Femur Flute was discovered in 1995 in the cave of Divje Babe near Cerkno in Slovenia, and was dated to 82,000 years ago.[10] Recently, this date has been called into question, but I've decided to include it because the electron spin resonance dates on bear teeth found in the same level as the flute are this old. The Paleolithic Bear Clan is one of the oldest clans on Earth. We see it emerging all the way through the Fifth Underworld, and it is global during the Neolithic, as established by Dr. Felicitas Goodman.[11] This flute establishes that Neanderthal was musical during the Fifth Underworld, probably right back to Day Two. A beautifully carved piece of red ochre was found in the Blombos Cave in South Africa that has been dated to 77,000 years before the present.[12] Furthermore, Drachenloch Altar in Switzerland was built by Neanderthals 75,000 years ago during Night Two, and it contains thirteen bear skulls.[13]

Seven skulls point toward the cave entrance, and six skulls are in niches cut in the back of the cave. *I wonder if this sacred Bear Clan cave is an altar for the Seven Days and Six Nights of the Fifth Underworld.* Do not underestimate what these people knew. The Fifth Underworld time acceleration was a very dramatic change, and Neanderthal was very psychic and in tune with spirits.

Day Three (*sprouting*) opened in 61,200 BC, and by this time Neanderthal is literally sprouting up everywhere. We have a great tracking on his development from 100,000 to 60,000 years ago in Shanidar Cave, which was occupied for 40,000 years! The anthropologist Ralph Solecki excavated Shanidar Cave in the Zagros Mountains in northern Iraq between 1951 and 1960, and he calls it the "Cave of Flowers."[14] This site has the first accepted evidence that Neanderthal used flowers as well as red ochre in his burial practices. Solecki comments, "No longer can we deny the early men the full range of human feelings and experience."[15] La Ferrassie is a Neanderthal cave in southwestern France that has the earliest art—cupules—petroglyphs that look like finger indentations. I have personally investigated many cupules in Mesoamerica, Chile, and lately at a site outside Evora, Portugal, and they often look like renditions of the Pleiades star system, as the cupules of La Ferrassie appear to be. This could be *very* significant, because La Ferrassie is also famous for the early twentieth-century discovery of the most complete Neanderthal skeleton. This man was around forty to fifty-five years old, and he had such bad osteoarthritis that his people had to care for him until he finally died. So, add love and compassion to the list of Neanderthal traits.[16] La Ferrassie Man's dating is still controversial, but it seems highly likely he was buried 60,000 to 70,000 years ago, probably during Day Three. Indeed, Day Three was a sprouting of consciousness, and then Night Three was a time of processing.

Day Four (*proliferation*) was 53,300 to 45,400 BC, and the midpoint was 49,350 BC, when we find something truly astonishing. The midpoint is always the peak of the whole cycle, and Neanderthal built *blast furnaces* 50,000 years ago in Spain for making their tools, which is a sign of advanced skill.[17] Next, during Night Four, a change is coming, because Cro-Magnon left Africa and came north.

Day Five (*budding*) was 37,500 to 29,600 BC—the *Upper Paleolithic Revolution*—when there was an explosion of more advanced tool-making, art, and the interbreeding of Neanderthal and Cro-Magnon. Until recently, this idea has been anathema to researchers, but DNA research indicates this is what happened, and to me it is only logical. They would have needed each other then, yet eventually Cro-Magnon dominated. When Cro-Magnon arrived around 45,000 years ago during Night Four, Neanderthal occupied territory from the tip of Gibraltar to Siberia.[18] The Upper Paleolithic Revolution was a great flowering of art and culture, such as the incredible cave art that is usually attributed to Cro-Magnon man. I think a better approach is to see that this evolution in art and consciousness came about in the *mixing* of these two ancestors, even though Cro-Magnon ended up dominating. The real struggle over domination seems to have occurred during Night Five—29,600 to 21,700 BC—which was to be expected, because the Fifth Night of all Nine Underworlds are the most destructive phases. We take a major step forward during the Days, and then sometimes during the Nights, something has to go to make room for the new things. In this case, it was Neanderthal and his psychic and dreaming imaginative brain. Like all true primitives, such as the Australian aboriginals, Neanderthal probably did not value Cro-Magnon's drive, especially into his territory. In any case, the extinction of Neanderthal may have been the first extinction of humans, which is one reason it is worth remembering him. This also may have been the beginning of valuing rationality over psychic intelligence.

Day Six (*flowering*) was 21,700 to 13,800 BC, the flowering of the global maritime civilization. Cro-Magnon was a seafarer who built cities by the sea, which I covered in detail in the text. Then Night Six—13,800 to 5900 BC—opened with the early signs of climatic disturbances attributable to the fragments of the Vela Supernova, and we have the rest of the story in this book. Viewing the cataclysms as events that would be expected during the Sixth Night of any Underworld, we can see that things were radically altered and cleared away during Night Six, and then Day Seven (*fruition*) begins 7,900 years ago, when we see the emergence of the Holocene agricultural civilization.

It is quite fascinating to put the last 102,000 years into the context of the Days and Nights of the Fifth Underworld; it offers a fresh perspective on a period that is very hard to penetrate. *The purpose of the Fifth Underworld was the evolution of the sensitive and compassionate human.* Might this offer some thoughts about what we are becoming now? This idea is enriched by brief comments about the agendas of the subsequent Underworlds, the Sixth, Seventh, Eighth, and Ninth. The Sixth Underworld—3115 BC to AD 2011—is the National Underworld, when civilization flowered all over the planet. The Seventh Underworld—AD 1755 to 2011—is the Planetary Underworld, when industry swept the globe. We became workers instead of farmers, which organized us into hierarchical economic units. The agenda of the Eighth Underworld—AD 1999 to 2011—is technology, which is unifying humankind. And the Ninth Underworld occurs during 2011, when we are to experience the simultaneous completions of all Nine Underworlds, the total recall of humanity's wisdom as we become one with each other and with nature. Let us hope this vision is a true one.

NOTES

Chapter 1. Seizing the Cycles of the Stars

1. Milton, *Paradise Lost,* 254.
2. Calleman, *Mayan Calendar.*
3. Cruttenden, *Lost Star of Myth and Time,* 80–81.
4. Allan and Delair, *Cataclysm!,* 15, 207–11.
5. Krupp, *Beyond the Blue Horizon;* North, *Stonehenge.*
6. Schoch, *Voices of the Rocks,* 33–51; West, *Serpent in the Sky.*
7. Malkowski, *Ancient Egypt.*
8. J. B. Delair, letter to the author, August 3, 1999.
9. Bauval and Gilbert, *Orion Mystery,* 179–96.
10. Giamario, "May 1988 and the Great Galactic Alignment," 57–64; Jenkins, *Maya Cosmogenesis,* 105–14, 324–26; Fiorenza, *Erection of the Holy Cross,* 14; Kushi, *Era of Humanity,* 98–100.
11. Kushi, *Era of Humanity,* 104.
12. Sesti, *Glorious Constellations,* 447.
13. Ryan and Pitman, *Noah's Flood;* Oppenheimer, *Eden in the East.*
14. Kushi, *Era of Humanity,* 105.
15. Allan and Delair, *Cataclysm!,* 83–137.
16. Goodman, *Where the Spirits Ride the Wind,* 19–23.
17. Calleman, *Mayan Calendar;* Calleman, *Solving the Greatest Mystery;* Clow, *Mayan Code.*
18. Ibid.
19. Yarris, "Fossil Records Show Biodiversity Comes and Goes."

Chapter 2. The Great Cataclysm and the Fall

1. von Dechend and de Santillana, *Hamlet's Mill,* 145.
2. Allan and Delair, *Cataclysm!,* 149–51, 161–64.
3. Lockyer, *Dawn of Astronomy;* North, *Stonehenge;* Sullivan, *Secret of the Incas.*
4. LaViolette, *Earth Under Fire.*
5. Allan and Delair, *Cataclysm!,* 149–68. See also Flem-Ath and Flem-Ath, *When the Sky Fell,* 53–72.

6. Allan and Delair, *Cataclysm!,* 263.

7. Ibid., 265–69.

8. Van Andel, *New Views on an Old Planet,* 107–8; Stewart, *Drifting Continents,* 29–34, 181.

9. Allan and Delair, *Cataclysm!,* 267.

10. Ibid., 267–68.

11. Ibid., 268.

12. Flem-Ath and Flem-Ath, *When the Sky Fell,* 1–6; Hapgood, *Maps of the Ancient Sea Kings,* 174–88; Hapgood, *Path of the Pole,* 1–45, 185–92.

13. Kuhn, *Structure of Scientific Revolutions.*

14. Guy Berthault, quoted in Richard Milton, *Shattering the Myths,* 78.

15. Allan and Delair, *Cataclysm!,* 12–17.

16. Kushi, *Forgotten Worlds,* 64.

17. Allan and Delair, *Cataclysm!,* 14.

18. Ibid., 54.

19. Ibid., 136–37.

20. Ibid., 135.

21. Ibid., 136.

22. Hapgood, *Maps of the Ancient Sea Kings.*

23. Ibid., 188–202.

24. J. B. Delair, letter to the author, August 3, 1999.

25. Hancock, *Fingerprints of the Gods,* 22–23.

26. Hapgood, *Maps of the Ancient Sea Kings,* 178.

27. Ibid., 188, brackets mine.

28. Flem-Ath and Flem-Ath, *When the Sky Fell,* 73–88.

29. Hapgood, *Maps of the Ancient Sea Kings,* 187.

30. Ibid.

Chapter 3. The Bicameral Brain and the Sphinx

1. Jaynes, *Origin of Consciousness,* 46.

2. Ibid., 104–5.

3. Ibid., 101–25.

4. Mounts, "Brave New World of Antidepressants"; Whitaker, "The Scourge of Prozac," 1–6.

5. Jaynes, *Origin of Consciousness,* 255–92.

6. Lynch, "Unreasonable Unity of God," pt. 3, chapter 20; Carter, *Mapping the Mind.*

7. Velikovsky, *Mankind in Amnesia,* 28–35.

8. Bauval and Gilbert, *Orion Mystery,* 69, 189–96.

9. Clark, *Myth and Symbol in Ancient Egypt,* 246–63.

10. Hancock, *Fingerprints of the Gods*, 383–87. See also Emery, *Archaic Egypt*, 21–37.

11. Bauval and Gilbert, *Orion Mystery*, 187.

12. Hancock, *Fingerprints of the Gods*, 382.

13. Plato, *Timaeus and Critias*, 33–36.

14. Hoffman, *Egypt Before the Pharaohs*, 102.

15. Bauval and Brophy, *Black Genesis*, 87–89; Brophy, *The Origin Map*.

16. West, *Serpent in the Sky*, 196–232.

17. Hancock, *Fingerprints of the Gods*, 396.

18. Hoffman, *Egypt Before the Pharaohs*, 102.

19. Butzer, *Early Hydraulic Civilization*, 56.

20. Hoffman, *Egypt Before the Pharaohs*, 40.

21. Butzer, *Early Hydraulic Civilization*, 35.

22. Ibid., 39.

23. Ibid., 12–56; Lockyer, *Dawn of Astronomy*, 235–42.

24. Butzer, *Early Hydraulic Civilization*, 26–36.

25. Hapgood, *Fingerprints of the Gods*, 407–8.

26. Hoffman, *Egypt Before the Pharaohs*, 28.

27. Settegast, *Plato Prehistorian*, 97–101; Lhote, *Tassili Frescoes*, insert between 88 and 89; insert between 96 and 97.

28. Cooper, "Why We Must Now Rethink Civilization," 26–27.

29. Temple, *Sirius Mystery*.

30. Butzer, *Early Hydraulic Civilization*, 23.

31. Bauval and Gilbert, *Orion Mystery*, 196.

32. Ibid., 97–104.

33. Lawton and Ogilvie-Herald, *Giza*, 323–25.

34. Lockyer, *Dawn of Astronomy*.

35. Bauval and Hancock, *Keeper of Genesis*, 194.

36. Dick, *Biological Universe*, 215.

37. Sellers, *Death of the Gods*, 251.

38. Lockyer, *Dawn of Astronomy*, 352–53.

39. Bauval and Gilbert, *Orion Mystery*, 179–96.

40. Sellers, *Death of the Gods*, 93.

41. von Dechend and de Santillana, *Hamlet's Mill*, 63.

42. Sellers, *Death of the Gods*, 94.

43. Ibid., 93.

44. Dunn, *Giza Power Plant*, 134–50.

45. Clow, *Alchemy of Nine Dimensions*.

46. Naydler, *Temple of the Cosmos*, 80; Lamy, *Egyptian Mysteries*, 35–46.

47. Scranton, *The Science of the Dogon*.

48. Dunn, *Giza Power Plant,* 125–50.

49. Clow, *Alchemy,* 19–31.

Chapter 4. The Story of the Prediluvial World

1. Velikovsy, *Mankind in Amnesia,* 30–31.

2. Editors of Pensée, *Velikovsky Reconsidered,* 7.

3. Velikovsky, *Mankind in Amnesia,* 30.

4. Ellis, *Thoth,* 205.

5. Benford, *Deeptime,* 8.

6. Flem-Ath and Flem-Ath, *When the Sky Fell,* 14.

7. Dillehay, *Settlement of the Americas,* 36.

8. Flem-Ath and Flem-Ath, *When the Sky Fell,* 61.

9. Ibid.

10. Allan and Delair, *Cataclysm!,* 133–34; Hapgood, *Maps of the Ancient Sea Kings,* 182.

11. Settegast, *Plato Prehistorian,* 17.

12. Flem-Ath and Flem-Ath, *When the Sky Fell,* 107–8; Hapgood, *Maps of the Ancient Sea Kings,* 126–36.

13. Kreisberg, ed., *Lost Knowledge of the Ancients,* 145–67.

14. "Cave Painting: Rethinking Our Ancient Past," *Epoch Times.*

15. Hancock, *Fingerprints of the Gods,* 409.

16. Doumas, *Wallpaintings of Thera,* 68–83.

17. Plato, *Timaeus and Critias,* 38.

18. Settegast, *Plato Prehistorian,* 27.

19. Rudgley, *Lost Civilizations,* 69–71.

20. Settegast, *Plato Prehistorian,* 28–29.

21. Ibid.

22. Ibid., 106

23. Ibid., 107–11.

24. Goodman, *Where the Spirits Ride the Wind,* 20–23, 58–60.

25. Oppenheimer, *Eden in the East,* 430.

26. Clottes and Courtin, *Cave Beneath the Sea,* 34–35.

27. Settegast, *Plato Prehistorian,* 109.

28. Ibid. See also Hapgood, *Maps of the Ancient Sea Kings,* 124–33.

29. Oppenheimer, *Eden in the East,* 441–74.

30. Settegast, *Plato Prehistorian,* 110.

31. Clark, "Gemini: Searching for the Missing Twin."

32. Settegast, *Plato Prehistorian,* 110.

33. Goodman, *Where the Spirits Ride the Wind,* 23.

34. Hitching, *World Atlas of Mysteries,* 77.

35. Ibid.

36. Ibid., 80.

37. Gooch, *Neanderthal Legacy*, 48–52.

38. Richer, *Sacred Geography*, xxii.

39. Michell and Rhone, *Twelve-Tribe Nations*.

40. Hitching, *World Atlas of Earth Mysteries*, 77.

41. Settegast, *Plato Prehistorian*, 17.

42. Hapgood, *Maps of the Ancient Sea Kings*, 175.

43. Ibid.

44. Flem-Ath and Flem-Ath, *When the Sky Fell*, 40.

45. Plato, *Timaeus and Critias*, 156.

46. Van Andel, *New Views on an Old Planet*, 85–87.

47. Hapgood, *Maps of the Ancient Sea Kings*, 4–68, 177–81.

48. Collins, *Gateway to Atlantis*, 288–89.

49. Dillehay, *Settlement of the Americas*.

50. Walter Neves quoted in Larry Rohter, "An Ancient Skull Challenges Long-Held Theories."

51. Sourcebook Project, *Science Frontiers* 1, no. 126.

52. Oppenheimer, *Eden in the East*.

53. Hapgood, *Maps of the Ancient Sea Kings*, 218.

54. Allan and Delair, *Cataclysm!*, 101.

55. Settegast, *Plato Prehistorian*, 93–96; Plato, *Timaeus and Critias*, 37.

56. Gimbutas, *Language of the Goddess*, 321.

57. Plato, *Timaeus and Critias*, 35–36.

58. Lockyer, *Dawn of Astronomy*, 329, 414–18.

59. Rudgley, *Lost Civilizations*, 100.

60. Plato, *Timaeus and Critias*, 36–37.

Chapter 5. Geomancy and Primordial Memory

1. Gimbutas, *Language of the Goddess*, 321.

2. Michell, *Old Stones*, 6.

3. Michell, *New View over Atlantis*, 83–105.

4. Cowan and Silk, *Ancient Energies*, 8–23.

5. Michell, *Old Stones*, 11–27.

6. John Burke and Kaj Halberg, *Seed of Knowledge*, 2005.

7. Michell, *Old Stones*, 11.

8. Graves, *Needles of Stone*, 99–100. See also Hitching, *Earth Magic*.

9. Michell, *New View over Atlantis*, 47–58.

10. Dames, *Silbury Treasure*.

11. Ellis, *Thoth*, 104–29.

12. Michell, *New View over Atlantis,* 50.

13. Sullivan, *Secret of the Incas,* 23–24.

14. Michell, *New View over Atlantis,* 94.

15. Clow, *Mind Chronicles,* 45; Mills, *History of Saginew County Michigan,* 29–30.

16. Michell, *New View over Atlantis,* 39.

17. Feuerstein, Kak, and Frawley, *Cradle of Civilization,* 76–99.

18. Van Flandern, *Dark Matter,* 155–236.

19. Rudgley, *Lost Civilizations,* 8–9. See also Goodman, *Where the Spirits Ride the Wind,* 219–23.

20. Naydler, *Temple of the Cosmos,* vii.

21. Michell, *New View over Atlantis,* 94.

22. Bauval and Brophy, *Black Genesis,* 219–32.

23. Ibid., 222–24; and Clow, *Mind Chronicles.*

24. Hancock, *Fingerprints of the Gods,* 400–7.

25. Lichtheim, *Ancient Egyptian Literature,* 197–99.

26. Meeks and Favard-Meeks, *Egyptian Gods,* 26.

27. Lichtheim, *Ancient Egyptian Literature,* 149–61.

28. Frankfort, *Kingship and the Gods,* 101–23.

29. Ibid., 19.

30. Ibid., 21.

31. Ibid., 23.

32. Ibid., 112, 126.

33. Ibid., 128–29.

34. Ibid., 91–129.

35. Ibid., 130.

36. Ibid., 133.

37. Ibid., 134.

38. Ibid., 79.

39. Fagan, *Black Land to Fifth Sun,* 74.

40. Frankfort, *Kingship and the Gods,* 79–87, 83–85.

41. Ibid., 86.

42. Sety and El Zeini, *Abydos,* 102.

43. Alford, *Phoenix Solution,* 321–23.

44. Ibid., 327.

45. Ibid., 322.

46. Naydler, *Temple of the Cosmos,* 13.

Chapter 6. Çatal Hüyük and Noah's Flood

1. Settegast, *Plato Prehistorian,* 30–34; Gimbutas, *Language of the Goddess,* 116–17.

2. Emery, *Archaic Egypt,* 152, fig. 8, and 165–93.

3. Barnett, "Written in Stone," 11.

4. Collins, *Gods of Eden,* 327–66.

5. Collins, *Ashes of Angels,* 327–47.

6. Ibid., 344.

7. Pellegrino, *Unearthing Atlantis,* 246. See also Hoffman, *Egypt Before the Pharoahs,* 23–32.

8. Rapp and Hill, *Geoarchaeology,* 159.

9. Settegast, *Plato Prehistorian,* 46.

10. Ibid., 46–49.

11. Ibid., 50.

12. Plato, *Timaeus and Critias,* 134.

13. Settegast, *Plato Prehistorian,* 42.

14. Ibid., 51.

15. Ibid., 67, 141.

16. Ryan and Pitman, *Noah's Flood.*

17. Ibid., 188–201.

18. Collins, *Gods of Eden,* 312–17; Oppenheimer, *Eden in the East,* 60–61.

19. Hapgood, *Maps of the Ancient Sea Kings,* 186–87; Ryan and Pittman, *Noah's Flood,* 145.

20. Hapgood, *Maps of the Ancient Sea Kings,* 187; Pittman, *Noah's Flood,* 145.

21. Feuerstein, Kak, and Frawley, *Cradle of Civilization,* 87–99.

22. Galanopoulos and Bacon, *Atlantis,* 112.

23. Mavor, *Voyage to Atlantis,* 46.

24. Plato, *Timaeus and Critias,* 36.

25. Delair, "Planet in Crisis."

26. Settegast, *Plato Prehistorian,* 128.

27. Ibid.

28. Ibid., 163–71.

29. Mellaart, *Çatal Hüyük,* 24.

30. Ryan and Pitman, *Noah's Flood,* 184.

31. Collins, *Ashes of Angels,* 266–70.

32. Settegast, *Plato Prehistorian,* 189.

33. Ibid., 201–3.

34. Ibid., 189.

35. Fagan, *Black Land,* 69.

36. Settegast, *Plato Prehistorian,* 201, 215–16.

37. von Dechend and de Santillana, *Hamlet's Mill,* 62–63.

38. Settegast, *Plato Prehistorian,* 9, 215–21.

39. Ibid., 201. See also Ulansey, *Mithraic Mysteries,* 9.

40. Settegast, *Plato Prehistorian*, 9, 215–16.

41. Browne, "Harnessing a Molecule's Explosive Powers."

42. Rudgley, *Lost Civilizations*, 50–57.

43. Ibid., 86–105.

44. Ibid., 87.

Chapter 7. The Fallen Angels and the Stones of Ica

1. *The New Jerusalem Bible.*

2. Kushi, *Era of Humanity*, 100.

3. Ibid., 65–69.

4. Ibid., 105.

5. Ibid., 104.

6. Ibid., 104–5.

7. Scott, *Kundalini*, 236–37.

8. Collins, *Ashes of Angels*, 10.

9. Icke, *Biggest Secret;* Knight and Lomas, *Hiram Key;* Pauwels and Bergier, *Morning of the Magicians;* Ravenscroft, *Spear of Destiny.*

10. Collins, *Ashes of Angels*, 10.

11. Collins, *Gods of Eden*, 261.

12. Collins, *Ashes of Angels*, 279–85.

13. Ibid., 287.

14. Allan and Delair, *Cataclysm!*, 183–90.

15. Collins, *Ashes of Angels*, 286–87.

16. Mellaart, *Çatal Hüyük*, 66.

17. Collins, *Ashes of Angels*, 286.

18. Ibid., 345.

19. Allan and Delair, *Cataclysm!*, 183–90; Van Andel, *New Views on an Old Planet*, 36, 86, 96–97.

20. Collins, *Ashes of Angels*, 286–90.

21. Collins, *Beneath the Pyramids.*

22. Picknett and Prince, *Stargate Conspiracy*, 89–94.

23. Delair and Oppé, "The Evidence of Violent Extinctions in South America," 280–97; Shanks, "Everything You Ever Knew About Jerusalem Is Wrong," 20–29.

24. Collins, *Ashes of Angels*, 102.

25. Ibid., 92.

26. Ibid., 98; Settegast, *Plato Prehistorian*, 211–25.

27. Collins, *Ashes of Angels*, 100–101.

28. Ibid., 103.

29. Ibid., 105.

30. Ibid., 116.

31. Ibid., 51–54.

32. Robinson, *Nag Hammadi Library.*

33. Collins, *Ashes of Angels,* 23–24.

34. Ibid., 24–25.

35. Ibid., 63.

36. Ibid., 62–73.

37. Ibid., 38–45.

38. Ibid., 41.

39. Fox, *Original Blessing,* 18, 232–38.

40. Collins, *Ashes of Angels,* 109–22.

41. Ibid., 110–16.

42. Ibid., 114.

43. Ibid., 111–15.

44. Ibid., 112.

45. Ibid., 127–34.

46. Ibid., 140.

47. Ibid., 205–7.

48. O'Brien and O'Brien, *Genius of the Few,* 68–70.

49. Collins, *Ashes of Angels,* 244.

50. Ibid., 245.

51. Ibid., 247–49.

52. Collins, *Gods of Eden,* 267–84.

53. Lamy, *Egyptian Mysteries,* 7.

54. Cabrera, *Engraved Stones of Ica.*

55. Ibid., 14.

56. Delair and Oppé, "Violent Extinctions," 280–97.

57. Cabrera, *Engraved Stones of Ica,* 87–102.

58. Ibid., 40–42.

59. Ibid.; Bellamy, *Built Before the Flood,* 35; Hancock, *Fingerprints of the Gods,* 76.

60. Cabrera, *Engraved Stones of Ica,* 25.

61. Delair and Oppé, "Violent Extinctions," 286–92.

62. Calleman, *Mayan Calendar.*

63. Cabrera, *Stones of Ica,* 87–102.

64. Ibid., 64–74, 200.

65. Delair and Oppé, "Violent Extinctions," 281–94.

66. Cabrera, *Stones of Ica,* 24.

67. Ibid., 87–102.

68. Gaddis, *American Indian Myths,* 9–10; Rudgley, *Lost Civilizations,* 100.

69. Cabrera, *Stones of Ica*, 64–74, 200.

70. Allan and Delair, *Cataclysm!*, 207–11.

71. Ibid., 317.

72. Collins, *Gods of Eden*, 338–41.

73. Cabrera, *Stones of Ica*, 164–67.

74. Ibid., 166.

75. Malkowski, *Ancient Egypt*, 191.

76. Ibid., 192.

77. Ibid., 192–96; Burke and Halberg, *Seed of Knowledge*, 9–21, 141–69.

78. Malkowski, *Ancient Egypt*, 196.

79. Cabrera, *Stones of Ica*, 152.

80. Ibid., 152.

81. Ibid., 142.

82. Hancock, *Fingerprints of the Gods*, 76.

83. Cabrera, *Stones of Ica*, 157–58, 256.

84. Ibid., 110–34.

85. Hapgood, *Mystery in Acambaro*, 72–153.

86. Ibid., 93.

87. Ibid., 96 (italics mine).

88. Dunn, *Giza Power Plant*, 103–70.

89. Ibid., 87.

90. Ibid., 105.

91. Ibid., 109–19.

92. Ibid., 109–24.

93. Ibid., 134–35.

94. Ibid., 138–39.

95. Ibid., 151.

96. Malkowski, *Ancient Egypt*, 8.

97. Ibid., 83–86.

98. Ibid., 93.

99. Ibid., 95.

Chapter 8. The Stargate Conspiracy and the Kosmokrater

1. Edgar Cayce as cited in Picknett and Prince, *Stargate Conspiracy*, 59.

2. Lawton and Ogilvie-Herald, *Giza*, 214–16, 476–78; Christopher Dunn, "Petrie on Trial," *Atlantis Rising* 24 (2000): 24–25, 60–61.

3. Hapgood, *Path of the Pole*, xiv–xv.

4. Picknett and Prince, *Stargate Conspiracy*, xv.

5. Ibid., 59.

6. Ibid.

7. Temple, *Sirius Mystery.*

8. Picknett and Prince, *Stargate Conspiracy,* 34.

9. Clow, *Pleiadian Agenda,* xix–xxi; Clow, *Alchemy,* 83–99.

10. Picknett and Prince, *Stargate Conspiracy,* xiv.

11. Ibid., 28.

12. Ibid., 59.

13. Ibid., 105.

14. Ibid., 106–7.

15. Ibid., 255–302.

16. Ibid., 63, 191.

17. Ibid., 84.

18. Hurtak, *Book of Knowledge.*

19. Picknett and Prince, *Stargate Conspiracy,* 87.

20. Ibid.

21. Ibid., 81–115.

22. Ibid., 100.

23. Ovason, *Secret Architecture.*

24. Hancock, *Mars Mystery,* 91–92.

25. Picknett and Prince, *Stargate Conspiracy,* 117–19.

26. Ibid., 121.

27. Ibid., 135.

28. Ibid., 128.

29. Hoagland and Bara, *Dark Mission.* See the book's cover.

30. Ibid., 247.

31. Allan and Delair, *Cataclysm!,* 226.

32. Hancock, *Mars Mystery,* 48.

33. Hoagland and Bara, *Dark Mission,* 124.

34. Van Flandern, *Dark Matter,* 155–65.

35. Ibid., 155–59.

36. Ellis, *Thoth,* 104–31.

37. Wilford, "Replying to Skeptics, NASA Defends Claims About Mars."

38. Picknett and Prince, *Stargate Conspiracy,* 157–59; Hancock, *Mars Mystery,* 21–22.

39. Chandler, "Clinton Touts Mars Project."

40. Hancock, *Mars Mystery,* 23.

41. Wilford, "Replying to Skeptics."

42. Allan and Delair, *Cataclysm!,* 205.

43. Ibid.

44. Milne, *Doomsday,* 33–34; Mann, *Shadow of a Star,* 56–64, 81–98.

45. Picknett and Prince, *Stargate Conspiracy,* 162.

46. Ibid., 164; Hurtak, *Book of Knowledge.*

47. Picknett, *Stargate Conspiracy,* 162–69.

48. Ibid., 167–69.

49. Ibid., 169–72.

50. Ibid., 173.

51. Clow, *Alchemy of Nine Dimensions.*

52. Picknett and Prince, *Stargate Conspiracy,* 206.

53. Ibid., 170.

54. Ibid., 239.

55. Ibid., 41.

56. Goodman, *Alternate Reality,* 25.

57. Ulansey, *Mithraic Mysteries,* 4.

58. Ibid.

59. Ibid., 88.

60. Ibid., 68–69.

61. Ibid., 71–73.

62. Ibid., 75.

63. Ibid., 76.

64. Ibid., 78.

65. Ibid., 83.

66. J. B. Delair, letter to the author, November 22, 2000.

67. Settegast, *Plato Prehistorian,* 220.

68. Ibid., 225.

69. Ibid., 219.

70. Ibid., 240–51.

71. Collins, *Ashes of Angels,* 95.

72. Ibid., 185–87.

73. Ulansey, *Mithraic Mysteries,* 32–33, 47–49.

74. Ibid., 57.

75. Lash, *Not in His Image,* 271.

Chapter 9. Goddess Alchemy and the Heliopolitan Mysteries

1. Clow, *Pleiadian Agenda,* 54.

2. Ibid., 73; Clow, *Alchemy,* xxix.

3. Lomas, *Hiram Key,* 75–95.

4. Icke, *Biggest Secret.*

5. McLaren, *Language of Emotions,* 11.

6. Ibid., 61–63.

7. Meeks and Favard-Meeks, *Egyptian Gods,* 58.

8. Clow, *Mind Chronicles,* 4.

9. Ibid.

10. Jaynes, *Origins of Consciousness*, 379–432.

11. Clow, *Chiron*, 1–12.

12. Allan and Delair, *Cataclysm!*, 204, 222.

13. Gore, *Ecstatic Body Postures*, x.

14. Ibid., ix.

15. Ibid.

16. Goodman, *Where the Spirits Ride the Wind*, 107.

17. Ibid., 3–5.

18. Gore, *Ecstatic Body Postures*, 16.

19. Ibid., xii.

20. Sherratt, "The Origins and Spread of Agriculture and Pastoralism in Eurasia," 133–40.

21. Gore, *Ecstatic Body Postures*, 18.

22. Picknett and Prince, *Stargate Conspiracy*, 346–51.

Appendix A. Egyptian Timeline

1. Hancock, *Fingerprints of the Gods*, 381–87. The very ancient date is from Manetho, the Turin Papyrus, Diodorus Siculus, Herodotus, and the Palermo Stone.

2. Collins, *Gods of Eden*.

3. Hoffman, *Egypt Before the Pharaohs*; Emery, *Archaic Egypt*.

Appendix B. Earth Changes during the Holocene Epoch

1. J. B. Delair, "Planets in Crisis," 6–9.

Notes from J. B. Delair's article:

40. Barton, P & Wood, *Geophys. Journ.*, vol. 79, 1984, pp. 987–1022.

41. Manley, J., *Atlas of Prehistoric Britain*, Oxford, 1989.

42. Gresswell, RK, *Sandy Shores in South Lancashire*, Liverpool, 1953, see fig. 6.

43. Manley, *op cit.*

44. Kuenen, PH, *Marine Geology*, New York, 1950.

45. Van Bemmelen, RW, *The Geology of Indonesia*, The Hague, 1949.

46. Geyh, MA, Kudrass, HR and Strief, *Nature*, vol. 278, 1979, pp. 441–443.

47. Hantoro, WS, Faure, H. Djuwansah, R, Faure-Denard, L & Pirazzoli, PA. *Quat.Intern.*, vol. 29/30, 1995, pp. 129–34.

48. Van Andel, TH, Heath, GR, Moore, TC & McGeary, DRF, *Amer.Journ.Sci.*, vol. 265. 1961, pp. 737–758.

49. Smart, J, *Geology*, vol. 5, 1977, pp. 755–759.

50. Torguerson, T, Jones, MR, Stephens, DE & Ullman, WJ, *Nature*, vol. 313, 1985, pp. 785–787.

51. Bloom, A, *Quaterneria,* vol. xii, 1970.

52. Piazzolli, PM & Montaggioni, F, *Palaeogeogr.Palaeoclimat.Palaeoecol.,* vol. 68, 1988, pp. 153–175.

53. Piazzoli, PM, Montaggioni, F, Delibrias, G, Faure, G & Salvet, B, *Proc. 5th Intern.Coral Reef Cong.* (Tahiti), 1985, vol. 3, pp. 131–136.

54. Wadia, DN, *Geology of India,* 1953, p. 37.

55. Holmes, A, *Principles of Physical Geology,* London, 1944, pp. 417–418.

56. Lees, GM & Falcon, NL, *Geogr.Journ.,* vol. 118, 1952, pp. 24–39; see p. 28 fn.

57. Grant, DR, *Canad.Journ.Earth Sci.,* vol. 7, 1970, pp. 676–689.

58. King, PB, *The Evolution of North America,* Princeton, NJ, 1937.

59. Fillon, RH, *Quat. Res.,* vol. 1, no:4, 1971, pp. 522–531.

60. Putnam, WC, *Geology,* New York, 1964.

61. Bergvist, B, *Geologiska Forengingen I Stockholm Forhandlinger,* vol. 99, 1977, pp. 347–357.

62. Velichko, AA (ed.), *Late Quaternary Environments of the Soviet Union,* London, 1984.

63. Kyasov, DD, *Late Quaternary History of Major Lakes and Inland Seas of Eastern Europe,* Leningrad, 1975.

64. Kolp, O, *Quaestiones Geogr.,* vol. 13/14, 1990, pp. 69–86.

65. Klakegg, O and Rye, N, *Norsk.Geolog.Tidskrift.,* vol. 70, 1990, pp. 47–59.

66. Svensson, N-O, *Terra Nova,* vol. 3, 1991, pp. 359–378.

67. Gams, H and Nordhagen, R, *Mitteilungen der Geographischen Gessell,* Munchen, vol. xvi, 1923, heft.2, pp. 13–348.

68. Moon, H, (trans.), *Linn.Soc.Lond.,* ser. 3, vol. 1, pt. 1, 1939.

69. Wirrmann, D & de Oliveira Almeida, LF, *Palaeogeogr.Palaeoclimat.Palaeoecol.,* vol. 58, 1987, pp. 315–323.

70. Holmes, A, op. cit.

71. Wright, HE Jr., *Bull.Res.Council Israel,* no. 7g, 1958, pp. 53–59.

72. Flint, RF, *Glacial Geology and the Pleistocene Epoch,* New York, 1947, p. 382.

73. Sayce, AH, *Hibbert Lectures,* London, 1887, p. 21.

74. Oppenheim, L, *Ancient Mesopotamia,* Chicago, 1963, p. 161.

75. Gams & Nordhagen, *op. cit.*

76. Gregory, JW, 1911. *Rep.Brit. Assoc. Adv. Sci.,* Portsmouth, pp. 445–446.

77. Brelsford, V, *Geogr.Journ.,* vol. 83, 1934, pp. 48–50.

78. Fowler, G, *Geogr.Journ.,* vol. 79, 1932, pp. 210–212.

79. Fowler, G, *Proc.Cambs.Antiq.Soc.,* vol. xxxiii, 1933, pp. 109–128.

80. St Joseph, JK, *Antiquity,* vol. xviii, 1974, pp. 295–298.

81. Kendall, HGO, *Proc.Prehis.Soc.E. Anglia,* vol. 1, pt. 2, pp. 135–139, n.d.

82. Harris, M, *Cannibals and Kings,* New York, 1976.

83. Holmes, A, op. cit.

84. Mulcahy, MJ, in Jennings, JN and Marbutt, JA (eds.), *Landform Studies from Australia and New Guinea,* Cambridge, 1967, pp. 211–230.

85. Dury, GH & Logan, MI, *Studies in Australian Geography,* London, 1968, pp. 14–15.

86. Selby, MJ, Hendry, CH & Seeley, MK, *Palaeogeogr.Palaeoclimat.Palaeoecol.,* vol. 26, 1978, pp. 37–41.

87. Boocock, C & Van Straten, OJ, (trans.,) *Proc.Geol.Soc.S.Afr.,* vol 65, 1962, pp. 125–171.

88. Wright, op. cit.

89. Holm, DA, *Science,* vol. 132, 1960, pp. 1369–1379.

90. McClure, *Nature,* vol. 263. 1976, pp. 755–756.

91. Al Sayari & Zotl, JG (eds.), *Quaternary Period in Saudi Arabia,* New York, 1978.

92. Kropelin, S & Soulie-Marsche, I, *Quat.Res.,* vol. 36, 1991, pp. 210–223.

93. Pachur, J-J & Kropelin, S, *Science,* vol. 237, 1987, pp. 298–300.

94. NcCauley, JF, Schaber, GG, Breed, CS, Grolier, MG, Haynes, CV, Issawi, B, Elachi C & Blom, A, *Science,* vol. 218, 1982, pp. 1004–1020.

95. Geyh, MA & Jakel, D. *Palaeogeogr.Palaeoclimat.Paleoecol.,* vol. 15, 1974, pp. 205–208.

96. Gautier, EF, *Geograph. Rev.,* vol. 16, 1926, pp. 378–394.

97. Harvey, CPD & Grove, AT, *Geogr.Journ.,* vol. 148, pp.327–336, n.d.

98. Bowen, R, & Jux, U, *Afro-Arabian Geology: A kinematic view,* London & New York, 1987.

99. Gardner, EW, *Geol.Mag.,* vol. 64, 1927.

100. Ritchie, JC & Haynes, CV, *Nature,* vol. 330, 1987, pp. 645–647.

101. Murray, GW, *Geogr.Journ.,* vol. 117, 1951, pt. 4, pp. 422–434.

102. Ibid.

103. Ibid.

104. Murray, GW, *Journ.Egypt.Archaeol.,* vol. 17, 1931.

105. Twitchell, KS, *Saudi Arabia,* 3rd edn., New Jersey, 1958.

106. Thesiger, W, *Arabian Sands,* London, 1959.

107. Kutzbach, JE, *Science,* vol. 214, 1981, pp. 59–61.

108. Kutabach, JE & Otto Bliesner, BL, *Journ.Atmosph.Sci.,* vol. 39, no.6, 1982, pp. 1177–1188.

109. Eden, MJ, *Journ.Biogeogr.,* vol. 1, 1974, pp. 95–109.

110. Prance, GT, *Acta Amazonica,* vol. 3, no. 3, 1973, pp. 5–28.

111. Haffer, J, *Science,* vol. 165., 1969, pp. 131–137.

112. Vanzolini, PE & Williams, EE, *Archos.Zool.Est.Sao Paulo,* vol. 19, 1970, pp. 1–124.

113. Meggers, BJ, pp. 493–496 in Prance, GT (ed.), *Biological Diversification in the Tropics,* New York, 1982.

114. Mousinho de Meis, MR, *Bull.Geol.Soc.Amer.*, vol. 82, 1971, pp. 1073–1078.

115. Flemley, JR, *The Equatorial Rain Forest: A Geological History*, 1979.

116. Campbell, KE Jr. & Frailey, D. *Quat.Res.*, vol. 21, 1984, pp. 369–375.

Appendix C. Holocene Chronological Highlights

1. J. B. Delair, "Planet in Crisis," 8.

Appendix D. Reflections on Earth's Tilting Axis

1. J. B. Delair, "Planet in Crisis," 2–11. Sections of the article are excerpted only.

2. Marshack, *Roots of Civilization*, 9–16.

3. Ibid., 27–32, 35, 39–41, 53, 89, 217, 269, 360–61; Rudgley, *Lost Civilizations*, 103–4.

4. Rudgley, *Lost Civilizations*, 102.

5. Ibid., 102–4

6. Ibid., 104.

7. Brennan, *Stars and the Stones*.

8. Temple, *Crystal Sun*.

9. Ellis, *Thoth*, 104–31.

10. Knight and Lomas, *Uriel's Machine*, 152–82.

11. Ibid., 213–32.

12. Lockyer, *Dawn of Astronomy*, 108.

13. Temple, *Crystal Sun*, 412–14.

Notes from J. B. Delair's article:

28. Lambeck, K, *The Earth's Variable Rotation: Geophysical Causes and Consequences* (Cambridge, 1980).

29. Rochester, MG, *Phil.Trans.Roy.Soc.Lond.*, vol. A306, 1984, pp. 95–105.

30. Ray, RD, Eames, RJ & Chao, BF, *Nature*, vol. 391, 1996, n. 65831, pp. 595–597.

31. Dahlen, FA, *Geophys.Journ.Roy.Astron.Soc.*, vol. 52, 1979.

32. Guinot, B, *Astron.Astrophys.*, vol. 19, 1972, pp. 207–214.

33. Ibid., 20.

34. Harris, J, *Celestial Spheres and Doctrine of the Earth's Perpendicular Axis*, Montreal, 1976.

35. Warren, RF, *Paradise Found; The Cradle of the Human Race at the North Pole. A Study of the Prehistoric World*, Boston, 1885, p. 181.

36. Allan, D. S., and Delair, J. B., *When the Earth Nearly Died*, Bath, 1995.

119. Keaney, P., (ed.), *The Encyclopedia of the Solid Earth Sciences*, Oxford, 1993, p. 134.

120. Whaler, K & Holme, R, *Nature*, vol. 382, no. 6588, 1996, pp. 205–206.

121. Ramalli, G, *Rheology of the Earth*, 2nd edn., London, 1995.

122. Pellegrino, O, *Return to Sodom and Gomorrah*, New York, 1995.

123. Mansinha, L & Smylie, DL, *Journ.Geophys.Res.,* vol. 72, 1967, pp. 4731–4743.

124. Dahlen, FA, Geophys. *Journ.Roy.Astron.Soc.,* vol. 32, 1973, pp. 203–217.

125. Yatskiv, YS & Sasao, T, *Nature,* vol 255, no. 5510, 1975, p. 655.

126. Whiston, W, *A New Theory of the Earth,* London, 1696.

127. Catcott, A, *A Treatise on the Deluge,* London, 2nd edn., 1761.

128. Donnelly, I, *Ragnarok: The Age of Fire and Gravel,* 13th edn., New York, 1895.

129. Beaumont, C, *The Mysterious Comet,* London, 1932.

130. Bellamy, HS, *Moons, Myths, and Men,* London, 1936.

131. Velikovsky, I, *Worlds in Collision,* London, 1950.

132. Patten, DW, *The Biblical Flood and the Ice Epoch,* Seattle, 1966.

133. Muck, O, *The Secret of Atlantis,* London, 1978.

134. Englehardt, WV, *Sber.Heidel.Akad.Wiss.Math.Nat.KL.,* 2 abh, 1979.

135. Clube, V, and Napier, WR, *The Cosmic Serpent,* London, 1982.

Appendix E. The Paleolithic Revolution and the Fifth Underworld

1. Calleman, *Mayan Calendar.*

2. Schmid, "Skull Hints at Human Neanderthal Interbreeding."

3. McIlroy, "Neanderthal Cave Changes Thinking About Extinction."

4. Callaway, "Neanderthal Genome Reveals Interbreeding with Humans"; Wade, "Scientists Hope to Unravel Neanderthal DNA and Human Mysteries."

5. Calleman, "The Tortuguero Monument 6 and the Maya End Date."

6. Calleman, *Purposeful Universe.*

7. Gooch, *Cities of Dreams,* 9.

8. Baigent, *The Jesus Papers,* 166.

9. Wilson, *Atlantis and the Kingdom of the Neanderthals,* 15.

10. Bahn and Vertut, *Journey Through the Ice Age,* 84.

11. Goodman, *Where the Spirits Ride the Wind,* 107.

12. David Lewis Williams, *The Mind in the Cave,* 98; Tellinger and Heine, *Adam's Calendar,* 11–12.

13. Gooch, *Cities of Dreams,* 99–100.

14. Solecki, *Shanidar: The Humanity of Neanderthal Man.*

15. Ibid., 178.

16. Encyclopedia of Irish World Art, online. www.visual-arts-cork.com /prehistory/ferrassie-cave-neanderthal-burial.htm

17. Gooch, *Neanderthal Legacy,* 46.

18. Hall, "Last of the Neanderthals," 34–59.

SUGGESTED
READING

Allan, D. S., and J. B. Delair. *Cataclysm! Compelling Evidence of a Cosmic Catastrophe in 9500 B.C.* Santa Fe: Bear & Company, 1997.

Calleman, Carl Johan. *The Mayan Calendar and the Transformation of Consciousness.* Rochester, Vt.: Bear & Company, 2004.

Clow, Barbara Hand. *The Alchemy of Nine Dimensions: The 2011/2012 Prophecies and the Nine Dimensions of Consciousness.* Charlottesville, Va.: Hampton Roads, 2010.

Collins, Andrew. *From the Ashes of Angels: The Forbidden Legacy of a Forgotten Race.* London: Signet, 1997.

Dunn, Christopher. *The Giza Power Plant: Technologies of Ancient Egypt.* Santa Fe: Bear & Company, 1998.

Flem-Ath, Rand, and Rose Flem-Ath. *When the Sky Fell: In Search of Atlantis.* New York: St. Martin's Press, 1995.

Goodman, Felicitas D. *Where the Spirits Ride the Wind: Trance Journeys and Other Ecstatic Experiences.* Bloomington: Indiana University Press, 1990.

Gore, Belinda. *Ecstatic Body Postures: An Alternate Reality Workbook.* Santa Fe: Bear & Company, 1995.

Hapgood, Charles. *Maps of the Ancient Sea Kings: Evidence of Advanced Civilization in the Ice Age.* London: Turnstone Books, 1966.

Jaynes, Julian. *The Origin of Consciousness in the Breakdown of the Bicameral Mind.* Boston: Houghton Mifflin, 1976.

Lash, John Lamb. *Not in His Image: Gnostic Wisdom, Sacred Ecology, and the Future of Belief.* White River Junction, Vt.: Chelsea Green Publishing, 2006.

Malkowski, Edward F. *Ancient Egypt: 39,000 BCE.* Rochester, Vt.: Bear & Company, 2010.

McLaren, Karla. *The Language of Emotions.* Boulder, Colo.: Sounds True, 2010.

Picknett, Lynn, and Clive Prince. *The Stargate Conspiracy.* London: Little, Brown, 2000.

Ryan, William, and Walter Pitman. *Noah's Flood: The New Scientific Discoveries About the Event That Changed History.* New York: Touchstone, 1998.

Settegast, Mary. *Plato Prehistorian: 10,000 to 5,000 BC—Myth, Religion, Archaeology.* Hudson, N.Y.: Lindisfarne Press, 1990.

Ulansey, David. *The Origins of the Mithraic Mysteries.* Oxford, U.K.: Oxford University Press, 1989.

von Dechend, Hertha, and Giorgio de Santillana. *Hamlet's Mill: An Essay on Myth and the Frame of Time.* Boston: David R. Godine, 1977.

For the sacred postures discussed in chapter 9, write to the Cuyamungue Institute, Route #5, Box 358-A, Santa Fe, New Mexico 87501.

The video of the author working with Abdel Hakim, *Nine Initiations on the Nile,* is available for $35 from Wiseawakening.com.

Bibliography

Aeschylus. *Prometheus Bound,* trans. E. H. Plumptre, 1868. Full citation not available, but an alternate translation can be found in Albert Cook and Edwin Dolan, *Greek Tragedy.* Dallas, Tex.: Spring Publications, 1972.

Alford, Alan F. *The Phoenix Solution: Secrets of a Lost Civilisation.* London: Hodder and Stoughton, 1998.

Allan, D. S., and J. B. Delair. *Cataclysm! Compelling Evidence of a Cosmic Catastrophe in 9500 B.C.* Santa Fe: Bear & Company, 1997.

Bahn, Paul G., and Jean Vertut. *Journey Through the Ice Age.* Berkeley: University of California Press, 1997.

Baigent, Michael. *The Jesus Papers: Exposing the Greatest Cover-up in History.* San Francisco: Harper Collins, 2006.

Barnett, Adrian. "Written in Stone." *New Scientist* (October 4, 1997).

Bauval, Robert, and Thomas Brophy. *Black Genesis: The Prehistoric Origins of Ancient Egypt.* Rochester, Vt.: Bear & Company, 2011.

Bauval, Robert, and Adrian Gilbert. *The Orion Mystery: Unlocking the Secrets of the Pyramids.* New York: Crown Publishers, 1994.

Bauval, Robert, and Graham Hancock. *Keeper of Genesis: A Quest for the Hidden Legacy of Mankind.* London: Heinemann, 1996.

Bellamy, H. S. *Built Before the Flood: The Problem of the Tiahuanaco Ruins.* London: Faber and Faber, 1947.

Benford, Gregory. *Deep Time: How Humanity Communicates Across Millennia.* New York: HarperCollins, 2000.

Bond, Alan, and Mark Hempsell. *A Sumerian Observation of the Köfel's Impact Event.* Great Britain: Alcuin Academics, 2008.

Brennan, Martin. *The Stars and the Stones: Ancient Art and Astronomy in Ireland.* London: Thames and Hudson, 1983.

Brophy, Thomas Y. *The Origin Map: Discovery of a Prehistoric Megalithc Astrophysical Map and Sculpture of the Universe.* New York: Writer's Club Press, 2002.

Browne, Malcolm W. "Harnessing a Molecule's Explosive Powers." *New York Times,* 25 January, 2000.

Burke, John and Kaj Halberg. *Seed of Knowledge, Stone of Plenty.* San Francisco: Council Oaks Books, 2005.

Butzer, Karl W. *Early Hydraulic Civilization in Egypt: A Study in Cultural Ecology.* Chicago: University of Chicago Press, 1976.

Cabrera, Javier Darquea. *The Message of the Engraved Stones of Ica.* Lima: privately published, 1989.

Callaway, Ewen. "Neanderthal Genome Reveals Interbreeding with Humans." *New Scientist* (May 6, 2010).

Calleman, Carl Johan. *The Mayan Calendar and the Transformation of Consciousness.* Rochester, Vt.: Bear & Company, 2004.

———. *The Purposeful Universe.* Rochester, Vt.: Bear & Company, 2009.

———. *Solving the Greatest Mystery of Our Time.* London: Garev, 2001.

———. "The Tortuguero Monument 6 and the Maya End Date." www.calleman.com. August 19, 2009.

Carter, Rita. *Mapping the Mind.* Berkeley: University of California Press, 2010.

"Cave Painting: Rethinking Our Ancient Past." *Epoch Times.* Vancouver, B.C.: *Bulletin de la Societé Préhistorique de France* (1957), no. 10. December 15, 2008.

Chandler, David L. "Clinton Touts Mars Project." *Boston Globe,* 8 August, 1996.

Christy-Vitale, Joseph. *Watermark: The Disaster That Changed the World and Humanity 12,000 Years Ago.* New York: Paraview Pocket Books, 2004.

Clark, Brian. "Gemini: Searching for the Missing Twin." *The Mountain Astrologer Magazine* 91 (2000).

Clark, R. T. Rundle. *Myth and Symbol in Ancient Egypt.* London: Thames and Hudson, 1991.

Clottes, Jean, and Jean Courtin. *The Cave Beneath the Sea: Paleolithic Images at Cosquer.* New York: Harry N. Abrams, 1996.

Clow, Barbara Hand. *Alchemy of Nine Dimensions: The 2011/2012 Prophecies and the Nine Dimensions of Consciousness.* Charlottesville, Va.: Hampton Roads, 2010.

———. *Chiron: Rainbow Bridge Between the Inner and Outer Planets.* St. Paul, Minn.: Llewellyn Publications, 1987.

———. *The Mayan Code: Time Accleration and Awakening the World Mind.* Rochester, Vt.: Bear & Company, 2007.

———. *The Mind Chronicles.* Rochester, Vt.: Bear & Company, 2007.

———. *Nine Initiations on the Nile.* Infinite Eye Productions, 1996. Video.

———. *The Pleiadian Agenda: A New Cosmology for the Age of Light.* Santa Fe: Bear & Company, 1995.

Clube, Victor, and Bill Napier. *The Cosmic Winter.* Oxford, U.K.: Basil Blackwell, 1990.

Cochran, Gregory, and Henry Harpending. *The 10,000 Year Explosion: How Civilization Accelerated Human Evolution.* New York: Basic Books, 2009.

Collins, Andrew. *Beneath the Pyramids: Egypt's Greatest Secret Uncovered.* Virginia Beach, Va.: A.R.E. Press, 2009.

———. *From the Ashes of Angels: The Forbidden Legacy of a Fallen Race*. London: Signet, 1997.

———. *Gateway to Atlantis: The Search for the Source of a Lost Civilization*. London: Headline, 2000.

———. *Gods of Eden: Egypt's Lost Legacy and the Genesis of Civilization*. London: Headline, 1998.

Cook, Albert, and Edwin Dolin. *Greek Tragedy*. Dallas, Tex.: Spring Publications, 1972.

Cooper, Glenda. "Why We Must Now Rethink Civilization." *London Daily Mail*, 28 December, 2000.

Cooper, Milton William. *Behold a Pale Horse*. Sedona, Ariz.: Light Technology Publishing, 1991.

Cornford, Francis M. *Plato's Cosmology: The Timaeus of Plato*. Indianapolis, Ind.: Hackett Publishing, 1997.

Cowan, David, and Anne Silk. *Ancient Energies of the Earth*. London: Thorsons, 1999.

Cruttenden, Walter. *Lost Star of Myth and Time*. Pittsburgh, Pa.: St. Lynn's Press, 2006.

Cumont, Franz. *The Mysteries of Mithra*. New York: Dover, 1956.

Dames, Michael. *The Silbury Treasure: The Great Goddess Rediscovered*. London: Thames and Hudson, 1976.

de Lubicz, R. A. Schwaller. *The Temple of Man*. Rochester, Vt.: Inner Traditions, 1998.

Delair, J. B. "Planet in Crisis," *Chronology and Catastrophism Review* (2), 1997.

Delair, J. B., and E. F. Oppé, "The Evidence of Violent Extinctions in South America," in *The Path of the Pole*, ed. Charles Hapgood. Kempton, Ill.: Adventures Unlimited Press, 1970.

Dick, Steven J. *The Biological Universe: The Twentieth Century Extraterrestrial Life Debate and the Limits of Science*. Cambridge: Cambridge University Press, 1996.

Dillehay, Thomas D. *The Settlement of the Americas: A New Prehistory*. New York: Basic Books, 2000.

Doumas, Christos. *The Wallpantings of Thera*. Athens: The Thera Foundation, 1992.

Dunn, Christopher. *The Giza Power Plant: Technologies of Ancient Egypt*. Santa Fe: Bear & Company, 1998.

Editors of Pensée. *Velikovsky Reconsidered*. New York: Doubleday, 1976.

Ellis, Ralph. *Thoth: Architect of the Universe*. Dorset, U.K.: Edfu Books, 1997.

Emery, W. B. *Archaic Egypt*. London: Penguin Books, 1961.

Encyclopedia of Irish World Art, online. www.visual-arts-cork.com/prehistory/ferrassie-cave-neanderthal-burial.htm.

Fagan, Brian. *From Black Land to Fifth Sun.* Reading, Mass.: Perseus Books, 1998.

Faulkner, R. O. *The Ancient Egyptian Coffin Texts,* vol. 1. Warminster, U.K.: Aris & Phillips, 1973.

———. *The Ancient Egyptian Pyramid Texts.* Oxford, U.K.: Oxford University Press, 1969.

Feuerstein, Georg, Subhash Kak, and David Frawley. *In Search of the Cradle of Civilization.* Wheaton, Ill.: Quest Books, 1995.

Fiorenza, Nick Anthony. *Erection of the Holy Cross: Astronomical Earth-Grid Spacetime Mapping.* Fort Collins, Colo.: IANS, 1995.

Fischer, Steven Roger. *Glyph-Breaker.* New York: Copernicus, 1997.

Flem-Ath, Rand, and Rose Flem-Ath. *When the Sky Fell: In Search of Atlantis.* New York: St. Martin's Press, 1995.

Fox, Matthew. *Original Blessing: A Primer in Creation Spirituality.* Santa Fe: Bear & Company, 1983.

Frankfort, Henri. *Kingship and the Gods: A Study of Ancient Near Eastern Religion and the Integration of Society and Nature.* London: University of Chicago Press, 1948.

Gaddis, Vincent H. *American Indian Myths and Mysteries.* New York: Indian Head Books, 1977.

Galanopoulos, A. G., and Edward Bacon. *Atlantis: The Truth Behind the Legend.* New York: Bobbs-Merrill, 1969.

Giamario, Daniel. "May 1988 and the Great Galactic Alignment." *The Mountain Astrologer* 82 (May/June 1998).

Gimbutas, Marija. *The Language of the Goddess.* San Francisco: Harper & Row, 1989.

Gooch, Stan. *Cities of Dreams: The Rich Legacy of Neanderthal Man Which Shaped Our Civilization.* London: Ryder, 1989.

———. *The Neanderthal Legacy.* Rochester, Vt.: Inner Traditions, 2008.

Goodman, Felicitas D. *Ecstasy, Ritual, and Alternate Reality.* Bloomington, Ind.: Indiana University Press, 1992.

———. *Where the Spirits Ride the Wind: Trance Journeys and Other Ecstatic Experiences.* Bloomington, Ind.: Indiana University Press, 1990.

Gore, Belinda. *Ecstatic Body Postures: An Alternate Reality Workbook.* Santa Fe: Bear & Company, 1995.

Graves, Tom. *Needles of Stone.* London: Granada, 1980.

Halberg, Burke. *Seed of Knowledge, Stone of Plenty.* San Francisco: Council Oak Books, 2005.

Hall, Stephen S. "Last of the Neanderthals." *National Geographic* (October 2008).

Hamblin, Jane, and the Time-Life editors. *The First Cities.* New York: Time-Life Books, 1973.

Hancock, Graham. *Fingerprints of the Gods.* New York: Crown, 1995.

———. *The Mars Mystery.* New York: Crown, 1998.

———. *Underworld: The Mysterious Origins of Civilization.* New York: Crown, 2002.

Hancock, Graham, and Santha Faiia. *Heaven's Mirror: Quest for the Lost Civilization.* New York: Crown, 1998.

Hapgood, Charles. *Maps of the Ancient Sea Kings: Evidence of Advanced Civilization in the Ice Age.* London: Turnstone Books, 1966.

———. *Mystery in Acambaro.* Kempton, Ill.: Adventures Unlimited Press, 2000.

———. *The Path of the Pole.* Kempton, Ill.: Adventures Unlimited Press, 2000.

Harris, David R., ed. *The Origins and Spread of Agriculture and Pastoralism in Eurasia.* Washington, D.C.: Smithsonian Press, 1996.

Hitching, Francis. *Earth Magic.* New York: William Morrow, 1977.

———. *The World Atlas of Mysteries.* London: Pan Books, 1981.

Hoagland, Richard C., and Mike Bara. *Dark Mission: The Secret History of NASA.* Los Angeles: Feral House, 2007.

Hodder, Ian. *The Leopard's Tale: Revealing the Mysteries of Catalhoyuk.* London: Thames and Hudson, 2006.

Hoffman, Michael A. *Egypt Before the Pharaohs: The Prehistoric Foundations of Egyptian Civilization.* New York: Dorset Press, 1979.

Hurtak, J. J. *The Book of Knowledge: The Keys of Enoch.* Los Gatos, Calif.: The Academy for Future Science, 1977.

Icke, David. *The Biggest Secret.* Scottsdale, Ariz.: Bridge of Love Publications, 1999.

Jaynes, Julian. *The Origin of Consciousness in the Breakdown of the Bicameral Mind.* Boston: Houghton Mifflin, 1976.

Jenkins, John Major. *Maya Cosmogenesis 2012.* Santa Fe: Bear & Company, 1998.

King, L. W. *Enuma Elish: The Seven Tablets of Creation.* London: Luzac, 1902.

Knight, Christopher, and Robert Lomas. *The Hiram Key: Pharaohs, Freemasons, and the Discovery of the Secret Scrolls of Jesus.* Boston: Element, 1999.

———. *Uriel's Machine: The Prehistoric Technology That Survived the Flood.* Boston: Element, 1999.

Kreisberg, Glenn, ed. *Lost Knowledge of the Ancients.* Rochester, Vt.: Bear & Company, 2010.

Krupp, E. C. *Beyond the Blue Horizon: Myths, Legends of the Sun, Moon, Stars, and Planets.* New York: HarperCollins, 1991.

———. *Echoes of the Ancient Skies: The Astronomy of Lost Civilizations.* New York: Harper & Row, 1983.

Kuhn, Thomas S. *The Structure of Scientific Revolutions.* Chicago: Chicago University Press, 1962.

Kushi, Michio. *The Era of Humanity.* Berkeley: East West Journal, 1974.

———. *Forgotten Worlds: Guide to Lost Civilizations and the Coming One World.* Becket, Mass.: One Peaceful World Press, 1992.

Lamy, Lucie. *Egyptian Mysteries: New Light on Ancient Knowledge.* London: Thames and Hudson, 1981.

Lash, John Lamb. *Not in His Image: Gnostic Wisdom, Sacred Ecology, and the Future of Belief.* White River Junction, Vt.: Chelsea Green Publishing, 2006.

LaViolette, Paul A. *Earth Under Fire: Humanity's Survival of the Ice Age.* Rochester, Vt.: Bear & Company, 2005.

———. *The Talk of the Galaxy: An ET Message for Us?* Alexandria, Va.: Starlane Publications, 2000.

Lawton, Ian. *Genesis Unveiled.* London: Virgin Books, 2003.

Lawton, Ian, and Chris Ogilvie-Herald. *Giza: The Truth.* London: Virgin Publishing, 2000.

Lewis-Williams, David. *The Mind in the Cave.* London: Thames and Hudson, 2002.

Lhote, Henri. *Tassili Frescoes.* New York: Dutton, 1959.

Lichtheim, Miriam. *Ancient Egyptian Literature* (3 vols.). Berkeley: University of California Press, 1980.

Lockyer, J. Norman. *The Dawn of Astronomy.* London: Macmillan, 1894.

Lomas, Robert. *Turning the Hiram Key.* Gloucester, Mass.: Fair Winds Press, 2005.

Lynch, Raymond. "The Unreasonable Unity of God." Unpublished manuscript, December 14, 2010.

Malkowski, Edward F. *Ancient Egypt: 39,000 BCE.* Rochester, Vt.: Bear & Company, 2010.

Mann, Alfred K. *Shadow of a Star: The Neutrino Story of Supernova 1987A.* New York: W. H. Freeman, 1997.

Marschak, Alexander. *The Roots of Civilization.* New York: McGraw-Hill, 1972.

Mavor, James W. *Voyage to Atlantis.* Rochester, Vt.: Park Street Press, 1990.

McIlroy, Anne. "Neanderthal Cave Changes Thinking About Extinctions," *Globe and Mail,* 14 September, 2006.

McLaren, Karla, *The Language of Emotions.* Boulder, Colo.: Sounds True, 2010.

Meeks, Dimitri, and Christine Favard-Meeks. *Daily Life of the Egyptian Gods.* Ithaca, N.Y.: Cornell University Press, 1993.

Mellaart, James. *Çatal Hüyük: A Neolithic Town in Anatolia.* New York: McGraw-Hill, 1967.

———. *The Neolithic of the Near East.* New York: Charles Scribner's Sons, 1975.

Mendelssohn, Kurt. *Riddle of the Pyramids.* London: Thames and Hudson, 1974.

Mills, James Cook. *History of Saginew County, Michigan.* Saginew, Mich., 1918.

Michell, John. *The New View over Atlantis.* San Francisco: Harper & Row, 1983.

———. *Old Stones of Land's End.* Bristol, U.K.: Pentacle Books, 1979.

Michell, John, and Christine Rhone. *Twelve-Tribe Nations and the Science of Enchanting the Landscape.* London: Thames and Hudson, 1991.

Merekhovsky, D. S. *The Secret of the West.* London: np., nd.

Milne, Antony. *Doomsday: The Science of Catastrophic Events.* London: Praeger, 2000.

Milton, John. *Paradise Lost.* Norwalk, Conn.: Easton Press, 1976.

Milton, Richard. *Shattering the Myths of Darwinism.* Rochester, Vt.: Park Street Press, 1992.

Mounts, Linda. "Brave New World of Antidepressants." *After Dark Magazine* (July 1999).

Naydler, Jeremy. *Temple of the Cosmos: The Ancient Egyptian Science of the Sacred.* Rochester, Vt.: Inner Traditions, 1996.

Neves, Walter in Larry Rohter's article "An Ancient Skull Challenges Long-Held Theories." *New York Times,* 26 October, 1999.

The New Jerusalem Bible. New York: Doubleday, 1985.

North, John. *Stonehenge: A New Interpretation of Prehistoric Man and the Cosmos.* New York: The Free Press, 1996.

O'Brien, Christopher, and Barbara Joy O'Brien. *The Genius of the Few: The Story of Those Who Founded the Garden in Eden.* Northhamptonshire, U.K.: Turnstone, 1985.

Oppenheimer, Stephen. *Eden in the East: The Drowned Continent of Southeast Asia.* London: Weidenfeld and Nicolson, 1998.

Ovason, David. *The Secret Architecture of Our Nation's Capital.* New York: HarperCollins, 2000.

Pauwels, Louis, and Jacques Bergier. *The Morning of the Magicians.* New York: Stein and Day, 1964.

Pellegrino, Charles. *Unearthing Atlantis: An Archaeological Odyssey.* New York: Vintage Books, 1993.

Pensée, Editors of. *Velikovsky Reconsidered.* New York: Doubleday, 1976.

Picknett, Lynn, and Clive Prince. *The Stargate Conspiracy.* London: Little Brown, 2000.

Plato, *Timaeus and Critias.* Translated by Desmond Lee. London: Penguin, 1965.

Rapp, George Jr., and Christopher L. Hill. *Geoarchaeology: The Earth-Science Approach to Archaeological Interpretation.* New Haven, Conn.: Yale University Press, 1998.

Ravenscroft, Trevor. *The Spear of Destiny.* York Beach, Me.: Weiser, 1982.

Reich, Wilhelm. *Cosmic Superimposition.* Rangeley, Me.: Wilhelm Reich Foundation, 1951.

Richer, Jean. *Sacred Geometry of the Ancient Greeks.* Albany: State University of New York Press, 1994.

Ridley, Matt. *Genome: The Autobiography of a Species in 23 Chapters.* New York: HarperCollins, 1999.

Robinson, James M., ed. *The Nag Hammadi Library.* San Francisco: Harper & Row, 1977.

Rudgley, Richard. *The Lost Civilizations of the Stone Age.* New York: The Free Press, 1999.

Ryan, William, and Walter Pitman. *Noah's Flood: The New Scientific Discoveries About the Event That Changed History.* New York: Touchstone, 1998.

Schmid, Randolph E. "Skull Hints at Human Neanderthal Interbreeding." *Vancouver Sun,* 16 January, 2007.

Schoch, Robert M. *Voices of the Rocks: A Scientist Looks at Catastrophes and Ancient Civilizations.* New York: Harmony Books, 1999.

Scott, Mary. *Kundalini in the Physical West.* London: Routledge & Kegan Paul, 1977.

Scranton, Laird. *Sacred Symbols of the Dogon: The Key to Advanced Science in the Ancient Egyptian Hieroglyphs.* Rochester, Vt.: Inner Traditions, 2007.

———. *The Science of the Dogon: Decoding the African Mystery Tradition.* Rochester, Vt.: Inner Traditions, 2006.

Sellers, Jane B. *The Death of the Gods of Ancient Egypt.* London: Penguin Books, 1992.

Sesti, Giuseppe Maria. *The Glorious Constellations.* New York: Harry N. Abrams, 1987.

Settegast, Mary. *Plato Prehistorian: 10,000 to 5,000 BC—Myth, Religion, Archaeology.* Hudson, N.Y.: Lindisfarne Press, 1990.

Sety, Omm, and Hanny El Zeini. *Abydos: Holy City of Ancient Egypt.* Los Angeles: LL Company, 1981.

Shanks, Hershel. "Everything You Ever Knew About Jerusalem Is Wrong (Well, Almost)." *Biblical Archaeology Review* (65), no. 6 (1999).

Sherratt, Andrew. *The Origins and Spread of Agriculture and Pastoralism in Eurasia.* Washington, D.C.: Smithsonian Press, 1996.

Solecki, Ralph S. *Shanidar: The Humanity of Neanderthal Man.* New York: Alfred K. Knopf, 1971.

Stewart, John A. *Drifting Continents and Colliding Paradigms.* Bloomington, Ind.: Indiana University Press, 1990.

Sullivan, William. *The Secret of the Incas: Myth, Astronomy, and the War Against Time.* New York: Crown Publishers, 1996.

Tellinger, Michael, and John Heine. *Adam's Calendar: Discovering the Oldest Manmade Structure on Earth: 75,000 Years Ago.* Johannesburg: Zulu Planet Publishers, 2008

Temple, Robert K. G. *The Crystal Sun.* London: Century Books, 2000.

———. *The Sirius Mystery.* New York: St. Martin's Press, 1976. (See also the revised edition, Rochester, Vt.: Destiny Books, 1998.)

Tompkins, Peter. *Secrets of the Great Pyramid.* New York: Harper & Row, 1971.

Ulansey, David. *The Origins of the Mithraic Mysteries.* Oxford, U.K.: Oxford University Press, 1989.

Van Andel, Tjeerd H. *New Views on an Old Planet: A History of Global Change.* Cambridge: Cambridge University Press, 1994.

Van Flandern, Tom. *Dark Matter, Missing Planets, and New Comets: Paradoxes Resolved, Origins Illuminated.* Berkeley: North Atlantic Books, 1993.

Velikovsky, Immanuel. *Ages in Chaos.* New York: Doubleday, 1952.

———. *Mankind in Amnesia.* New York: Doubleday, 1982.

von Dechend, Hertha, and Giorgio de Santillana. *Hamlet's Mill: An Essay on Myth and the Frame of Time.* Boston: David R. Godine, 1977.

Wade, Nicholas. "Scientists Hope to Unravel Neanderthal DNA and Human Mysteries." *New York Times,* 21 July, 2006.

West, John Anthony. *Serpent in the Sky.* New York: Harper & Row, 1979.

Whitaker, Julian. "The Scourge of Prozac." *Health and Healing Magazine* (September 1999).

Wilford, John Noble. "Replying to Skeptics, NASA Defends Claims About Mars." *New York Times,* 8 August, 1996.

Williams, David Lewis. *The Mind in the Cave.* London: Thames & Hudson, 2002.

Wilson, Colin. *Atlantis and the Kingdom of the Neanderthals.* Rochester, Vt.: Bear & Company, 2006.

Yarris, Lynn. "Fossil Records Show Biodiversity Comes and Goes." *Research News/ Berkeley Lab* (March 11, 2005).

INDEX

Page numbers in *italics* refer to illustrations.